Narrating *the* Management Guru

Tom Peters' work is important and too often under-estimated. David Collins provides a unique perspective on why Tom Peters matters.

Stuart Crainer, editor of *Business Strategy Review* and *Financial Times Handbook of Management*

Twenty-five years ago Tom Peters entered and altered the billion-dollar industry that provides advice on the business of management with the publication of *In Search of Excellence*. In this book David Collins provides a critical reappraisal of Tom Peters; a man dubbed *the* management guru. The book provides a critical analysis of the key works of Tom Peters and offers a critical review of Peters' detractors. Yet the book goes beyond the simple chronological mode of analysis that has previously been used to weigh up the contribution of this guru. Thus the text proposes a narrative review and reanalysis of Tom Peters.

Collins focuses on Peters' changing narratives and proposes a fourfold narrative typology to explore this guru's changing account of the business of management. Pursuing this narrative concern Collins argues that Peters' success as a guru derives from his abilities as a storyteller. Reviewing Peters' storytelling the author notes a decline in Peters' storytelling and an increasing reliance on certain story types. Furthermore he observes that this guru now tends to place himself at the centre of his narratives of business and change. On the strength of this analysis Collins concludes that Peters has 'lost the plot' and argues that new, and more appropriate, narratives must be sought and developed.

This book will be of great interest both to undergraduates and postgraduates engaged with change management and organization analysis. It will also be of interest to managers seeking new and innovative narratives.

David Collins is Reader in Management in the Department of Accounting, Finance and Management at the University of Essex.

Routledge advances in management and business studies

Narrating *the* Management Guru

In search of Tom Peters

David Collins

Routledge
Taylor & Francis Group

LONDON AND NEW YORK

First published 2007
by Routledge
2 Park Square, Milton Park, Abingdon, Oxon OX14 4RN

Simultaneously published in the USA and Canada
by Routledge
270 Madison Ave, New York, NY 10016

Routledge is an imprint of the Taylor & Francis Group, an informa business

© 2007 David Collins

Typeset in Times by Wearset Ltd, Boldon, Tyne and Wear
Printed and bound in Great Britain by TJI Digital, Padstow, Cornwall

Every effort has been made to contact copyright holders for their permission to reprint material in this book. The publishers would be grateful to hear from any copyright holder who is not here acknowledged and will undertake to rectify any errors or omissions in future editions of this book.

British Library Cataloguing in Publication Data
A catalogue record for this book is available from the British Library

Library of Congress Cataloging in Publication Data
A catalog record for this book has been requested

ISBN10: 0-415-41666-3 (hbk)
ISBN10: 0-203-96178-1 (ebk)

ISBN13: 978-0-415-41666-5 (hbk)
ISBN13: 978-0-203-96178-0 (ebk)

Made in Kilmarnock

Contents

Acknowledgements

When I completed my first book way back in 1998 I took a few moments to record, in print, my gratitude to my older brother, Chik Collins. My sister, Christine, read this acknowledgement and chided me – gently. 'What about the rest of us?', she inquired.

'We all helped in different ways!', she protested, before launching into a familiar refrain involving nappies, bed-time stories, one very runny nose, countless tissues and an assortment of special treats. She was right of course. Better to mention none than single out, just, one sibling. But I know she will forgive me for what follows. Exceptions prove the rule and the one sister that I will now single out for special attention was indeed, truly, exceptional.

The last time I saw my sister Joan was on a wet October night in 2005. Joan had travelled from her adopted home in North Carolina to make her, annual, pilgrimage to Scotland. Each autumn I, too, travelled home to Scotland to see my sister, my mother and the rest of the clan.

At one time I had made this journey alone. In 2005 I was accompanied by my wife and by our two young children. To ease the journey to and from Scotland we had elected to travel by car at night. On the last night of our stay in Scotland the boys had gone to bed as normal around eight o'clock. Mindful of the journey ahead of us my wife and I had both retired soon afterwards.

At midnight I arose to make final preparations for the journey home. As I entered my mother's living room I found my sister (and my mother) waiting for me. I was surprised but, in hindsight, the presence of Joan and my mother in the living room is not at all surprising.

We had all said our goodbyes earlier in the evening but Joan had waited up so that she could have another – and as it turns out, her very final opportunity to say farewell to my wife, myself and to my two boys. That's the sort of person she was.

I have many, many special memories of my sister. It was she who taught me to tie my shoes and to tell the time. I can still hear her voice whenever I recall her favourite words and phrases. But my final memory of Joan is special. This small but caring and thoughtful act sums up Joan's character and her approach to life in general. Our parents did a very good job with Joan.

On the morning of Thursday 3 November 2005, Joan was getting ready to go to Young Howard Elementary School where she had worked for a dozen years as a teacher. That morning two of her four daughters were with her in the family home in Fayetteville. Alerted by a sudden crash her daughters rushed through the house in search of the noise. They found their mother lying on the bathroom floor.

Joan had suffered a ruptured aneurysm. She was taken to hospital where she confounded all medical expectations, simply, in continuing to live.

When news of Joan's stroke reached Scotland (and soon after England) we were deeply shocked, but hopeful. Michael my eldest brother had, previously, suffered a similar attack and survived. Indeed he survives to this day – good job Mike! – so we, each, hoped for the best and yet steeled ourselves in preparation for the worst.

In Scotland my sisters Elaine and Barbara, promptly, volunteered to travel to America to be with Joan and her girls. It took a few days to arrange flights and the necessary time off from work but when they arrived in North Carolina Joan was still clinging to life. Despite the facts each of us dared to hope that this was 'a good sign'.

Elaine and Barbara did much to help Joan's children but, in the end, nothing could be done for Joan. The hospital records that she died on Friday 18 November, just 12 days short of her 52nd birthday. Barbara, however, insists that Joan died on the morning of 3 November on her own bathroom floor, in the arms of her children.

Each of us must cope with the pain of grief in our own way. In an attempt to recognize Joan's contribution to the field of education and, somehow, carry on her work, her daughters have established *The Joan Polumbo Pre-Kindergarten Memorial Fund* within the Cumberland County Education Foundation, which can be found at 308 Green Street, Fayetteville, NC 28301.

I dedicate this book to my sister Joan. In her memory, all royalties from this work will go directly to the fund established in her name.

Yet having, now, mentioned six of my eight siblings I feel that I must point out that my brother Tom and my sister Maureen together with Christine, Michael, Barbara, Elaine, Chik and, of course, Joan all made very telling contributions to this text. And for this – and much, much more – I am truly grateful.

As for my wife, Katy and our boys Jack and Daniel: For the most part, it must be said, this trio acted to delay the completion of this text . . . and well done for that. George Orwell has suggested that delay is best thought of as a natural part of the craft of writing. A child sitting stationary on a swing, however, *should* be regarded as an offence against nature!

Introduction

This book is about Tom Peters. It has been produced to coincide with the 25th anniversary of the publication of the text, *In Search of Excellence* (Peters and Waterman, 1982), which transformed Peters from a mere 'management consultant' to *the* 'business guru'. Yet unlike other books (see Kennedy, 1996, 1998; Crainer, 1998a), which exist primarily to celebrate the wit and wisdom of writers such as Tom Peters, this text is no simple exercise in hagiography. Instead this book has been designed to provide an even-handed, yet critical and analytical, review of the works of Tom Peters. This aim, to produce an even-handed, critical review of Tom Peters' contribution to the business of management, makes this book distinctive.

Accounts of the works of Tom Peters tend to be either hagiologic or apoplectic. The difficulty being that those who fawn over Tom Peters fail to recognize the problems associated with his accounts of managing, whereas those who fall over themselves to attack the works of this author, too often, fail to acknowledge his impact on the world of management and the insight he has brought to this complex arena. Recognizing both the limits of hagiology and the dangers of simple apoplexy this book offers a distinctive appreciation of Tom Peters. It attempts to till the fertile analytical ground that lies between the opposing camps that have grown up around Tom Peters in the hope of:

- providing a fresh look at the works of this famous pundit,
- generating fresh insights on the track record and future prospects of a man labelled as *the* management guru.

Life before Peters?

If you are over 40 you may struggle to remember a time before Tom Peters. Like the character, George Bowling[1] who appears in the novel *Coming up for Air* (Orwell, 1990), you may vaguely recall a simpler time; a time before celebrity gurus and celebrated managers (see Huczynski, 1993); a time before booksellers stocked large sections on 'Management'; a time when airport booksellers sold novels and travel guides rather than the musings of management's gurus. You may even be able to remember a time in your own life when politicians and managers spoke, clearly and plainly, unhindered by buzzwords and three letter acronyms (see Grint, 1997a).

If you are under 30 you may well be puzzled by these comments. Unlike your older colleagues and siblings you may be untroubled by what others term buzz-words (see Collins, 2000). Indeed you may think of these terms as naturally occurring resources, which facilitate transparent communication. You may well regard 'three letter acronyms' as indispensable to modern conversation. You may even employ an acronym when you speak of such acronyms (see Grint, 1997a). Yet because you will probably know little of Tom Peters – indeed my guess is that you are reading this book now, only, because someone over 40 has told you that you have to – you may not appreciate the ways in which the busi-ness of management and the language of organization have changed in the last 25 years.

But you needn't worry if you are reading this book only because someone else has instructed you to do so. There are good reasons to read this book beyond the compulsion of your elders because, like it or not, (and many do not) Tom Peters is an important figure in the world of business and in our cultural lives more generally. Indeed, without realizing it, you probably pepper your everyday speech and/or your written work – whether this work takes the form of a student essay or a management report – with ideas and concepts that, to a greater or lesser degree, can be traced back to Tom Peters.

In one way or another Tom Peters has been at the leading edge of manage-ment thought for 25 years. Many, as we shall see later in this book, would grudge Peters this accolade or would, instead, complain that his position, at the forefront of such developments in management thought and practice, is no cause for celebration. Nevertheless any objective analyst would have to concede that in the short space of time, that is a quarter of a century, Tom Peters has pro-duced or popularized ways of thinking that have altered the way we view the world. Furthermore any objective analysis of the last quarter century would have to acknowledge that these new ways of thinking have facilitated alternative ways for managers to act that have, in turn, precipitated wider changes in the way we live our lives.

At root many of these adjustments are a product of the fact that Peters – in concert with others – has changed the way we speak of management (see Foltz and Resener, 1985; *The Economist* 15/06/1985).

The language of business

Commentators tend to debate and dispute the value of Tom Peters' accounts of the business of management. Yet all tend to accept that some 25 years ago Tom Peters entered and altered the daily vocabulary of management.

Big deal! I hear you respond. He talks big – all sorts of people do – but does he back this talk with action?

This riposte is understandable at one level. In everyday speech we tend to make a distinction between 'talk' and 'action'. Indeed we tend to denigrate talk and vaunt action. Thus the challenge: 'You talk the talk but can you walk the walk?'.

Yet in recent years a number of academics have suggested that such attempts to privilege 'action' above 'talk' are flawed and misleading (see Marshak, 1998; Westwood and Linstead, 2001; Grant *et al.* 2004, 2005a, 2005b). Looking specifically at managerial work a number of academics have argued that 'talk' and 'action' must be considered indivisible. Indeed a number of leading academics have argued that the work of management *is* talk because managing is a social and political process hinged on the arts of persuasion (see Hales, 1993 for an account of the socio-politics of managing).

Putting this another way we might say that the peculiar nature of managerial work obliges managers to 'walk the walk' by 'talking the talk'. Consequently academics such as Marshak (1998) suggest that those commentators who privilege 'action' above 'talk' do us a disservice because they deny students, academics and practitioners access to the very tools and processes of 'talk' that managers employ to facilitate action in organizations (see Gioia and Chittipeddi, 1991; Søderberg, 2003).

Viewed within the context of this discussion of talk and action, therefore, Tom Peters' entrance into the language of business *is* 'a big deal'. His entrance into the language of business *is* significant and has had far-reaching consequences because, in changing our patterns of speech, he has made space for new forms of thought, new modes of practice and novel methods of organizing (see Keenoy and Anthony, 1992).

A brief look at a number of management texts should help to illustrate this point.

Management texts

Reviewing academic representations of management and managing Knights and Willmott (1999) complain that academic textbooks on management are, in effect, in breach of the Sale of Goods Act. These texts, they warn us, are not fit for purpose because they, singularly, fail to reflect upon the complex processes that are generated and thrown up when individuals attempt to manage the efforts of others in the pursuit of gain. To overcome the limitations of such texts Knights and Willmott (1999) have produced an alternative, or transgressive, management textbook (see Fine, 1994; Czarniawska, 1999), which explores the nature and processes of managerial work by analysing selected writings of a few, key, novelists.

Discussing the limitations of normal textbook representations of management they complain that such books exist to prepare students to pass exams. The problem being that the examination papers, and the curricula that these texts reflect, produce limiting and distorted accounts of our organized worlds, which obscure the realities of managerial work. Consequently Knights and Willmott are forced to question the value of the traditional academic textbook on management *and* the applicability of the academic curriculum.

Reviewing the academic curriculum for business and management, Knights and Willmott suggest that student textbooks struggle to find adequate representations of managerial work because a top-down focus upon structures, strategies and systems tends – quite literally – to remove people from the equation. Thus Knights and Willmott protest that academic textbooks tend to represent 'management' in a disembodied way.

In an attempt to present a fuller appreciation of the work of 'managers', Knights and Willmott present an alternative rendering of managerial lives that is inspired by the works of novelists, whom, they argue, have offered more intimate and more human accounts of the processes and outputs of social organization.

Thus the transgressive text prepared by Knights and Willmott uses the work of novelists as it attempts to transport us from the textbook world of 'management' – where management is somehow other than human, to the novelist's world of 'managing', which is, sadly, often inhumane!

As we shall see the texts produced by novelists are, often, prescient as well as perceptive in their appreciation of the worlds of work!

Living management

In the novel *Office Life* Keith Waterhouse (1978) produces a rich and highly amusing account of a branch of the UK civil service. Anticipating the concern with corporate cultures that would soon come to dominate the field of management studies (see Deal and Kennedy, 1982), Waterhouse documents, skilfully, the rhythms, routines and processes of the workplace. Indeed he produces a deeply human account of what happens when people are thrown together for 8–10 hours each day. That is to say that Waterhouse skilfully portrays his civil servants as vain, petty and pompous – although we should point out that these characteristics are not peculiar to civil servants!

Waterhouse, however, does not simply blame his characters for their very obvious failings. For Waterhouse the curious behaviour of the staff – the behaviours that shape and undermine their interactions – is symptomatic of the basic irrationalities that characterize the modern workplace. To demonstrate this fact Waterhouse places his subjects in a bureaucracy whose primary function is self-reproduction. As the story of *Office Life* progresses, therefore, we discover that Waterhouse's bureaucrats are employed to produce nothing more and nothing less than bureaucracy.

The story of *Billy Liar* also penned by Keith Waterhouse (1960) has a similarly negative and mocking view of the modern workplace. To be fair we should concede that Billy's employers do have a final product. Unlike the case of *Office Life*, Billy's place of employment does have a purpose that goes beyond the simple reproduction and extension of bureaucracy – he is an accountant in a funeral parlour. Yet the point remains that, for our eponymous hero, work is boring and confining. Consequently Billy day-dreams of a life of chance and heroic adventure in an attempt to escape the hum-drum routine of his daily grind.

The film *The Rebel*, which was first released in 1960 and starred England's famous comic actor Tony Hancock presents a similar view of the workplace as a regime founded upon sacrifice and self-denial. In this film Hancock is a petty bureaucrat; a minor cog in the larger machine that ... well that's precisely the issue for Hancock's character because this man, who longs to live the romantic life of the artiste, finds his work to be empty and without meaning.

In different ways, then, each of these 'texts' allows us to pursue key elements of 'managing' that, Knights and Willmott argue, have been excluded from the conventional treatments of 'management'. Thus Waterhouse's (1960, 1978) novels signal the importance of key concepts such as power, identity and subjectivity in and at work.

Of course we could continue in this vein for some time. Clearly, authors such as Sinclair Lewis (1922), Upton Sinclair (1965). David Nobbs (1976. 1977) and more contemporary authors such as Jeff Torrington (1996) have all produced accounts of work and working which also (a) signal the importance of power, identity and subjectivity at work and (b) oscillate between mockery and lamentation.

Rather than continue with an analysis that risks merely cataloguing the novelists who have commented on the nature and meaning of work in a modern capitalist context therefore, we will, instead, conclude our very brief discussion of the ways in which management and managers have been represented in novels and film by noting the contribution of Jeremy Lewis (1992).

On love ... among the filing cabinets

In a compilation that, successfully, explores the ways in which men (and women) of letters have depicted work in fictional contexts Jeremy Lewis (1992) provides a useful summary of the pattern of thought that, so often, underpins fictional, yet nonetheless accurate and honest, portrayals of the experience of work (see Wright-Mills, 1978; Brawer, 1998; Knights and Willmott, 1999). In contrast to scholars of work and industry who have, typically, taken the automobile plant as the archetypal form of modern work (see Moorhouse, 1981 for a critique) Lewis's compilation focuses upon the office environment. Discussing the bizarre form of existence that is office life, Lewis produces an account of the world of work, which reveals its pace, its complexity and its banality. He notes:

> In a halfway rational world, I suppose, the office and office life would be something of an endangered species, exciting a similar start of surprise as an old-fashioned corner shop or a uniformed nanny pushing a penny-farthing pram. Most office workers, after all, claim to resent their way of life, rolling their eyes heavenwards at the mention of the boss's name, groaning and slapping their foreheads at the thought of that meeting on Monday morning, and dreaming of giving it all up in a sudden bid for freedom; modern technology should, in theory, make it easier to work at home, flashing faxes to and fro and attending meetings via a cordless telephone in the garden, while the cat picks its way between the print-outs and the baby

beams in the sun; given the strains of urban life, the horrors of commuter trains and inner-city rents, surely the office as most of us know it should soon become a thing of the past – to the relief of all concerned, except for a few power-crazed obsessives and workaholics, whose lives (or so the rest of us like to persuade ourselves, when feeling particularly harried or inadequate) are so starved of ordinary pleasures that only work can afford them any satisfaction.

(Lewis, 1992: 3)

What should we take from this?

In the context of our critical review of Tom Peters' works on management one thing seems clear: given the choice between textbooks, which portray managerial work as, somehow, less than human and novels, which tend either to mock or lament the inhumanity of managing, it should not surprise us that managers – before Peters – chose not to devote very much of their time to reading about the business of management. Indeed – if the best seller lists are a reliable guide to managerial reading habits[2] – it seems that when the managers of the 1970s chose to read something other than reports and ledgers they turned their attention to books that, variously, documented the lives of the Hollywood stars; offered advice on diet, weight loss and sexual performance; or to books that highlighted and/or explained the circumstances of recent scandals in Government (Foltz and Resener, 1985; *The Economist* 15/06/1985).[3]

But this picture changed in the early 1980s. Of course a review of today's best seller lists demonstrates that there is still a mass market for 'kiss and tell' biographies and for sex and diet manuals. But since the 1980s there has also been a mass market for books, which portray the business of management in a more positive light.[4]

Many of these texts are biographies written by, or on behalf of, senior management figures (see Crainer, 1998b; Anonymous, 1999). But perhaps more importantly there is a larger market segment produced by a celebrated elite of commentators. This group of commentators is often labelled (although not uncontroversially) 'management gurus' (see Huczynski, 1993; Collins, 2000).

The gurus of management

Huczynski (1993) observes that in recent years a huge industry has grown up to advise managers on the business of management. At the top of this industry is an elite grouping of pundits now known as the gurus of management. These gurus offer advice on a broad spectrum of topics including 'strategic management', 'change management', 'branding', 'marketing strategy' and 'self-development'. Yet despite the breadth of this offering Huczynski argues that the works produced by the gurus of management tend to exhibit a core of common features and attributes. Thus Huczynski suggests that the texts produced by management's gurus typically identify a looming crisis and/or missed opportunity in business and, simultaneously, spell out the (small number of) steps that must be taken to close the gap between practice and possibility. But this begs the question: Until the 1980s managers did not, routinely, choose to read about management matters. But now practitioners of all sorts of management are, clearly, of the opinion that what other managers do, and what they might learn from these managers, really does matter. What has changed?

The full picture is complex, of course (see Collins, 2000), but part of the change involves Tom Peters for he has been at the forefront of a movement, which:

- has provided a new vocabulary of (and for) managerial work,
- demonstrates a concern with 'managing' as a social and political process, and so, refuses to portray 'management' as a cold and rational science,
- represents work and management in cultural terms and so highlights the importance of storytelling and myth-making in management.

In short Tom Peters, in concert with other gurus and commentators, has provided an accessible account of management, which insists that managing others is no longer to be thought of as the reserve of the socially dysfunctional, bureaucratic functionary depicted in the work of Waterhouse (1978). Instead Peters has argued, persuasively, that management is synonymous with leadership. Furthermore his analysis of the problems and prospects of/for the US economy (see for example Peters and Waterman, 1982; Peters and Austin, 1985) positions these managerial leaders on a level with the, more commonly recognized, heroes of modern and ancient history – the sorts of heroes who tend to get books written about them; the kind of people who, at other times and in other contexts, previously dominated the best seller lists!

Venerable gurus?

Studying the etymology, or origins, of the term, guru, Jackson and Carter (1998) note that this often abused term derives from the Sanskrit word for venerable. Recognizing this Jackson and Carter suggest that gurus should be thought as individuals who inspire devotion in, and from, a following because they spread knowledge, understanding and enlightenment. This definition, however, makes it difficult for some to employ the term 'guru' in conjunction with the word management. Indeed I normally (see Collins, 2000) insist on rendering the term guru in inverted commas in an attempt to maintain some distance between my 'critical-practical' analysis of management's gurus and the, more hagiographic accounts prepared by commentators such as Kennedy (1996, 1998).

Yet despite such notes of dissent as regards the nature and value of management's gurus it is, nonetheless, clear that Peters and a few other commentators have engineered key changes in the way we:

- think about work
- talk about working
- manage ourselves and others.

We might not be overflowing with gratitude yet it is, nevertheless, true that thanks to Peters we now have a new way of speaking about management which insists that managing is, not so much a job as, an heroic way of life. And that's just for starters!

In praise of Peters?

Thanks to Peters – and given the disputed standing of Tom Peters you may choose to read this section in the raised tones that signal approval and celebration or in the monotone that every teenager knows signals sarcasm, borne of despair – we now have new ways of exploring the business of management, which, unlike previously popular representations, neither reduce it to rules and procedures, nor lament its nature. Thus we now tend to speak of work organizations more positively and in cultural terms, which highlight harmony, unity and leadership (Martin, 1992). Indeed managers, police officers (*Guardian*, 27/08/1998), educators, even footballers now speak, routinely, of cultural management and the need for cultural change.[5] Wherever and whenever an issue is defined as being big, deep-seated and/or especially problematic that issue is soon defined in cultural terms and is said to require (a) some form of long-term cultural management and (b) the intervention of an heroic, managerial leader schooled in the ways and means of managing by gurus such as Tom Peters.

Thanks to Peters we now share a common understanding that managers and their organizations are 'perfectible' (see Ackroyd and Thompson, 1999). Long before Bill and Ted[6] brought their tortured syntax to the silver screen; long before these characters exhorted the need to 'be excellent to one another', Tom Peters had shoe-horned this rather clumsy expression into our consciousness and into our patterns of speech. Indeed in, perhaps, his most famous work (Peters and Waterman, 1982) he suggested that 'excellence' should be regarded as the quest of all business people (he would probably have said businessmen). Furthermore, he claimed to have identified the necessary attributes that would allow organizations to achieve 'excellence' in their products and in their management processes. Similarly Peters should be recognized as either the progenitor or popularizer of other terms such as 'empowerment', 'management by wandering around' and 'skunk works' that have colonized the English language in general and the language of business in particular.

Taken as a whole this catalogue of achievement suggests that each of us, whether we realize it or not, owes more to Peters than we might realize. Recognizing this, the section that follows provides an overview of Peters' curriculum vitae and has been designed to serve two key purposes.

For those under the age of 30 the section will introduce Tom Peters as it looks back on his 25-year publishing career. For those over 40 the section should serve not so much as an introduction to this man's work as a reminder of this man's (debatable) achievements. For both parties, however, this section should be read as an attempt to provide the necessary background materials for the 'fresh look' at Tom Peters that follows in the remainder of this text. When we have concluded this brief review of Peters' curriculum vitae we will intro-duce the structure of the book, as a whole, and we will provide a basic outline of the book's intents and methods.

By convention introductory chapters normally conclude when the book's structure has been revealed to the reader. However we must prolong our intro-ductory comments beyond this normal point of conclusion.

Tom Peters, as will soon become very clear, tends to excite and polarize opinion. Given the controversy that surrounds Tom Peters we envisage that this book (if it is not ignored altogether) may well precipitate critical reviews, if not a hostile reaction, from many of those who have followed Peters' career as a guru.

Those in the thrall of Peters, for example, may accuse this work of being unfair. Indeed fans of Tom Peters may well seek to portray this work as an unwarranted, academic, intrusion into the 'practical affairs of business' (see Collins, 1996, 1998). Those who object, in principle, to Tom Peters, on the other hand, might protest that this book is largely irrelevant because this guru's account of management has already been subject to a programme of detailed academic scrutiny, which has effectively 'rubbished' this guru's thinking. And between these two camps there exists another group of more agnostic scholars (see Collins, 2000) who may well protest against both the subject matter of this work *and* the methods employed to track its subject.

Recognizing that these camps may well choose to voice their opinions, force-fully, this introductory chapter will attempt to anticipate some of the objections that might be raised against this project. To this end our prefacing comments are prolonged beyond the normal course of an introductory chapter to allow us to explore a number of the objections that might be raised against the subject and method of this text. Some readers, I concede, may find this analysis, and my protestations, an unhelpful distraction. In an attempt to maintain the flow of the text I have chosen to locate my discussion of these anticipated objections towards the end of our introductory commentary. Those who find this section, either, unhelpful or unnecessary should feel free to jump ahead to the opening chapter.

So who is Tom Peters?

In a survey undertaken for the publisher, Bloomsbury, Tom Peters was named as the 'third most important management thinker alive today'.[7] In the same survey his first major text on management, *In Search of Excellence* (Peters and Water-man, 1982) was lauded as the 'Greatest Business Book of All Time'. In a similar vein *The Economist* has granted Peters a title that is, at once, more elegant and ambiguous (see Collins, 2000).[8] For *The Economist*, therefore, Peters is not just a guru. He is, it seems, *the* guru; 'the uber-guru' of management. (Sometimes I fear that this may make me part of the 'untermenschen' of management – but that's my problem).

Fortune magazine has endowed Peters with a similarly grand title. For *Fortune*, therefore, Peters is the 'Ur-guru' of management.

The nature and standing of the business guru is, of course, debatable (see for example Huczynski, 1993; Hilmer and Donaldson, 1996; Micklethwait and Wooldridge, 1997; Kieser, 1997; Jackson and Carter, 1998; Collins, 2000 for reviews). However one thing is clear. Tom Peters has maintained his position atop the global market for advice on management for a quarter of a century. His seminars, for example, are extraordinarily expensive, yet they regularly sell-out. Furthermore his books on management have enjoyed international, volume sales for 25 years.

But we are getting ahead of ourselves. Tom Peters – the man feted world-wide as a, if not *the*, guru of business – was born in Baltimore in 1942. Since becoming a business guru he has – when not travelling the world to spread his message – tended to divide his time between a home in Palo Alto and his 1,600 acre farm in rural Vermont. However a recent biographical sketch (see Peters, 2003) suggests that he and his family now divide their home-life between their farm in Vermont and an island retreat off the coast of Massachusetts. Clearly it pays to be a guru!

Peters has built his career as management guru by lambasting corporations for their dependence on hard data and committee decision-making. Given this his academic and intellectual background may come as a surprise: he holds two engineering degrees from Cornell University (BCE, MCE) and two business degrees from Stanford University (MBA, PhD). In addition he holds a number of honorary degrees including an honorary doctorate from the State University of Management in Moscow, which was awarded in 2004.

Yet despite his academic pedigree Peters, like Knights and Willmott (1999), remains sceptical as regards the relevance and capacity of formal educational qualifications – in the managerial field at least.

In his most recent, major, work Peters (2003) reports that in 2002 he tried (and failed) to return his Stanford MBA following the scandal which surrounded Enron's collapse. Peters took this decision to attempt to have his degree award withdrawn, he tells us, after he had watched Robert Jaedicke – an Enron Board member and chair of the Board's Audit Committee – insist, in a live television broadcast, that he knew nothing of the peculiar transactions and accounting methods that brought this company down.[9]

Commenting on this, apparently, extreme reaction to Jaedicke's protestations of innocence Peters observes that, 30 years previously, this man had been the Professor on the 'Advanced Accounting' course on his MBA curriculum. Consequently he is forced to question the value of his formal training in management:

> When a guy who served as Enron's *audit* boss ... the last bastion of bean counting ... invokes the 'Clueless' defense, it makes you wonder: Did he have any clue as to the usefulness of the curriculum at the school where he'd been dean? Did he have any clue as to what lessons I'd extract from his 'advanced' accounting course?
>
> (Peters, 2003: 8; emphasis and ellipses in original)

Yet Peters' knowledge of work and management is not, solely, derived from the instruction he received at Stanford University. Between 1966 and 1970 Peters served in the US Navy. During this time he made two active service deployments to Vietnam where he served with the Navy's construction battalion (commonly known as the Seabees). In addition Peters also spent some time on secondment with Britain's Royal Navy. Indicating a sense of humour that is not always readily apparent in his written work this former sailor points out that during his Navy career he also survived a gruelling tour of duty in the Pentagon.

Following his time in the Navy, Peters worked for the consulting firm Peat Marwick Mitchell in its Washington office (Blackhurst, 2003). Although we should point out that Peters' own on-line biography makes no mention of this. Following this brief sojourn with Peat Marwick Mitchell, Peters took up a post in the White House as a Senior drug-abuse advisor.

The McKinsey years

In 1974 Tom Peters – then known as Thomas J Peters – left the White House to join the, now, famous consultancy firm McKinsey and Company. Between 1974 and 1976 he worked on a variety of consulting projects for this firm. However, his career with McKinsey was interrupted in January 1976 when a kidney complaint forced him to take some time off. Actually 'taking time off' probably misrepresents what Peters really did with this sick leave for he used this period of, enforced, absence from work to complete the PhD thesis in 'Organizational Behaviour', which he had begun while studying for his MBA at Stanford University.

Having completed this, previously, stalled programme of research Peters returned to McKinsey and Company in early 1977 and was made a partner of the company in that same year. He remained with the McKinsey organization until 1981.

During this second period with McKinsey and Company, Peters began work on a project which in 1982 would propel him to instant and lasting fame. This programme of work, whose genesis and orientations we will examine in more detail in the chapter that follows, sought to explore 'organizational effectiveness'.

In 1981 Peters resigned from McKinsey and Company and settled down to write-up the findings of this research into organizational effectiveness. In this same year Peters invited a former McKisney colleague, Bob Waterman, to help him to tame what had become a rough and unstructured book manuscript running to some 1,300 pages. In 1982 this now condensed and tidied manuscript was released by the publisher Harper and Row as a book entitled *In Search of Excellence.*

Given the reading habits of the general public, both, authors and publishers were sanguine about the potential of this book. Crainer (1997) notes that the publishers reckoned that *In Search of Excellence* might sell somewhere between 10,000 and 20,000 copies nationwide, and so, commissioned an initial print run of 15,000 books for the US market. To the surprise of all concerned, however, *In Search of Excellence* quickly became a best seller in the United States. Indeed in April 1983 this text became the first (non-biographical) guru book directly concerned with the nature and processes of managing to top the prestigious *New York Times* best seller list. *In Search of Excellence* remained atop this list for two years until it was toppled by Peters' next book entitled *A Passion for Excellence* (Peters and Austin, 1985), which was released in 1985.

It would not be an exaggeration to suggest that *In Search of Excellence* defined and created a new market segment for the publishing industry. It was, and remains, a world-wide phenomenon. Despite focusing on American companies and on the American economy the book achieved mass sales in Britain, in Continental Europe and in the Far East (see Lorenz, 1986a; Huczynski, 1993). Indeed Crainer (1997) reports that when Tom Peters travelled to China, for the first time, in 1988 he was greeted by five publishers each of whom had produced best selling Chinese editions of *In Search of Excellence!*

Biographies

Tom Peters has now produced 15 books on management (see Table I.1). In addition he has written many articles for the popular business press and he has inspired many, many more academic and journalistic analyses of his (debatable) contribution to the business of management (see Chapters 1 and 2). For a time he also produced a popular newspaper column that was widely syndicated.

This author's reputation and notoriety has also led to the production of two 'professional biographies'. I call these texts 'professional biographies' because they are focused, almost exclusively, upon matters that relate, narrowly, to the working life of Tom Peters. Accordingly, Tom Peters' private life remains for the most part, just that. Consequently those elements of Peters' life which may have had an important impact on his work as a writer and commentator – his

Table I.1 A catalogue of Tom Peters' books on the business of management

(1982) *In Search of Excellence* (joint with Robert Waterman)
(1985) *A Passion for Excellence* (joint with Nancy Austin)
(1987) *Thriving on Chaos*
(1992) *Liberation Management*
(1993) *The Tom Peters Seminar: Crazy Times Call for Crazy Organizations*
(1994) *The Pursuit of Wow!*
(1997) *The Circle of Innovation: You can't Shrink your Way to Greatness*
(2003) *Re-imagine! Business Excellence in a Disruptive Age*
(1999a) *The BrandYou 50*
(1999b) *The Project50*
(1999c) *The Professional Service Firm50*
(2005a) *Tom Peters Essentials: Design* (joint with Marti Barletta)
(2005b) *Tom Peters Essentials: Talent* (joint with Marti Barletta)
(2005c) *Tom Peters Essentials: Leadership* (joint with Marti Barletta)
(2005d) *Tom Peters Essentials: Trends* (joint with Marti Barletta)

early days, his many marriages, his time in therapy (Durman, 1997) – remain, for the most part, beyond the purview of the biographers of his career.

The first of these 'professional biographies' was penned by the British business journalist Stuart Crainer (1997) in 1997. This book has acted as a key source of reference for this current reappraisal of the works and project of Tom Peters. Given this it is important to point out that this insightful text offers a very good account of the genesis of the excellence project and of the birth of the modern guru that is Tom Peters. Importantly this work also provides occasional glimpses of Peters' complex character.

The second 'professional biography' written some three years later by the British journalist, and founding editor of the journal *Management Today*, Robert Heller (2000) is, for our current purpose, less satisfactory.

Reading Crainer's biography of Peters one senses in the author a frustration. I have read this work on numerous occasions and I always conclude my reading with a sense that the author was slightly disappointed with this book. It seems to me that despite Crainer's attempts to find out something about the man behind the myth, the subject of this professional biography chose to remain aloof throughout the production of the text. Consequently Tom Peters appears as a complex, yet elusive and somewhat enigmatic presence throughout what is, actually, a fairly lengthy book (see also Postrel, 1997).

When I read Heller's account of Tom Peters I am, likewise, struck by a sense of frustration. Yet in this case the frustration is mine alone. Heller's text is shorter and is, altogether, less substantial than that produced by Crainer. Yet there is nothing in this work to suggest that Heller is less than completely content with a text, which tends to lack both critical intent and insight.

Frequent flyer

In addition to writing books Tom Peters still travels the globe giving seminars on the business of management. This probably explains why his horse is called 'Frequent Flyer'. Peters' schedule is now less ambitious and less frenetic than in the early years of his guru career. Nevertheless he still offers between 70 and 100 seminars each year.

He is, and has for many years been, one of the most highly paid speakers on this very lucrative lecture circuit. Sources (who have asked to remain anonymous) suggest that a booking agent based in the UK would have to pay Tom Peters around US$85,000 to deliver a 60-minute, keynote, conference speech to an audience in London.

Structure and layout

Now that we have a sense of the impact and continuing influence of Tom Peters I can reveal the structure that we will employ in the remainder of this text as we attempt our critical review of the work of this author.

In Chapters 1 and 2 we offer a critical review of Tom Peters' key works on management. Charting the pattern and development of his work over the past 25 years we will deal with the texts that he has produced, from 1982 until the present day, in a chronological fashion.

In keeping with the aims and orientations of an earlier work (Collins, 2000) these chapters have been designed to allow readers to locate, understand and critique the work of Tom Peters. To this end, and recognizing the need to locate Peters' various texts in the time and place of their original production, these chapters are structured around '3Cs' as we set out to examine the *content* and *context* of these works and the *criticisms* that each text invites.

Chapter 1 deals with Peters' first two texts, which were co-authored by Bob Waterman (Peters and Waterman, 1982) and Nancy Austin (Peters and Austin, 1985) respectively. In addition this chapter looks, in depth, at the academic comment and criticism which the first of these books, in particular, precipitated.

Chapter 2 deals with six of the texts produced by Peters between 1987 and 2003. The apparent imbalance in these chapters reflects, as we shall see, a growing academic consensus that Peters is not to be taken seriously. Consequently Chapter 2 is able to deal with six of Peter's texts (whereas Chapter 1 had space to consider only two), in part because this author's post-1985 texts have failed to secure the attention of academics and as a result have not been subject to sustained, critical, academic review.

In Chapter 3 we withdraw somewhat from the chronological form of analysis developed in Chapters 1 and 2. While conceding that such chronological analyses offer a convenient and economic means of (a) developing our concerns and (b) disseminating information on Peters' ideas and concerns we will, nevertheless, suggest that Tom Peters' works on management have been subject to changes that are not easily captured in a conventional chronological rendering of his works. To this end Chapter 3 will argue that, over the past 25 years, Peters' works on management have employed a variety of narrative formats which, while commented upon (see Crainer, 1997; Collins, 2000) have not been subject to detailed examination. In an attempt to explore the narrative experimentation that has characterized Peters' works on management this chapter will propose a narrative as opposed to a chronological analytical framework. Having detailed an alternative narrative typology for Tom Peters' works, Chapter 3 will suggest a number of possible explanations for the changes observed in this pundit's work.

In Chapter 4 we continue to develop our concern with narrative while changing focus slightly. Thus Chapter 4 is focused upon stories and storytelling in the work of Tom Peters.

This chapter acknowledges the growth of a narrative concern with organization and management (see Czarniawska, 1997, 1999; Westwood and Linstead, 2001; Grant *et al.* 2004) and offers an outline of the literature concerned with storytelling in organizations before proceeding to develop a fresh analytical perspective on the works of Tom Peters that draws upon this tradition. Recognizing Peters' interest in and commitment to storytelling, Chapter 4 will re-examine the key works of Peters that were analysed in Chapters 1, 2 and 3 from a storytelling perspective. On the strength of this examination we will chart the stories that Peters has employed to breathe life and meaning into his attempts to reshape management. Based upon this charting we will suggest that a story-telling approach provides interesting perspectives on Peters' concerns, orientations and mode(s) of representation. Furthermore, we will argue that our storytelling review generates fresh and interesting insights on this pundit's future prospects as a guru. Finally Chapter 5 reviews and recounts the arguments developed in Chapters 1 to 4 and signals a few issues for future research and development.

Anticipating objections

Before we move on to reflect on the works of Tom Peters we must first consider a number of objections that might be raised by those inclined to harbour reservations as regards the subject and/or method of this text. To this end we will consider four potential objections that, we anticipate, might be raised by readers and reviewers in opposition to this particular attempt to offer fresh insights on the work of Tom Peters.

The first three objections that we will consider relate to the subject matter of our text. The fourth objection, as we shall see, relates more directly to the method of this text.

Objection one: Why bother?

Many academics plainly regard the works of Tom Peters (and his guru counter-parts) as superficial. Indeed the works of management's gurus are generally regarded as being too flimsy to merit sustained academic investigation. Brad Jackson's (1996) analysis of business process reengineering (BPR) captures this sentiment rather well. Commenting on the academic reaction to the gurus of management, he notes:

> The management guru phenomenon has received only limited attention by the academic community. What little attention it has received has been incomplete and invariably dismissive. The gurus' work is generally con-sidered to be too philosophically impoverished, theoretically underdevel-oped and empirically emaciated to warrant serious academic scrutiny.
>
> (Jackson, 1996: 572)

However Jackson is clear that this, academically purist, reaction to manage-ment's gurus is both limited and limiting. Taking our lead from Brad Jackson, therefore, we raise three counterpoints to this first objection to the subject matter of our text.

First, as Jackson suggests, the academically pure, yet socially condescending, account of management's gurus that is rendered by the rebuttal: 'Why bother?', fails to acknowledge that Tom Peters has generated, entered and sustained, over a 25-year period, a mass market for his commentaries. Are we to ignore this? Are we seriously suggesting that this, sustained, mass-market success is unworthy of academic inquiry? What does it say about the approach of 'critical' academic inquiry when we, cavalierly, label all those who have sought inspiration from Peters as being either dopey or easily duped (see Collins, 2001)?

This leads to our second concern: that academic attempts to dismiss Tom Peters' work as being unworthy of sustained academic inquiry singularly fail to provide managers and students with the tools and understanding they would require in order to form a more critical appreciation of the nature and standing of this commentator's work (see Abrahamson, 1996; Jackson, 1996; Abrahamson and Eisenman, 2001; Mohrman, 2001; Collins 2004a, 2005).

Third we must consider the consequences of the academic detachment that is, at least, implicit in our first anticipated objection. Despite academic attempts to mock and lambast the gurus of management it is clear that other actors in our economies and polities do not regard Peters, and his ilk, as horrors best avoided. Quite the contrary, in fact, many politicians and business executives clearly value the advice and exhortation that gurus such as Tom Peters provide.[10] The fact that these influential actors are prepared to listen to, and to act upon, the advice of management's gurus means that the academy's apparent desire to remain aloof from the gurus and their concerns is not cost free. Indeed we might suggest that the academically purist response, which Jackson bemoans, imposes externalities on other constituencies who, for the want of a more critical awareness, lack the means to resist having the tools and processes of guru thinkers thrust upon them (see Collins, 2001, 2004b, 2005).

Objection two: **Tom Peters is passé**

This second objection to our text also relates to the subject matter of this work and might well be viewed as a diluted version of the first objection considered above. Thus our second objection seems to concede that, at a particular point in time, Tom Peters might well have been worthy of sustained critical inquiry, but protests that, nowadays, he should be regarded as a fading star; a man whose ideas and orientations are now passé.

At one level, of course, we should concede that Tom Peters' recent, single-authored works have failed to achieve the massive sales volumes of his texts of 1982 and 1985. In this respect it may be fair to suggest that Peters may be past the zenith of his career as a writer and commentator. Yet to concede this point does not demonstrate that Peters and his work are to be regarded as being passé. Indeed a number of counterpoints may be raised against the suggestion that Peters is 'past it'.

First we should remember that Peters commands a fee of $85,000 for a 60-minute conference speech, delivered to a London audience. This is hardly the level of compensation payable to a commentator who is either 'past it' or passé!

Second we would do well to note that while Peters' recent texts have not matched the sales figures he achieved in the mid-1980s, his current level of sales remains impressive and pales only in comparison to the unprecedented sales racked up by his early works. Third we should acknowledge that Peters' most recent key work on management (Peters, 2003) has already racked up sales in excess of 100,000 copies and appeared on the *Business Week* best seller list at number six on 30 January 2004. Yet in the name of balance we should also acknowledge that the book had slipped to number 13 on this chart by 1 March of that same year.

Fourth it is worth pointing out that Peters' text of 2003 represents the first in a series of 25 books that this author will produce for his new publishers, Dorling Kindersley, over the next few years (Reingold, 2003). Authors who are 'past it' do not generally conclude 25 book deals with major international publishers!

Fifth, we should point out that while the suggestion that Peters' work is passé may hold currency in certain networks, there exist other networks of scholars, practitioners and policy-makers who would reject such knowledge claims (see Lilley, 1997 and Latour, 1987 for a more general discussion). With this point in mind we would do well to note that while academic journals have often chosen to ignore Peters' recent contributions to the business of management, popular but nonetheless respected and highly influential publications such as *Business Week*, *Forbes*, *The Economist*, *The Times*, the *Independent*, the *Evening Standard* and the *Christian Science Monitor*, to name but a few, have carried broadly favourable reviews of his recent works and clearly continue to regard this man as a commentator of some significance.

Objection three: We won't learn much from this 'fresh look' because Peters does not write his own books anyway!

It is clear that many of those who have been labelled as management gurus do not actually pen their own books (Crainer, 1998b; Furusten, 1999; Clark, 2004). Writing for the journal *Inc.com* an anonymous (1999) 'ghost writer' gives a candid assessment of the role, nature and prevalence of 'ghosting' in the segment of the publishing industry that tenders advice to management. Indeed, this anonymous 'ghoster' suggests that would-be gurus will happily pay ghost writers $20,000 to pen a *Harvard Business Review* article. Furthermore this anonymous, but apparently wealthy, author suggests that those keen to take on the mantle of 'guru' will pay $200,000 (plus a sales royalty) to have a ghost writer produce a complete book in their name.

Given this, it is perhaps unsurprising that people would voice the charge that Peters – who has been at the top of this industry for 25 years – does not actually produce his own words. The problem with this allegation being, however, that it does not apply to Tom Peters.

Tom Peters is, by his own admission, a talker rather than a writer. Like many in this field he is, it would be fair to say, no literary craftsman. When producing his books on management he has often depended upon the skills of professional editors and collaborators. In addition it is also true that this writer has, at times, contracted-out the research for his texts and has sometimes used the case reports produced by his researchers in a verbatim fashion within his accounts of the business of management (Crainer, 1997). However it would not be accurate to suggest that Peters', key works are simply written by another on his behalf. Indeed there are, clearly, some reviewers who would lament the fact that Peters *did not* choose to have his books ghost written. Thus reviewers in recent years have often complained that this author's works are ill-structured and just too long!

Crainer (1997; see also Durman, 1997), for example, remarks acidly that *Thriving on Chaos* is true to its title. In addition he suggests that *Liberation Management* is poorly structured and, consequently, largely unreadable. Similarly Christopher Lorenz (1992) has produced a review of *Liberation Management* which gives vent to his frustrations regarding the size and lay-out of this text.

While conceding that *Liberation Management* contains some interesting ideas which would, perhaps, set the agenda for debate in managerial circles for some time to come, Lorenz asks, somewhat plaintively: Why did it have to be 834 pages in length? Indeed he concludes 'Peters' rampaging new tome will delight more people than it maddens, and instruct almost everyone ... The only pity is that the covers of the book are so damned far apart'.

The defence against the charge that Peters' works are ghost written, therefore, is simple and straightforward. Peters *does* receive editorial assistance and he does reach out to colleagues for both guidance and inspiration – who among us does not? But it would be a terrible exaggeration to suggest that Peters has simply employed others to produce the key texts that we will analyse in this work. In short, Peters writes his own books, although we have to indulge a rather elastic definition of 'writing' here because the first drafts of Peters' seminar text (Peters, 1993) and his most recent major work (Peters, 2003) were, in fact, dictated (see Chapter 2). But, in truth, the most clear-cut defence we can offer Peters against the charge of 'ghosting' is this. We can feel confident that Peters is the author of the key texts that are analysed in this monograph because:

- No professional writer would produce such lengthy and jumbled works.
- No ghost writer would produce a text such as *Liberation Management*, which devotes 22 of its 834 pages to displaying its contents.
- No professional writer would have produced a text with the shrill tone (see *The Economist*, 20/12/2003) of *Re-imagine* (Peters, 2003).

Objection four: **We cannot come to a proper understanding of management's gurus from an analysis of their texts alone!**

This point of objection is, in the main, an argument against the method of this text, although we should point out that this line of argument would tend to occur in tandem with the third objection listed above. Indeed those inclined to raise this fourth objection to our method of analysis might suggest that, *because* gurus have their texts written for them, academics should not seek to judge these commentators on the strength of their written works, but should instead reflect upon the other important ways in which practitioners and policy-makers encounter their gurus.

We have, of course, already countered the idea that Peters' key works have been ghost written. Nevertheless in response to this fourth objection we must concede that it would be accurate to suggest that Peters is at his best when he communicates directly on a face-to-face basis.

Recognizing the importance of such live forms of communication to the projects of management's gurus, Clark and Greatbatch (2002) have argued that we can learn much about the ways in which these commentators exercise their effects by analysing the ways in which they stage and structure their performances. Analysing Peters' performances (among others), Clark and Greatbatch tell us that Peters, the performance artiste, uses humour and storytelling:

- to break down the defences of his audience,
- to establish his legitimacy as a commentator,
- to maintain audience affiliation to his overall project.

This work on guru performances is both engaging and significant insofar as it reminds us of the ploys and stratagems which those who would inscribe our realities tend to employ (see also Latour, 1987; Jackson 1996; 2001). Yet I cannot accept that the existence of this literature or the expression of its central claim – that we need to recognize that management's gurus tend to attract an audience and publicity through live performances, which are staged to bring about a desired effect – necessarily invalidates the method of this text. Indeed there are good reasons to suggest that this book is complementary to the work on live guru performances that has been developed by Clark and Greatbatch. A few points are worthy of note in this respect.

First we should note that while Clark and Greatbatch argue, quite correctly, that we can learn much about the ways in which gurus construct meaning through an analysis of their live performances, they do not treat such performances in isolation. Indeed in keeping with Fincham's and Clark's (2002) analysis of the 'advice industry' (see also Kipping and Engwall, 2003; Collins, 2006), Clark and Greatbatch argue that the guru's live performance is but one component of an overall marketing strategy (which would also include such things as book and journal publications, chat show appearances and the production of merchandise such as t-shirts and audio-tapes). Thus Clark and Greatbatch suggest that the study of gurus as performers provides an *additional* dimension to our appreciation of these actors rather than *the* preferred alternative mode of analysis.

Second our focus upon stories and storytelling in the written works of Tom Peters means that we share with Clark and Greatbatch an understanding that audiences are wilful and obstinate, liable to develop (from the author's point of view) readings and understandings that are perverse and obstructive (see Latour, 1987). In common with Clark and Greatbatch, therefore, our narrative review of

Peters' texts is centrally concerned with the staging and framing of ideas and with the ways in which ploys involving humour (and tragedy) are used to massage the sympathies and understanding of the reader.

Third, and a little more prosaically, it is worth pointing out that while the performances of gurus are an important component of their overall marketing strategy, and while academic treatises on the nature and structure of these performances are instructive, we should not overlook the fact that most people – even those who know something of Tom Peters – will have no direct experience of his seminars and will know of this man only through his written work and through newspaper and television reports of his conduct at seminars. Thus we might argue that our method of analysis – which focuses upon the stories that Peters tells in his textual representations of management – reflects more fully and more accurately the ways in which the majority of 'ordinary' people encounter gurus such as Tom Peters.

Summary

In this chapter we have introduced the man who is Tom Peters. In providing a general overview of Peters' contribution to the field of management studies, we have attempted to demonstrate that this commentator has had a serious and lasting impact upon our appreciation of the business of management. Yet we have also acknowledged that Peters' ideas on management matters tend to excite and polarize opinion. Recognizing this we have attempted to anticipate (and counter) the objections, which we envisage might be raised in opposition to both the subject matter and the method of this text.

Given our response to these objections we feel confident that we have established a robust case for the subject and the method of this text. In summary, then, we believe that the account of Tom Peters developed in this text is viable and sensible insofar as it:

- deals with an important and influential actor who has done much to shape our appreciation of the business of management,
- develops a narrative account of Peters' key works to explore important changes in this author's works that, hitherto, have not been subject to detailed and sustained academic scrutiny,
- employs a storytelling perspective to generate fresh insights on a key international commentator,
- complements those approaches that are at the leading edge of academic inquiry in this field.

1 The early works of Tom Peters

Introduction

In the chapter that introduced this work we observed that Tom Peters has had a profound impact upon the world of business and on our daily lives more generally. Indeed we argued that Tom Peters has *entered and altered* the way we speak of managerial matters whether these be related to the management of large-scale business concerns, the management of schools (Peters and Austin, 1985) or to the management of the self (see Peters, 1999c; 2003; Peters and Barletta, 2005a; 2005b). In addition we suggested that in making such changes to the language of business Tom Peters has made space for new forms of action and for new modes of organizing.

Yet we also suggested that it would be a mistake to assume that everyone recognizes the part which Peters has played in shaping the language and practice of business. Some readers will know nothing of the life and works of Tom Peters. Others may have an intimate knowledge of his musings on management but may well doubt his contribution to this arena. However, I suspect that most readers will fall somewhere between these two poles. That is to say that my experience suggests that most people connected with business have heard of Tom Peters but are not really qualified to venture an opinion as to the nature and quality of his overall project because they have read little of his work and, consequently, have no detailed knowledge of the ideas and orientations that underpin his account of the business of management.

Recognizing that most readers will have only a very limited appreciation of the life and works of this key management commentator, this chapter, and the one which follows, will offer a review of Tom Peters' main published works on management. To this end Chapter 1 will focus upon Peters' texts of 1982 and 1985, whereas Chapter 2 will focus upon the six key texts produced by Peters since 1987.

At first glance this division of Peters' work into two chapters – the first dealing with only two texts while the second wrestles with a further six – might appear unbalanced. Yet first impressions can deceive. In fact Chapters 1 and 2 have been structured to bring balance to this text when it is considered as a whole. Thus Chapters 1 and 2 have been crafted in a manner that allows us to produce an account of the works of Tom Peters which divides (more-or less) evenly into two chapters dealing with:

- jointly *versus* single-authored texts,
- early *versus* later 'guru works' (Crainer, 1997),
- the early texts that have excited academic commentary and analysis *versus* the later texts that have, in contrast, generated little in the way of academic commentary or review.

Taken together, however, Chapters 1 and 2 should be read as an attempt to:

- explore the key ideas and arguments underpinning this author's works,
- facilitate the narrative review of Tom Peters' work that will be undertaken in Chapters 3 and 4.

Let us begin our exploration of the ideas and arguments of Tom Peters with a few words from his biographers – Stuart Crainer and Robert Heller

Peters' biographers

Prefacing his rather gushing tribute to the wit and wisdom of Tom Peters, Robert Heller (2000) describes this commentator as a 'business *master*mind' (original emphasis) who has 'transformed the world of business'. Indeed Heller suggests that Tom Peters stands at the top of an industry which he, in effect, created. Thus Heller notes:

> Tom Peters built his reputation as the archetype of the evangelical guru on one book, *In Search of Excellence*. Published in 1982, this title has outsold all other management books by millions of copies.
>
> (Heller, 2000: 5)

Stuart Crainer (1997) in his professional biography (see Introduction) of Peters offers a similar account of this man's project and legacy. He observes that:

> Tom Peters has spawned an industry – the management guru business – populated by an array of top academics, consultants, a sprinkling of former executives and a fair share of charlatans. Competition [in this industry] is fierce and the pace fast. The world's managers demand a constant stream of books, seminars, conferences, and videos. And they want more. Ideas are packaged and repackaged. Names become brands and every grain of innovative thinking is exploited for all it is worth. The bitchiness of academia is combined with the ruthlessness of the world of management consultancy.
>
> (1997: 7)

Recognizing, only too keenly, 'the bitchiness of academia' *and* the ruthless world of the management consultant, we will not seek to add (unnecessarily) to the vitriol that has so often been heaped on the work (and character) of Tom Peters. Instead we hope to provide a fair and balanced assessment of this individual's contribution to the business of management. Yet in doing this we must work to separate Peters' contributions to the publishing industry and to, what might be termed, 'management theatre' (*The Economist* 24/09/1994) from his contributions to management thought and practice.

Theatre of hate?

Tom Peters' contribution to the business of publishing is clear and enduring. He has enjoyed mass-market sales for 25 years. He has, in effect, spawned and raised a market niche that now successfully straddles the industry segments of publishing devoted to 'Business' and 'Self-help' (Micklethwait and Wooldridge, 1997). His contribution to 'management theatre' is similarly clear and uncontested. In Heller's terms Tom Peters *is* 'the archetype of the evangelical [business] guru' (2000: 5).

Yet when it comes time to weigh up Peters' contribution to management thought and practice, the tone of the discourse changes. Many who readily concede that Peters is an evangelist and a performer of world renown, stubbornly insist that Peters' self-belief and stage-craft serve only to mask the fact that his thinking is cloudy, that his analyses are limited, and that his contribution to managerial practice is limited and limiting.

The 3Cs

In an attempt to give due weight to these competing perspectives on the nature and worth of Tom Peters' contribution to the business of management, this chapter offers an analysis of Peters' works of 1982 (Peters and Waterman, 1982) and 1985 (Peters and Austin, 1985) that, in the best alliterative traditions of guru commentary, is concerned with 3Cs. Namely:

- Context
- Content
- Critique

We are concerned with *context* simply because it is impossible to understand the *content* of any work on the business of management in isolation. For example we will argue that *In Search of Excellence* (Peters and Waterman, 1982) can only be understood, in context, as a product of more general discussions that took place in Europe and the US throughout the 1970s concerning (a) America's decline as a manufacturing power and (b) Japan's concomitant rise as an economic powerhouse (see Kahn, 1970; Kahn and Pepper, 1978). By the same token our discussion of the *content* of Peter's key books is shaped by a recognition that this author's ideas and arguments need to be explained, not simply as products, but as products in (and of) space and time. Our analysis of Peters' texts, therefore, appreciates that the content of Peters' works needs to be recognized as the product of particular social and economic contexts which:

- made certain ideas 'thinkable',
- transformed particular forms of thought into candidates for management action and organizational policy.

The third of our 3Cs – *critique* – seeks to place these readings of 'content in context' within an appropriately critical framework. In adopting this critical tone we recognize that, for many practitioners, Peters is above reproach. Yet we recognize, too, that for some in academia Peters is beneath contempt. Thus in offering a critical review of Peters' contribution to the business of management we will seek to strike a balance. While seeking to avoid the charge of academic bitchiness therefore, we will, nevertheless, work to provide a critical assessment of Peters' contribution to management thought and practice.

An unnecessary endeavour?

Many readers will doubtless be familiar with the academic and journalistic criticisms which were heaped on *In Search of Excellence* in the 1980s and 1990s, and so may feel that this appraisal of Tom Peters is unnecessary and, indeed, 'old hat'. In response to this charge, however, it is important that we consider the following observations.

First, while it is undoubtedly true that many readers will be conversant with *In Search of Excellence* and may be familiar with some of the criticisms made of this text, few readers are likely to be familiar with the content of Peters' later works and may have little appreciation of either the context of their development or of the criticisms that might be attached to these texts. Recognizing this, Chapters 1 and 2 have been designed to provide readers with a comprehensive analytical review of the key works that, as I see it, constitute the way-points in Peters' 25-year career as a management guru.

Our second observation concerning the reader's supposed familiarity with the works of Tom Peters relates to the quality of the criticism that has been voiced in the face of Peters' proposals and prognostications.

Peters' friends?

Many of the criticisms made of Tom Peters' works are accurate and well put. However, it would be a mistake to assume that all Peters' critics are equally well informed. Some critics, as we shall see, plainly misread and/or misunderstand this author's work, while others might, more accurately, be charged simply with failing to read this guru's works.

For example, writing for *The Times* (5/12/1992) Carole Leonard offers a review of *Liberation Management* (Peters, 1992). She tells us that *Liberation*

Management is the follow-up to Peters' second text *Thriving on Chaos*, which was produced in 1989. The problem for Leonard's review, however, is that *Thriving on Chaos* was Peters' third text and was published in 1987!

In the inaugural edition of the journal *Critical Perspectives on International Business*, Joanne Roberts (2005) makes similar errors. Casting a critical eye over the works of Tom Peters, Roberts attacks the publishing interests which, as she sees it, shape and distort the market for management knowledge. In this account of the business of publishing she argues that publishers of business books have a taste for particular forms and formats of work (which she disparages). Furthermore she argues that these publishers, like their commissioning counterparts in the cinematic industry, seem to prefer the familiar to the original, and so prefer to produce sequels to previously successful 'blockbusters'. Thus she observes that:

> management gurus, assisted by their publishers, adopt certain well-formulated methods to ensure the successful sale of their book. Such methods include the production of sequels to successful books. For instance, Peters and Waterman's (1983) *In Search of Excellence* was followed by *The Passion for Excellence* (Peters and Austin, 1994) and most recently by *Re-imaging! Business Excellence in a Disruptive Age* (Peters, 2003).
>
> (Roberts, 2005: 57–58)

Yet there are a few problems with this statement; problems which suggest that Roberts is, perhaps, not best qualified to lambast Tom Peters:

1   The 1994 text to which she refers is actually entitled *A Passion for Excellence* and was first published in 1985.
2   The 2003 text which Roberts lists is actually entitled *Re-imagine!* and not *Re-imaging!*
3   It is difficult to view *Re-imagine!* as a simple sequel to *A Passion for Excellence*. A sequel is commonly defined as a continuation of an earlier story. Now while it might be accurate to portray *A Passion for Excellence* as a sequel to *In Search of Excellence* and while there are certain thematic continuities that link Peters' first to his later book (doubtless similar continuities also appear in the works of Roberts), it is difficult to view *Re-imagine!* as a sequel to *A Passion for Excellence* since this work (as we shall see in Chapter 3) is quite unlike the other texts listed by Roberts in terms of layout, tone *and* narrative.

Recognizing the limitations of Peters' texts *and* the limitations of those commentaries that would seek to engage with the labours of Tom Peters, therefore, this chapter seeks to provide:

- a critical review of the works of this author *and*
- a critical review of the commentaries produced by Peters' detractors.

In this endeavour, and for ease of exposition, we will offer a chronological analysis of Tom Peters' main published texts on management.

Table 1.1 offers a list of Tom Peters' main texts on management while Table 1.2 lists those texts which, for want of a better term, we will label as 'minor works'. These minor works are excluded from our present analysis on the understanding that they tend to offer either condensed versions of ideas and arguments that have been developed in one or more of the main texts or 'signature' products developed by lesser members of the Tom Peters Group (TPG), which this guru has built up to service his personal brand (see also Golberg, Notkin and Dutcher, 1995).

Table 1.3 attempts to give some indication of Tom Peters' appeal as an author as it cites US sales figures for his key texts. These sales figures were generously provided by the Tom Peters Group.

Given our concern with chronology, our analysis commences with an account of perhaps Peters' most famous contribution – *In Search of Excellence* – which was published with a colleague in 1982.

In Search of Excellence

Context

In Search of Excellence was first published in 1982 as the collaborative product of Tom Peters and his McKinsey consulting colleague, Bob Waterman. Critical

Table 1.1 A catalogue of Tom Peters' 'major' or 'key' texts on management

(1982) *In Search of Excellence* (joint with Robert Waterman)
(1985) *A Passion for Excellence* (joint with Nancy Austin)
(1987) *Thriving on Chaos*
(1992) *Liberation Management*
(1993) *The Tom Peters Seminar: Crazy Times Call for Crazy Organizations*
(1994) *The Pursuit of Wow!*
(1997) *The Circle of Innovation: You can't Shrink your Way to Greatness*
(2003) *Re-imagine! Business Excellence in a Disruptive Age*

Table 1.2 A catalogue of Tom Peters' 'minor' texts on management

(1999a) *The BrandYou 50*
(1999b) *The Project50*
(1999c) *The Professional Service Firm50*
(2005a) *Tom Peters Essentials: Design* (joint with Marti Barletta)
(2005b) *Tom Peters Essentials: Talent* (joint with Marti Barletta)
(2005c) *Tom Peters Essentials: Leadership* (joint with Marti Barletta)
(2005d) *Tom Peters Essentials: Trends* (joint with Marti Barletta)
(Not dated) *Project 04: Snapshots of Excellence in Unstable Times*
(Not dated) *Women Roar: The New Economy's Hidden Imperatives*
(Not dated) *We Are in a Brawl with No Rules*
(Not dated) *The Death Knell for 'Ordinary': Pursuing Difference*
(Not dated) *Re-inventing Work: The Work Matters!*

Table 1.3 Sales figures for the main works of Tom Peters

Text	Date of first publication	Hardback sales US[a]	Paperback sales US	Total sales US
In Search of Excellence	1982	1,400,000	2,800,000	4,200,000
A Passion for Excellence	1985	515,000	550,000	1,065,000
Thriving on Chaos	1987	450,000	430,000	880,000
Liberation Management	1992	152,000	64,000	216,000
Tom Peters Seminar	1993	N/A	186,000	186,000
The Pursuit of Wow	1994	N/A	353,000	353,000
The Circle of Innovation	1997	122,000	64,000	186,000
Re-imagine	2003	No sales data available[b]	–	–

Source: The Tom Peters Group 2005.

Notes

a No reliable comprehensive sales figures are available for territories outwith the US.

b Contacts within the Tom Peters Group suggest that this text had, by 2005, sold 'in excess of 100,000 copies'.

commentaries on this text tend to highlight the peculiarities of the socio-economic context that characterized America – and much of Western Europe – during the 1970s and early 1980s.

It is, of course, important to highlight the ways in which the socio-economic context of America acted to shape the content of this text. Likewise it is important to acknowledge the ways in which particular readings of this context helped to facilitate the acceptance of the core message contained in this text. But this is only a part of the story. To gain a fuller appreciation of the nature of *In Search of Excellence* we need briefly to trace its genesis within McKinsey and Co, and to do this we need first to consider the nature of the management consulting industry.

The consulting industry

Commentaries on management consulting (see Clark and Fincham, 2002; Kipping and Engwall, 2003) suggest that, unlike other industries where cost or location may be of primary concern, the industry, which provides advice to managers, is driven primarily by reputation because the main consulting product – advice – is distinctive.

What do management consultants do? No this is not a joke. I do know a lot of jokes about management consultants but this is not the place for these. I am serious. What do consultants do?

Advocates for the management consultancy industry such as the Institute of Management Consultants (IMC) and the Management Consultancies Association (MCA) tend to suggest that consultants provide managers with specialist knowledge, information and skills that will allow the organization to develop value, and so move forward in a positive manner. But can we test this proposition?

Let us assume that a company hires a consultancy firm to change its corporate culture – not an uncommon commission in the field of consulting – and let's assume that six months into the programme people within the organization begin to comment that the company feels different; somehow more positive and energized. Can we be sure that the organizational effect we perceive is actually a product of the consultant's intervention? Can we be certain that this effect would not have occurred in the absence of the vast expenditure that has been committed to the consulting project?

The short answer is that we cannot be sure that our perceptions of this new and improved environment have been brought about by the actions of the consultants. Clearly the relationship between the consultants and the organizational effect perceived is coincidental, but we have no means to judge whether it is causative because the provision of advice and/or the intervention of consultants effectively precludes the objective evaluation of the outcomes and benefits of the consulting intervention. Those purchasing consultancy services, therefore, can never feel assured that the consultant's intervention actually caused the changes observed.

Perhaps unsurprisingly this uncertainty would – if left unmanaged – tend to make the consumers of consultancy services somewhat anxious. I would certainly feel queasy at the prospect of signing a seven-figure cheque for a service whose benefit cannot be fully evaluated or properly accounted! Wouldn't you?

Recognizing the anxiety that is a product of the uncertainties at the heart of the consulting contract, therefore, experts on the consulting industry suggest that, in marketing their wares, consultants must take steps to manage the concerns and anxieties of their clients. Kipping and Engwall (2003) have reflected on this. They suggest that consultancies are obliged to take steps to demonstrate their value to clients before they seek entry to the client's organization. Thus Kipping and Engwall argue that successful consultancy firms must take steps to build a reputation in the marketplace, which signals that the firm is competent and can be trusted to deliver on its promises.

Recognizing this, some consulting firms have built reputations for hiring only the brightest graduates from the top universities. Other firms, meanwhile, have sought to cultivate reputations for being, variously, providers of leading edge thinking or market leading tools in the hope that the acquisition of this standing in the marketplace will be enough to persuade anxious consumers that the quality of their market offering can be taken on trust.

Troubled times at McKinsey

Discussing the genesis of *In Search of Excellence*, Crainer (1997) suggests that this book developed as Tom Peters' then employers, the consulting firm, McKinsey and Co sought to defend their company's market position and reputation against two competitors: namely the Boston Consulting Group and Bain and Co.

In the early 1970s the Boston Consulting Group (BCG) had developed and successfully marketed two management tools, 'The Experience Curve' (which suggested that those companies that accumulated significant experience in the production of particular goods and services would reap the benefits of collapsing unit costs) and the 'Boston Matrix' (which offered the managers of conglomerate organizations a tool that, it was claimed, would measure market growth potential for all companies in a particular industry).

Within McKinsey there were fears that market developments of this sort were raising the reputation and profile of competitors at their expense. In an attempt to forestall and, hopefully, reverse this process the senior management of McKinsey cast around for a tool, idea or technique that might serve to rebuild their reputation in the marketplace as leading-edge strategic thinkers.

In 1977 McKinsey launched three 'practices' on 'Strategy', 'Organization' and 'Operations', respectively. These practices had a brief (a) to consider the relationship between strategy, structure and effectiveness and (b) to rejuvenate and rekindle the reputation of the partnership.

Tom Peters, who had recently returned to McKinsey and Co. following a 'medical sabbatical' (*that's sick leave to you and me*), was recruited to the 'Organization Practice' and was duly sent on an eight-week trip to gather knowledge and information on the practices of effective organizations. On the strength of this and other such knowledge-gathering activities, the 'Organization Practice' soon began to develop what was for McKinsey and its clientele a rather radical proposal. That is to say that the 'Organization Practice' argued that focusing upon 'strategy' and 'structure' was unproductive in the absence of a more detailed appreciation of the organizational processes that put structures to work and strategies into action.

Defining the problem in such negative terms was, of course, relatively easy for the 'Organization Practice'. Stating a positive solution to the problem identified, however, proved to be more problematic.

In an attempt to bring some greater coherence to these stirrings concerning the limitations of what Peters is wont to dismiss as 'conventional' thinking on strategy and structure (see Peters and Waterman, 1982), McKinsey first paired Peters with a senior colleague – Bob Waterman – and then drafted in two academics, Anthony Athos, a pioneer in the field of corporate culture, and Richard Pascale.

While the precise mechanics of the process are disputed (see Crainer, 1997; Peters, 2001), all the involved parties do tend to agree that, in time, this quartet (with the help of Julien Phillips, a McKinsey Associate) settled on seven words, beginning with the letter 's' (alliteration is a big deal in this industry!) that reflected their thinking as regards the organizational practices that allow businesses to develop and to act upon strategic plans. Thus the 'McKinsey 7-S model', which detailed a concern with (1) systems, (2) strategy, (3) structure, (4) style, (5) skills, (6) shared values and (7) staff, was formed.

Early reaction to this model among McKinsey's partners and clientele was mixed. However one organization – Siemens – was sufficiently intrigued by a presentation on 'excellence', which employed the 7-S framework, to commission a research project from the 'Organization Practice'. In response to this commission Peters, Waterman and another colleague, David Anderson, embarked on a programme of research between late 1979 and early 1980 that some two years later would constitute the backbone of the, now famous book, which was published in 1982.

In a nutshell this is the tale of how McKinsey and Co came to an appreciation of the core elements of what is now termed 'business excellence'. Yet to understand, properly, the genesis of the excellence project we must move from a consideration of McKinsey's internal machinations to examine the factors in the wider socio-economic context, which made the core message of *In Search of Excellence* both real and immediate to America's managers and decision-makers.

The external context

From 1981 to 1983 America endured a deep business recession. Hyatt (1999) paraphrasing Tom Peters has observed that, at this time, America had an unemployment rate in excess of 10 per cent, an inflation rate approaching 15 per cent and a banking interest rate in excess of 20 per cent.

This set of economic circumstances was the worst America had suffered in five decades and led to street scenes which many thought (or hoped) had been consigned to an earlier period of history. The *Observer* (quoted in Baskerville and Willett, 1985), for example, reported that in Washington DC 17,000 people had queued for up to five hours to receive food handouts. Similarly the American Bureau of Census Statistics published figures which show, only too painfully, the social impact of this economic dislocation. Thus the bureau observed that in 1983, 34.4 million Americans were living below the poverty line.

By the early 1980s, therefore, there was for many Americans the feeling that things were going badly wrong. This feeling was reinforced by the impression that America, and Americans, were suffering while others (mainly the Japanese) prospered.

The Japanese miracle

Fears regarding Japanese economic success and the growing dominance of the Asian economies more generally had, of course, been troubling a number of commentators and many ordinary Americans before the recession of 1981–1983. As early as 1970 Kahn (1970) had published *The Emerging Japanese Superstate* which argued that Japanese per capita income would exceed the per capita income of the US by the year 2000 as Japan rose, inexorably, to become an economic superpower. However, by 1978, Kahn, this time working with a co-author (Kahn and Pepper, 1978), had revised his forecast and was now suggesting that the Japanese economic mission – to catch up with the west – would be accomplished by 1980. This led a great number of people to ponder the reasons for the success of the Japanese economy.

Perhaps the most famous statement on the power and potential of the Japanese economy was written by Pascale and Athos (Peters' early collaborators in the development of the McKinsey '7-S framework') who, in 1981, applied the '7-S framework' to explore, and to explain, the reasons underlying what at the time was often referred to as 'the Japanese economic miracle'. Thus Pascale and Athos observed:

> In 1980 Japan's GNP was third highest in the world and if we extrapolate current trends, it would be number one by the year 2000. A country the size of Montana, Japan has virtually no physical resources, yet it supports over 115 million people (half the population of the United States), exports $75 billion worth more goods than it imports, and has an investment rate as well as a GNP growth rate which is twice that of the United States. Japan has come to dominate in one selected industry after another – eclipsing the British in motorcycles, surpassing the Germans and Americans in automobile production, wresting leadership from the Germans and Americans and overcoming the United States' historical dominance in businesses as diverse as steel, shipbuilding, pianos, zippers and electronics ... Japan is doing more than a little right. And our hypothesis is that a big part of that 'something' has only a little to do with such techniques as its quality circles and lifetime employment. In this book we will argue that a major reason for the superiority of the Japanese is their managerial skill.
>
> (Pascale and Athos, 1986 (1981): 20–21)

At root, then, Japanese economic success was said to be managerial. Japanese managers, it was argued, had become adept at managing organizational cultures (Fukuda, 1988) and it was this approach to management which had given Japan its economic advantage. In the early 1980s, therefore, there seemed two routes available to American management; either they could work *like* the Japanese or they could work *for* the Japanese (see Fucini and Fucini, 1990 for a more recent rendering of this concern).

Rejecting such forms of argument and analysis as distorted and unhelpful (in part, no doubt, because it would prove difficult to sell to American managers), Peters and Waterman produced *In Search of Excellence*, they tell us, to educate American managers in the distinctive capabilities of *American* management. In this regard *In Search of Excellence* might be thought of as an attempt to stimulate American managers to renew and to reinvigorate an indigenous, as opposed to a foreign-based or alien, approach to managing. To this end Peters and Waterman documented and, in so doing, encouraged managers to reflect upon, and to adopt, the practises of a number of important managers who presided over a range of 'excellent' American corporations.

Content

In Search of Excellence is based upon a simple, yet plausible idea: that successful organizations share common practices. Indeed Peters and Waterman suggest that it is what these organizations have in common that (a) explains their business success, their excellence and (b) sets them aside from less successful, less-than-excellent corporations.

Using the McKinsey '7-S' framework Peters and Waterman argued that their 'excellent' organizations had developed methods which allowed them to strike a balance between the 'hard-s' and the 'soft-s' factors of business. Indeed, Peters and Waterman argued that finding and maintaining an appropriate balance between the 'hard-s' and the 'soft-s' factors of business was the key to competitive success. For Peters and Waterman, therefore, the competitive slippage of corporate America was to be regarded as a product of imbalances in the American approach to management. These imbalances, they argued, had developed in the approach to management which had emerged in America during the 1950s and 1960s. Thus Peters and Waterman argued that in the post-Second World War era, many American managers (thanks in part to the peculiarities of the MBA curriculum and the tools provided by the consulting industry) had become fixated upon the 'hard-s' factors of business – *strategy*, *structure* and *systems* – and had lost sight of the importance of *staff*, *style*, *skill* and *superordinate* goals – the 'soft-s' factors required to breathe life into strategies, structures and systems.

To correct these failings, and so reinvigorate American business, Peters and Waterman advocated a more balanced approach to management. This more balanced approach to business, they argued, would depend upon the skills, energy and imagination of managerial leaders who would take responsibility for ensuring the productive alignment of the 'hard' and 'soft-s' factors of business.

Recognizing the central importance of this managerial work Peters and Waterman argued that excellent companies (even those from quite different industrial and commercial settings) would share attributes in common. According to the authors, therefore, each excellent company – despite differences in products, markets and technologies – would exhibit broadly similar forms of management. Indeed, they argued, that excellent companies would each have a culture displaying the eight attributes of excellence revealed by their research.

The eight attributes of excellence

(1) A bias for action

Excellent companies, Peters and Waterman argued, engage in traditional planning activities, but these neither bind them nor do they blind them to the importance of other managerial approaches. Recognizing this, Peters and Waterman argued that an excessive reliance on traditional forms of planning, and a reliance upon 'hard' data analysis, delays effective decision-making and discourages risk-taking. Thus the authors observed that excellent companies avoid 'paralysis by analysis' by scrupulously avoiding the use of committees, and by refusing to accept that all decisions have to be backed by 'hard' data analysis.

Instead of making excessive use of committees, Peters and Waterman argued that excellent companies maintain a bias for action, a willingness to try out new ideas and a willingness to take risks. This commitment to action, they argued, is maintained by excellent companies because these organizations form *ad hoc* groupings of people who 'love' to innovate and experiment. Furthermore the authors suggested that this tendency to action might be contrasted with the approach adopted by other companies who seem to form committees with a brief to *talk* about experimentation.

(2) Close to the customer

Excellent companies, Peters and Waterman argued, gear their innovation and their strategies, structures and systems to meeting and exceeding the expectations of the customer. Where a product or a system failed to satisfy customer needs, the excellent organization, Peters and Waterman insisted, would have a simple means of identifying this, and would have a channel to ensure that this information was fed back to the appropriate personnel within the organization, so that the problem would be remedied.

(3) Autonomy and entrepreneurship

Excellent companies value entrepreneurship. To encourage enterprise, to encourage people to develop and to try out new ideas, Peters and Waterman argued that excellent companies ensure that departments and units remain small enough to allow for *ad hoc* exchanges and informal networking. From such forms of exchange, new ideas and new products would be developed which would keep the company close to the customer.

(4) Productivity through people

While it is easy to mouth the words that people are the organization's key asset, Peters and Waterman argued that excellent companies pay more than lip service to this idea. Thus excellent companies work to ensure that people are recognized and rewarded for their contribution so that they in fact feel valued.

(5) Hands-on, value driven

Leaders of excellent companies are just that. They are leaders, not managers. In an attempt to refine the concept of leadership, Peters and Waterman argued that leaders are visible. They manage by walking about. They lead by example. Maintaining close contact with staff and with customers, leaders work to foster key values ('customers first', 'zero defects') which, we are told, help to bind people together in the pursuit of common goals.

(6) Stick to the knitting

Excellent companies, Peters and Waterman argued, remain focused upon the key skills of the organization. Contrary to the trend towards the construction of huge conglomerate organizations, Peters and Waterman suggested that excellent organizations thrive because they understand where their strengths lie, and build upon these strengths to delight their customers.

(7) Simple form, lean staff

Excellent companies are staffed by skilful, innovative and committed men and women. In an attempt to maximize the potential of their staff Peters and Water-man argued that excellent companies adopt simple, team-based structures designed to maximize interaction, and so innovation. Since the organization is value driven, and staffed by competent and committed employees, the organi-zation does not need to invest (divest?) money in the development and mainte-nance of a complex bureaucracy designed to oversee the efforts of others. Instead the excellent organization is able to adopt a simple (team-based) form and is able to operate successfully with a lean staff geared to meeting the needs of customers.

(8) Loose–tight properties

Excellent companies confront and conquer a key paradox. Excellent companies value innovation and risk-taking, and so they reward free-thinking people who have the courage, we might say, to reinvent the wheel. Yet to reap the rewards of innovation, to ensure that innovation remains customer-focused, a system of control is required. In seeking to channel and to control innovation, however, managers run the risk that they will actually stifle innovation. To overcome this paradox excellent companies, we are told, work carefully to ensure that staff understand the organization's values and are oriented to achieving these. In order to encourage innovation, therefore, the managers of excellent organi-zations make use of a 'loose' system of management. Yet because the organi-zation is value-driven, managers may employ this system of management, safe in the knowledge that the trust this places in their co-workers and subordinates will not be abused since the core values of the organization serve to integrate the diverse and autonomous contributions made by the various teams throughout the organizations. Thus excellent companies reward loyalty and foster commitment by granting freedom and autonomy!

On its own terms *In Search of Excellence* is a plausible, perhaps even a seduc-tive, piece of work. After all who could disagree with the idea that successful companies should direct their efforts towards meeting customer needs? Who could disagree with the idea that companies that desire innovation from their staff must be prepared to reward innovation? Who, now, would disparage the idea that companies need to strike a balance between the social and the tech-nical, between the 'soft-s' and the 'hard-s' factors, if they are to achieve excel-lence?

Yet in spite of all this seduction, and in spite of the fact that *In Search of Excellence* has, in effect, spawned a multi-million pound industry that includes:

*   journals (such as *Measuring Business Excellence* and *Total Quality Man-agement and Business Excellence*),
*   copycat texts such as Heller's (2002) *In Search of European Excellence* and
*   a general framework designed to promote and applaud key management practices such as the 'European Foundation for Quality Management Excel-lence Model'

there are key problems with the analysis offered by Peters and Waterman.

Dangerously wrong?

Perhaps the most commonly voiced criticism raised against the excellence project appeared in *Business Week* in November 1984 (5/11/1984) as a cover story entitled 'Oops: Who's excellent now?'. Reviewing the track record of the companies which Peters and Waterman had identified as 'excellent', this article observed that, just two years after the publication of *In Search of Excellence*, one-third of the 'excellent' firms celebrated by Peters and Waterman were suf-fering some degree of financial distress!

Of course we should not overlook the importance of this analysis and critique. It *is* important and it has hung around Peters' neck ever since. Yet this critique is actually rather limiting as the basis for a critical review of *In Search of Excellence*, for it seems to accept the core elements of the excellence project – that there is a separate and distinctive category of excellent firms who stand proud of their peers – but mocks Peters for backing the wrong horses! Others, however, have looked longer and harder at the work of Peters and Waterman and have generated critical reviews on the excellence project which question its outputs *and* the ideas, orientations and suppositions which constitute its inputs. One of the earliest of these more critical reviews was produced by Carroll (1983) just as the excellence phenomenon began to take off in the US.

A disappointing search

Discussing the 'conventional' account of management proffered by consultan-cies and, apparently, preferred by senior managers, Peters and Waterman counter that the accepted, or conventional, approach to management in the US is 'right enough to be dangerously wrong, and it has arguably led us seriously astray' (Peters and Waterman, 1982: 29). Noting this comment Carroll (1983) suggests that Peters' and Waterman's dismissal of American management as practised by earlier managerial 'pin-ups' – the likes of Robert McNamara (of Ford) and Harold Geneen (of IT and T) – is cavalier and is, furthermore, based upon sloppy scholarship.

David Guest (1992) has also drawn attention to this quotation. However, Guest turns these words back on the authors themselves. Thus Guest argues, in common with Carroll, that *In Search of Excellence* is plausible, yet flawed; seductive but ultimately dangerous. For Guest, therefore, it is *In Search of Excellence* that is 'right enough to be dangerously wrong'. It is *In Search of Excellence* that will lead us seriously astray.

In an attempt to substantiate this charge Guest and Carroll, in common with others (see also Aupperle, Acar and Booth, 1986; Van der Merwe and Pitt, 2003) analyse the many methodological and conceptual failings of the excellence project, which the *Business Week* article of November 1984 had either downplayed or overlooked.

The methodological critique

In Search of Excellence is based upon a sample of highly successful US firms. This book argues that these successful firms have attributes in common which define them and which separate them from their less successful counterparts. Yet Guest and Carroll, among others, argue that there are problems with the sampling technique adopted by Peters and Waterman.

For example both Carroll and Guest observe that, in preparing the sample of firms analysed in *In Search of Excellence*, Peters and Waterman employed unorthodox and largely unscientific methods. Thus critics of the excellence project have complained that the sample of 'excellent' firms selected for this programme of work has a rather subjective basis.

Peters and Waterman, these critics observe, developed their initial sample of firms by asking their McKinsey colleagues and other individuals connected to the world of business (such as journalists) to identify and to nominate those companies which they regarded as being at the leading edge of practice in a variety of industries. From this initial collection of firms the authors tell us that they proceeded to identify an initial group of 75 companies whose rating on six measures of financial performance, it is claimed, made them leaders in their respective fields.

From this grouping of 75 firms, Peters and Waterman tell us that they subsequently rejected 13 companies as failing to reflect the pattern of European business. Analysing the remaining 62 cases on a range of financial performance indicators, Peters and Waterman decided that 36 companies could be judged to be 'excellent'. However, by 'boosting' the scores awarded for innovation the authors tell us that they finally decided upon a sample of 43 excellent companies. From this grouping Peters and Waterman elected to conduct interviews in 21 of the remaining organizations. To supplement this sample of 21 companies, however, Peters and Waterman chose to study, in more depth, a further 12 organizations which they describe as 'near misses' on their criteria of excellence.

Perhaps unsurprisingly, both Carroll and Guest are dismissive of this approach to the calculation and codification of business excellence. They note that it begins with an *ad hoc* sample that reflects the orientations and predispositions of journalists and colleagues rather than, say, the structure of the market. Furthermore they suggest that this initial and *ad hoc* sample becomes progressively corrupted and skewed as the authors allow their own biases and orientations to adjust the population in a self-serving and thoroughly unscientific manner. Thus Carroll and Guest note that the authors dismiss 13 members of their sample as flunking a test of 'representativeness' but fail to discuss the actual mechanics of this test. Furthermore they note that Peters and Waterman blithely 'boost' scores for innovation to benefit another 12 members of their sample, which on the basis of their own criteria they had previously excluded.

Commenting on the outcomes of this questionable process Aupperle, Acar and Booth (1986) offer a very definite judgement on the validity of this so-called sampling mechanism. Thus they argue that Peters and Waterman have cobbled together an *ad hoc* and self-serving panel of firms that simply lacks the capacity to constitute a model of excellence.

In addition to the design problems noted above, Guest and Carroll also observe that the methodology of the excellence project is poorly executed. For example they argue that a great deal of weight is placed on anecdote and idiosyncratic recollection. Indeed, they observe that the data collected on the organizational practices of their 'excellent' organizations are undeserving of this grandiose and pseudo-scientific label, for it is too often the outcome of a simple chat with a senior executive, who would have obvious incentives to portray the organization, and his (very few women appear in this book!) role within the organization, in a positive light.

Finally on the issue of methodology, Carroll (1983) observes that Peters' and Waterman's failure to study a less-than-excellent population, in tandem with their supposed exemplars of excellence, means that we cannot be sure that the attributes of excellence *are peculiar to, and characteristic of, excellent firms*. In this sense the excellence hypothesis is 'non-falsifiable' insofar as the methodology is constitutionally incapable of uncovering information that would refute the idea that excellent firms (a) have attributes in common and that it is (b) these eight attributes which denote and deliver business excellence.

Together with such methodological failings, Guest and Carroll also cite a range of related conceptual shortcomings.

The conceptual critique

Guest and Carroll observe that *In Search of Excellence* makes what economists would term an 'heroic' assumption because it suggests that organizational success is solely a product of management's energy and commitment. Countering this assumption, which seeks to portray managers as the primary architects of organizational destiny, Carroll wonders why Peters and Waterman have been so dismissive of factors associated with the success of other notable companies and economies. Thus Carroll suggests that Peters' and Waterman's account of excellence is flawed because it fails to recognize the ways in which factors such as 'proprietary technology, market dominance, control of critical raw materials, and national policy and culture' (1983: 79) might have a bearing upon the fortunes of an organization. Indeed he continues:

> Unfortunately, the most perfect adherence to the eight lessons [of excellence] will probably not permit 20 years of success against an IBM unless there is some sort of protective technology. Similarly oil companies without access to lower-cost oil supplies will suffer regardless of how well they implement the lessons [of *In Search of Excellence*].
>
> (1983: 79)

In short Carroll argues that *In Search of Excellence* fails to acknowledge the range of contextual and environmental influences which intervene in the conduct of business, and which impact upon the opportunities for business excellence and success. Indeed he argues that in assigning organizations to a category marked 'excellent', it is unclear whether what Peters and Waterman have trumpeted as success in business due to the attributes of excellence might more usefully be considered as business success built upon technology, a patented process, geographic advantage, trade protection, or any one of a host of other environmental and contextual factors.

Writing in 1992 Guest also raises a criticism whose potential Carroll had foreseen in 1983. Noting that a number of Peters' and Waterman's companies soon fell from grace (the criticism voiced by *Business Week* which most readers recall), Guest observes that on the issue of implementing the attributes of excellence the authors fail to discuss whether in fact all of the eight attributes of Peters' and Waterman's excellent organizations are actually necessary for business excellence. Given that a number of the attributes do seem to overlap (for example attributes 1, 3 and 7 seem similar) might it be the case, that, say, six of the eight attributes of excellence constitute a sufficient basis for business success?

Van der Merwe and Pitt (2003) also question the extent to which firms would have to exhibit all eight of the attributes discussed by Peters and Waterman. However, the logic of the case put forward by Van der Merwe and Pitt is different to that advanced by Guest.

Reviewing the excellence project Van der Merwe and Pitt raise three important objections to the work of Peters and Waterman. First, they observe that, for Peters and Waterman, excellence is discussed in simple binary terms. Like pregnancy, it seems, that you are either excellent or *not* excellent, there being no 'in-between' set of circumstances. Disputing the character of excellence (rather than the character of pregnancy), therefore, Van der Merwe and Pitt suggest that business excellence might, more usefully, be construed as a continuum of possibilities.

Reflecting further on the nature of such possibilities, Van der Merwe and Pitt raise a second point of criticism. Noting that Peters and Waterman have produced a cultural appreciation of the business of management, which hinges around leadership, they question the efficacy of the authors' preferred cultural management strategies. Thus Van der Merwe and Pitt argue that Peters and Waterman portray excellent organizations as culturally unified collectives. However, they counter that this simple-minded celebration of common purpose prevents us from acknowledging conflict within the collective, and so effectively precludes the meaningful analysis of organizational politics. Accordingly Van der Merwe and Pitt suggest that the study of excellence needs a better appreciation of managerial and organizational politics.

On the strength of this more political reading of management and organization Van der Merwe and Pitt also raise a third point of criticism, which invites us to consider the wider costs and benefits of the excellence project. Thus they suggest that a desire to 'stick to the knitting' and to 'get close to the customer' might well visit costs – technically known as 'externalities' – on other groups and constituencies who have been excluded from the analytical frame by Peters' and Waterman's celebration of organizational unity and common purpose (see Collins, 2004b, 2005 for a discussion of the externalities of consulting).

Maidique (1983) offers a similar line of critique as she, too, focuses upon the design problems which limit the validity of the excellence project. In common with Guest, Maidique concedes that *In Search of Excellence* is a hugely popular text. Indeed, she argues that this text is successful because it has (a) a positive message that is (b) written in a conversational style with the aid of (c) colourful, evangelical prose (see also Mitchell, 1985; Hyatt, 1999). Yet, despite this, Maidique claims that *In Search of Excellence* does not stand up to sustained critical analysis. Indeed she argues that the agreeable, if superficial, characteristics of this text act to obscure the fact that Peters' and Waterman's argument is sloppy. Thus Maidique warns us that *In Search of Excellence* contains many sweeping generalizations and is, furthermore, marred by basic factual errors.

Karl Weick is one of the authors on the receiving end of at least one of these sweeping and dismissive generalizations. Perhaps this explains the tone of Weick's recent review of Peter's legacy.

Talk and action

Reviewing the managerial lessons of *In Search of Excellence*, Karl Weick (2004), like Guest, also argues that Peters and Waterman operate with a poor conceptualization of management. Noting that managing the efforts of others is a social and a political process, rooted in the arts of persuasion, and so hinged on verbal communication, Weick argues that *In Search of Excellence* is mistaken when it advocates a 'bias for action'. Instead Weick argues that successful managers have ' a bias for talk'.

As a comment on the nature of managerial work this is, of course, a perfectly sensible statement (see Grant *et al.* 1998; Westwood and Linstead, 2001; Grant *et al.* 2004). However, as a commentary on the work of Peters and Waterman it could not be more wrong since it is clear that in advocating what has become known as 'a bias for action', Peters and Waterman were, very clearly, telling managers that they would have to make real, personal and sustained efforts to *talk to* customers, colleagues and suppliers. Indeed, despite Weick's attack, the truth is that Peters and Waterman demonstrate, very clearly, their appreciation of the importance of talk and persuasion. Thus they suggest that in talking to customers, colleagues and suppliers, managers should work to create and to propagate stories that demonstrate the key attributes of excellence and their personal commitment to the quest for excellence. Viewed in these terms, it is quite clear that, for Peters and Waterman, the essence of management action means talking! Indeed it is important that we acknowledge that, for Peters and Waterman, such talk would necessarily imply storytelling and myth-making.

Despite Weick's attack on the supposedly limiting nature of the action orientation extolled by the excellence project, therefore, it is clear that, for Peters and Waterman, management action *means* managerial talk because the authors recognize that managing is, at root, a social and political process that depends upon myth-making and storytelling for the prosecution of its ends.

Set against what amounts to Weick's blatant misreading of *In Search of Excellence*, Watson's (2001) account of the legacy of the excellence project is more accurate, more balanced and ultimately far more perceptive in its reading of Peters and Waterman. While conceding that this (in)famous text has attracted deserved criticism for its conceptual and methodological failings, Watson, nevertheless, protests that *In Search of Excellence* is a significant work with hidden depths because it reminds us that management has a moral as well as a technical dimension insofar as it successfully portrays:

- employees as sentient humans; seekers and creators of meaning
- organizations as ambiguous and unpredictable.

Let us consider Watson's appreciation of *In Search of Excellence* in a little more detail.

Learning to manage

In the 1980s aspirant managers who wanted to garner some positive insight on the business of management had few (readable) texts to which they might refer. Previous best sellers concerned with management matters such as *The Peter Principle* by Peter and Hull (1969) and *Up the Organization* by Robert Townsend (1970), it would be fair to say, were less than adulatory in their treatment of management and managers. Indeed aside from the barbed and satirical renderings of management offered by the likes of Peter and Hull, reading options for the practising manager who wanted a serious, yet positive, account of the business of management were probably restricted to three texts penned by:

- A. P. Sloan the former Head of General Motors (Sloan with McDonald and Stevens, 1965)

- Harold Geneen the former Head of IT and T (Geneen with Moscow, 1986)
- Lee Iacocca the then Head of Chrysler and a former senior manager with Ford (Iacocca with Novak, 1986 (1984)).

Sloan's text had much to say on General Motors' 'hard' systems but made little mention of the 'soft-s' factors of business. Indeed, it would not be an exaggeration to say that Sloan's memoir amounts to a treatise on management *in the absence of people* (see Crainer, 1997).

Geneen's account of his career at IT and T does, at least, acknowledge the existence of people within this company. In that respect Geneen's text is an improvement on Sloan's. Yet in recounting his dealings with staff, Geneen appears in a guise that would unsettle Peters and Waterman.

Peters and Waterman, as we have seen, speak at length about the need to shape values and the need to foster commitment. But in his biography Geneen appears as the antithesis of the culturally sensitive leader. In this text Geneen seems to loom over IT and T in a menacing way. In his dealings with staff on a day-to-day basis he was, it seems to me, a bully; an egotistical man who regarded his colleagues and co-workers as so much cannon fodder for the 'hard-s' system which he, so clearly, venerated.

Unlike Geneen's text, Iacocca's account of his career, which was toppled from the top of the US best sellers lists by *In Search of Excellence*, does make some mention of 'values'. In this book Iacocca insisted that US workers and politicians would have to change their basic attitudes as regards such things as 'quality' and 'customers'. Yet the 'soft-s' factors of business are not, in truth, Iacocca's key concern. Instead much of Iacocca's text is devoted to recounting disputes with other managers (especially those from the Ford family) and to settling old scores. In this regard Iacocca's account of the managerial process is qualitatively different from that prepared by Peters and Waterman. Where Peters' and Waterman's text celebrates vision and leadership and stressed the need to inculcate a new set of organizational values, Iacocca's text is too often constrained by his desire to ensure that history records the quality of *his* vision and the accuracy of his judgement. Contrary to his aim, and contrary to Peters' and Waterman's account of the character attributes of the excellent manager, therefore, Iacocca often reveals himself to be somewhat lacking in grace.

Set against such accounts of the business of management it should be easier to understand just why Watson suggests that Peters and Waterman have done us a service through the production of *In Search of Excellence*. Thus in comparison with the biographies of Sloan, Geneen and Iacocca, and in comparison with the more light-hearted accounts of business produced by Townsend (1970) and by Peter and Hull (1969), *In Search of Excellence* is an important work for it:

- has popularized a basic and inescapable truth of management: that the meaning of management is, at root, the management of meaning,
- offers a new identity for management and, consequently, new ways for managers to be at work.

Mitchell (1985), however, sounds a note of dissent. Reviewing *In Search of Excellence* he concedes that this text is significant for it does, indeed, serve to remind managers that managing is a human endeavour. However, he protests that Peters' and Waterman's concern with cultural matters such as stories and symbolism is a triumph of form over substance. Thus he argues that *In Search of Excellence* has a concern with meaning and identity that is strictly manipulative.

Given the obvious limitations of this text how might we explain its market success?

Explaining success

Academic critics of *In Search of Excellence* often tend to suggest that it is a text largely without merit; a text that could appeal only to readers lacking taste and discernment. As an academic based in the UK I have often found myself having to justify an interest in Tom Peters to colleagues. Indeed a number of colleagues have been puzzled by my interest in Tom Peters and in recent years have chosen to quiz me on my reading of this guru. The implication of the normal line of questioning throughout these inquisitions being clear: why would someone with their critical faculties intact bother to read one let alone all of Tom Peters' texts?

My detailed response to this line of questioning is, of course, carried by this book as a whole. However, my shorter response – one designed for the sort of exchange that takes place over a coffee at a conference – runs something like this and mirrors Watson's (2001) comments as regards the appeal of the excellence project: leaving to one side the criticisms that have been raised with respect to the methodological design and analytical conceptualization that underpins *In Search of Excellence* we must not overlook the fact that this book has sold millions of copies. And before you interrupt, no it has not sold in millions because all managers are dim, ill-trained and/or easily corrupted (see Hilmer and Donaldson, 1996; Micklethwait and Wooldridge, 1997 for accounts of the supposed limits of management as an academic discipline). This text has sold millions of copies because it conveys an inescapable social truth. Namely that organizational life is complex, ambiguous and so difficult to navigate.

Thanks to Guest and Carroll most managers of a certain age can recount the flaws of the excellence project, but when quizzed these individuals often confess that they value the text despite its academic failings. Practitioners of management, it seems to me, actually like this text because as Maidique (1983) observes it is engaging and easy to read. But, perhaps more importantly, managers like *In Search of Excellence* because it (a) speaks to them directly about the trials they face in a manner which (b) suggests that managers and the corporations they represent are a force for good.

Of course this does tend to imply that managers employ *In Search of Excellence* in the same manner that a drunkard uses a lamp post – more for support than for illumination – but we should not overlook the fact that this insistence that business is part of a moral economy is (a) essentially truthful and (b) was, in 1982, a novel and distinctive message.

Yet having made this point as regards the true function, appeal and application of *In Search of Excellence* we must acknowledge that, by 1985, a significant proportion of Peters' audience was looking for more in the way of illumination on the prospects and processes of business excellence. Thus readers asked:

- How might the lessons of *In Search of Excellence* be acted upon?
- What might managers do to get things started?

In his second main text on managing, Peters, this time working with Nancy Austin (Peters and Austin, 1985), set out to provide a response to these thorny issues.

A Passion for Excellence

Peters, in common with other commentators who have been styled as management gurus, has often been attacked as a prescriptive writer. He is, it is claimed, too ready to offer glib solutions to problems that are simply too big and too complex to be addressed in such a simplistic and reductionist manner.

At one level, of course, this critique is perfectly accurate. Despite Peters' faith in the unifying benefits of cultural management, most organizations are characterized by conflicts over organizational goals, which remain, stubbornly, multiple and contested. Yet it would be a mistake to suggest that *In Search of Excellence* provides a simple prescription for excellence. True, Peters and Waterman do tell organizations what *sorts* of things they will have to do to become excellent. And it is equally true that Peters and Waterman do insist that organizations will have to take on all of their eight attributes of excellence if they are to retain their customer base. Yet this, generalized concern with structure and practice is, surely, a long way from a detailed and prescriptive account of 'how to be excellent'. Somewhat ironically, however, a prescription for excellence seems to be exactly what at least some of Peter's followers were asking for, following the publication of *In Search of Excellence.*

In a follow-up text Peters, working with Nancy Austin (Peters and Austin, 1985) set out to address this demand for additional guidance on what might be termed the implementation of models of business excellence. But rather than produce a glib and unhelpful prescription for excellence, Peters and Austin chose to reproduce a number of tales of excellence or 'implementation vignettes', which it was hoped would develop a heightened awareness of the organizational processes that underpinned the very best in organizational practice that they had observed.

Gates (1985) expresses this rather well. Reviewing *A Passion for Excellence* for the *Financial Post* (a Canadian newspaper) Gates comments:

> If you want a step-by-step solution for your company, forget it. On the other hand, if you want interesting anecdotes and funny asides, combined with what the authors have found to be common ingredients in excellent companies, then, *A Passion for Excellence* may be your kind of book.

Yet *A Passion for Excellence* sought to do more than simply add tales of triumph and endeavour to the excellence project. It also sought to modify the excellence project while reaffirming its core message. In this respect we might, while invoking a biblical metaphor, suggest that *A Passion for Excellence* should be considered to be the 'new testament' revision to the 'old testament' of *In Search of Excellence*. Like the Christian 'new testament', therefore, *A Passion for Excellence* extends, revises and simplifies the excellence credo. Thus in *A Passion for Excellence*, success in business is said to stem not from eight, but from just two key attributes:

1   Taking exceptional care of customers,
2   Innovating constantly.

Peters and Austin argue that, if organizations commit to taking exceptional care of their customers, and commit to innovation as the only constant, everything else should fall into place. Just as Christians committed to the single new testament commandment, to love others as thy self, do not need to be told not to steal and not to murder, so organizations committed to their customers and to innovation do not need to be told that productivity comes through people, or that they must be close to the customer, since these sentiments and ideas are subsumed within the two commandments of *A Passion for Excellence*.

A Passion for Excellence clearly exists as an attempt to extend, and to promote, the excellence project, yet it adopts a rather different mode of presentation and persuasion. Whereas *In Search of Excellence* was based upon empirical research (however poorly conceived and executed), *A Passion for Excellence* adopts a different tack, which all but rejects the idea that managers will require empirical proof to persuade them of the vitality, and validity, of the excellence project. In common with a range of business and management books written during the 1980s, therefore, *A Passion for Excellence* eschews theoretical reflection and methodological rigour, in favour of the logic of common sense (Collins, 1996, 1998).

Management as common sense

In 1985 Peters was, apparently, oblivious to the sociological problems of placing one's faith in simple facts and simply assumed that his simple facts would be the same as *my* simple facts and *your* simple facts. In a later text Peters (1989) seems to alter his position on the transparency of 'simple facts'. Indeed, in this later text, he concedes the existence of many forms of common sense and notes the ways in which concrete and practical experiences act to shape what is sensible. Discussing his growing frustration with the managers of America's 'blue chip' corporations, therefore, he looks back on his career as a guru and he confesses that:

Seminars with *Fortune 500* managers [came to fill] me with despair. They came. They applauded. They bought my books and tapes. But they were a desolate lot. Though I talked common sense ... it was not the kind of common sense their companies practised, and they knew what they were going back to.

However, in 1985, Peters and Austin took their cue from Thomas Paine, and so constructed an idealized and monotheistic account of common sense. Applauding Paine's simplistic commitment to common sense, and to plain talk, therefore, Peters and Austin insist that their book will offer the same: simple facts, plain arguments and common sense ungarnished by abstraction and theorization. They admonish us, too, that this should be enough to persuade anyone, with the courage to drop their defences and their prejudices, of the eloquence of their business mission and the commandments therein. With the aid of a sociological sleight of hand, therefore, Peters and Austin simultaneously excuse the fact that their book lacks the methodological and theoretical basis required to substantiate their claims, while disempowering those who might wish to dispute their ideas and claims. Perhaps it is this retreat from an explicitly theoretical base which explains the absence of scholarly reviews of *A Passion for Excellence!*

Yet before we proceed to analyse, more fully, the *content* of this work and the *criticisms* that might be voiced against it, we must, first, pause to consider the *context* of the production of *A Passion for Excellence.*

Context

In Search of Excellence was conceived and published during a time of social change and economic crisis and was shaped, in important ways, by the experience of recession. Published in 1985, *A Passion for Excellence* looked out on an altogether more buoyant and more optimistic economy than was visible from *In Search of Excellence* in 1982. Yet memories of the recession of 1981–1983, and the desire not to live through another period of such turbulence and dislocation, still loomed large in the text. Introducing *A Passion for Excellence*, Peters and Austin note:

> The battering American business took in the seventies and during the 1981–83 recession (is there anyone who thinks recovery means we're permanently out of the wood?) has humbled virtually every American manager.
>
> (Peters and Austin, 1985: xviii)

In this apparently innocuous statement Peters and Austin, I think, do two rather important things. First they encourage a particular reading of America's improving economic context. While conceding that America's recession ended in 1983 they are keen to remind us that the current experience of economic success will be fleeting in the absence of a continually renewing commitment to excellence. In effect, this apparently gentle warning as to the future amounts to an attempt to change the context of the US economy once and forever insofar as it makes the next recession (a) a heartbeat away and (b) an inevitability in the absence of 'a passion for excellence'.

Second, Peters and Austin pointedly observe that American management – or at least that variant of 'rational' American management which was roundly criticized in *In Search of Excellence* – has been 'humbled'. 'Rational' management, they inform us, has been brought down by the passage of history and by the course of world events. In pointing this out for the reader, Peters and Waterman signal their track-record and their superior knowledge and understanding of the world of business. In the vernacular they have 'put up'. Supporters of 'rational' management must now 'shut up' and must submit themselves, humbly, to a process of management re-education.

This recognition and reinforcement of the humbling of American management may also help to explain the *content* of this text, in particular, its self-confident proclamation as regards the virtues of 'plain talk' and 'common sense'.

Content

A Passion for Excellence, as we have seen, begins by acknowledging that the American economy was in a far healthier state by the middle years of the 1980s than it had been at the start of that decade. Yet Peters and Austin are keen to fend off complacency. The economy, they tell us rather pointedly, is not out of the woods.

In an attempt to extricate American managers from the metaphorical woods, which *A Passion for Excellence* identifies and which Peters and Austin render in the dark tones normally reserved for the Freudian analysis of folk tales and fairy stories, the authors advocate 'leadership'. Leaders and leadership, we are told, will provide the means of deliverance from current *and* future economic threat. Thus, in keeping with their simplified credo of excellence, Peters and Austin argue that leadership is to be regarded as the central, and key, component in achieving excellence. To ensure that customers receive exceptional care, and to ensure that organizations innovate constantly, leadership, they tell us, is required. Indeed, and according to their sub-title, it is leadership which makes *the* difference. In an attempt to bring substance to this claim, Peters and Austin (1985) produce page after page of stories designed to demonstrate that managerial leadership is a precondition of excellence *and* the means by which a passion for excellence will be sustained.

So what does leadership do? What do leaders do? Frankly, and from a reading of Peters and Austin, it would be easier to state what leaders cannot do – because, in truth, it seems that there is nothing that leaders cannot do, there is nothing that leadership cannot achieve. One problem, as we shall see in a moment, is that Peters and Austin do not pause to consider what leadership might be! But for the moment let us look at what 'leaders' do for Peters and Austin; let us examine *A Passion for Excellence* and its prescription for leadership.

The practice of leadership

For Peters and Austin the practice of leadership is based upon Management by Wandering Around (MBWA). This concept, of course, had been introduced to readers in Peters' first text, *In Search of Excellence*, where it had formed a component of the 'bias for action' attribute. However, in *A Passion for Excellence*, the concept of MBWA moves central stage to become the key factor underpinning managerial leadership, which in turn is the foundation upon which stand the two commandments of excellence.

The concept of MBWA states that mangers cannot lead from the boardroom. While managers can, and must, lead from the front, they cannot lead at a distance. Thus Peters and Austin argue that managers will only come to be viewed as leaders (and so, will only develop the followers required in value/vision-driven organizations) when they are able to connect with their staff. However, the authors warn us that for some members of the boardroom elite, this approach to leadership may prove to be a difficult and trying process. Thus in an echo of our earlier biblical allusion there is, within this account of the trials of managerial leadership, the suggestion that, for some, a passion for excellence may actually turn out to be a Christ-like passion.

Pattison (1997) takes this analysis of religious imagery somewhat further. Peters and Austin, he argues, do not simply allude to things that have religious connotations. Instead he tells us that these authors literally retell a famous biblical tale – albeit one from the Old Testament.

Religious metaphor and allusion

Discussing religious allusion and metaphor in the works of management's gurus, Pattison (1997) argues that *A Passion for Excellence* amounts to a modern secular retelling of the biblical story concerning Noah and the flood. Indeed, Pattison suggests that it is the familiarity of this religious tale which helps to make *A Passion for Excellence* substantial and persuasive in the absence of a programme of theoretically informed research.

The tale of Noah, as you will no doubt recall, begins by observing and recounting the ways in which the inhabitants of God's earth had fallen from grace to become degenerate. Recognizing this degeneracy the Old Testament tells us that God chose to recommence the business of creation. But to do this, to recreate Heaven on earth, we are told, God first had to cleanse His creation of sin.

Knowing that Noah and his family had remained true to His calling in the midst of the Godless depravity that had swept across the fabric of creation, God, the bible tells us, decides to spare Noah and his kin from the flood that he plans as the means of cleansing the earth. He instructs Noah to build an ark. In addition he tells Noah that he must herd animals on to the ark so that these, too, will be spared from the flood. To this end he issues precise instructions as to the size of the ark and the number and type of animals that should be gathered therein.

Noah, as a good and God-fearing man, does God's bidding and is spared from drowning. Those who failed to heed God's warnings and who, consequently, failed to atone for their failings and oversights, we are told, are denied entry to the ark and are simply left to perish in the deluge visited upon the fabric of God's creation.

Commenting on the rhetorical power of *A Passion for Excellence*, Pattison argues that this text follows and reproduces the essence of the biblical story of Noah, albeit in a secularized form. Reducing *A Passion for Excellence* to its elements, therefore, Pattison notes that, in this text, Peters and Austin warn their readers that:

- Changes in markets, technologies, regulation and consumer preferences are ushering in a new era of on-going change and turbulence.
- In the wake of this turbulent change there will be two types of organization: the drowned and the saved.
- Those who fail to heed the warnings, those who fail to prepare themselves for the future will be lost.
- Those who wish to be saved must 'get on board' with Tom Peters and his excellence project.

In an echo of the lesson of Noah, therefore, Peters and Austin warn us that there is no way to avoid the challenge, and no way to avoid the pain, which a passion for excellence may bring, because there is no means, aside from leadership, to solve the problems and paradoxes of modern management. And in this we have a further departure from the message of *In Search of Excellence*.

Soft and hard factors

In Search of Excellence, you will recall, argues that management needs to balance 'soft' and 'hard' analysis. However, *A Passion for Excellence* argues that 'soft' analysis is 'hard'! In fact, page after page of the Peters and Austin text celebrates 'soft' analysis. Thus in *A Passion for Excellence* managers are exhorted to follow their instincts, to do the obvious. Likewise they are encouraged to throw off the chains of statistical analysis, so that through 'naïve listening' they might see problems anew and from the perspective of the customer.

This, of course, does not mean that *A Passion for Excellence* is anti-analysis. What it does demonstrate is that Peters and Austin are attempting to undermine the privileged position of 'hard' 'number-crunching' as *real* analysis in order to show that 'soft' forms of analysis are equally (often more) reliable than 'hard' analysis. Or as Peters would say – if the guys who built it tell you that it walks like a duck and quacks like a duck, why would you need focus groups in 29 states to tell you that it is a duck?

So what do we do with all this information? Well it would be tempting to dismiss *A Passion for Excellence* as a technique-fixated (see Hilmer and Donaldson, 1996) approach to management. But, in truth, such a claim will not stick easily to this text. In fact there is much within the text of *A Passion for Excellence*, which, at one level, promotes careful, thoughtful and reflective management practice. Every few pages, in fact, Peters and Austin interrupt their 'implementation vignettes' to issue their readers with questions and topics for *analysis*. The question we must ask, however, is this; short of exhortation, anecdote and vignettes of excellence in practice, what has this text to say on the nature and practice of leadership? Unfortunately the answer is very little.

The leadership difference

Peters and Austin, as we have seen, argue that managerial leadership is *the* key to excellence. The problem being that, aside from making the claim that leadership is, in fact, the difference between conspicuous success and horrendous failure (see Pattison, 1997; Van der Merwe and Pitt, 2003), the authors actually offer little discussion of the debates which persist on the nature, meaning and effect of leadership.

In fact Peters and Austin seem studiously to ignore the controversies and complexities which have shaped serious scholarship on the nature and conduct of leadership for at least 50 years. How might we explain this omission? Two points come to mind.

First we might suggest that Peters' and Austin's stubborn and unbending support for the power of common sense reasoning means that *A Passion for Excellence* is, in fact, constitutionally incapable of providing a mature and balanced reflection on the nature and conduct of leadership. For to do this – to think through the complexities of leadership scholarship – the authors would have to embrace an approach to management rooted in an explicitly theoretical model. The problem being that the authors have already warned us that such academic theorizing is a crutch reserved for those who lack faith and vision.

Second we might argue that this disavowal of 'theory' allows Peters and Austin to produce a personal, and largely self-serving, notion of management that, on its own common sense terms, is complete and irrefutable. Yet for those schooled in the academic study of leadership, such faith in common sense is impudent and unacceptable.

Theorizing leadership

Commenting on the complexities of leadership and on the virtues of academic theorizing, Grint (1997b) states that men, like Peters, who place their faith in the virtues of common sense and who protest that such common sense reasoning is (a) superior to and (b) exists prior to academic theorizing are humouring a dangerous self-delusion (see also Collins, 1996). Indeed, Grint argues that those who protest that 'theory' is irrelevant to their mission and project have, unwittingly, adopted a theoretical position since to argue that theoretical analysis and reflection is irrelevant is to make assumptions (a) about the nature of the world and (b) about our abilities, as humans, to apprehend and to comprehend the world we inhabit. Thus it is clear that when Peters and Austin privilege 'facts' above 'theory' they are, whether or not they choose to acknowledge it, engaging in a form of theoretical analysis and reflection, for to reject the need for theory is to argue that 'facts' stand for themselves, that 'reality' is objective and self-evident to all (see Burrell and Morgan, 1979) and this is, itself, a view of the world that has been shaped and ordered by theoretical precepts and assumptions. However, we would also do well to note that this is a theoretical stance that few theorists accept, or in truth take seriously!

Given the theoretical nature of their practical aim and method, therefore, it is clear that when Peters and Austin assert that a passion for excellence is required, and when they assert that leadership is the difference between excellence and mediocrity (and mediocrity means failure), they invite the following inquiry: Which model of leadership do you have in mind?

Yet in reply *A Passion for Excellence* offers only a range of proverbial responses. Leaders listen; non-leaders talk. Leaders are humble; non-leaders are arrogant (see Peters and Austin, 1985: 354–361). Yet these aphorisms actually do little to answer our question. *And we do need an answer* because leadership is a theoretical construct, interpreted differently by various schools and scholars. Any attempt to analyse leader*ship*, therefore, reveals a veritable fleet of diverse accounts and models.

A fleet of theories

Grint (1997b) captures this diversity rather well. He offers an analysis that demonstrates both the depth and the breadth of that branch of scholarship concerned with the nature of leadership and with the conduct of leaders. Prefacing his analysis Grint notes that, between 1986 and 1996, at least 17,800 journal articles were written on leadership. Drawing out the significance of this figure he observes that this amounts to the production of 37 articles on leadership per week and suggests (although he exaggerates) that this means that those who were interested in the nature and practice of leadership during the decade 1986–1996 would have been obliged to read one article per hour of the working week just to keep abreast of current thinking. The problem being, as Grint observes, that there is no agreement as to what constitutes current thinking on leadership because scholarship in this area is subject to constant revision *and* regular reversals.

With leadership as with much else in life, therefore, it seems that the more one reads the less one can really know with certainty. Thus Grint notes:

> despite an enormous outpouring of material in the second half of the twentieth century, we appear to be little closer to understanding leadership than either Plato or Sun Tzu, who began the written debate several thousand years ago; certainly Chester Barnard's ... concerns that we should stop focusing upon the formal leader seem to have gone un-noticed. Since the post-war period we appear to have gone full circle: from assurances that personality traits were the key, through equally valid counter-arguments that

the situation was critical, to a controversy over whether the leader was person – or task-oriented, and back to hunting out the charismatics whose visions and transformational style would explain all.

(Grint, 1997b: 116)

Grint's analysis makes it clear, therefore, that when Peters and Austin advocate leadership in general they are, in fact, acting as advocates for a particular model of leadership, which remains unspoken in their analysis, yet contested and controversial in the wider arena.

Can we identify a preferred theorization of leadership in Peters' and Austin's celebration of common sense?

Previously when confronted with this question I have suggested (Collins, 2000) that Peters and Austin, in common with other management commentators, have opted for what amounts to a contingency model of leadership. Now, candidly, I am not so sure. Indeed I am now inclined to suggest that Peters' and Austin's disavowal of the benefits of 'theory' has led to the development of an account of leadership which straddles at least two of the frameworks identified by Grint (1997b).

A contingency model

For Peters and Austin, leadership is *the* difference between excellence and mediocrity, because in turbulent times when competition is fierce, when technologies change rapidly and when innovation in customer service is the key to survival, organizations need the vision of a leader to maintain energy and direction. This, in a nutshell, is the overarching message of *A Passion for Excellence*.

A leader for Peters and Austin, therefore, has two main roles to perform. The leader must:

1   diagnose the key contingencies facing the organization given the overarching problems identified by Peters and Austin,
2   fit the organization to these contingencies

However as Grint (1997b) has observed this contingent appreciation implies some level of consensus as regards the essence of leadership since it overlooks the controversies, which rage between:

* those who assume that leaders are born *versus* those who assume that leaders are everywhere only awaiting specialist training,
* those who assume that certain kinds of leader are suited only to certain situations *versus* those who assume that leaders (whether 'born' or 'made' by training) can adapt their attributes to a variety of situations.

Furthermore this support for leadership, in general, assumes that we can actually make sense of the situation confronting the organization. That is to say that this account of leadership assumes that we actually know how the contingent variables in the wider environment are moving *and* which of these contingencies we should respond to.

As I now see it the account of leadership produced by Peters and Austin attempts to side-step these analytical difficulties by (a) ignoring this controversy and (b) by forging, implicitly, an alliance between the 'contingent' and 'charismatic' tendencies identified by Grint. In a sense, then, the limitations of contingency thinking identified above scarcely intrude upon the work of Peters and Austin because these authors assume and protest that their leaders are special, passionate and, above all, charismatic individuals; people who possess the capacity to overcome the practical limitations that theorists of leadership have observed tend to undo the best intentions of *normal* individuals.

On its own terms this 'contingent-charismatic' account of leadership seems to provide a persuasive and substantial rendering of the problems and processes of managing. In Latour's (1987) terms this is a sweeping narrative, designed to carry us quickly downstream, away from the initial conditions and questionable suppositions that shape our understanding of the nature of leadership, to a place where all the elements of our knowledge are accepted tacitly and in silence.

It is the role of academic theorizing, however, to engineer 'negative modalities' in such streams of knowledge production. Accordingly, this chapter has sought to prise open the 'black box' of leadership promoted by Peters and Austin as a means of questioning the basic ideas, orientations and assumptions of the (revised and extended) excellence project. Thus we have sought to demonstrate that the excellence project as outlined in Peters' texts of 1982 and 1985 has currency only for so long as we allow Peters and his co-authors to:

* frighten us as regards the future,
* select and define our heroes,
* maintain apolitical models of organizational culture,
* ignore the existence of alternative explanations for business success,
* side-step questions concerning the virtues of academic theorization and the legitimacy of their common sense presumptions.

Summary

This chapter has reviewed Peters' first two books on the business of management that were co-written with Bob Waterman (Peters and Waterman, 1982) and Nancy Austin (Peters and Austin, 1985). The first of these texts – *In Search of Excellence* – was based upon a (dubiously constructed) sample of (supposedly) highly performing firms and claimed to have diagnosed the pre-conditions for business excellence and the practices that would sustain cultures of excellence.

This text effectively launched Peters' guru career *and* defined a new market for business publishing. Perhaps unsurprisingly, giving its academic pretensions, *In Search of Excellence* precipitated a large number of academic reviews. Many of these reviews sought to question the validity of the excellence project, and so reflected on the analytical and methodological shortcomings of this text. However, it is worth pointing out that this text also precipitated a body of more supportive academic and practitioner literature, which sought to apply the lessons of excellence to specific industries (see Miller, 1993; Barter, 1994; Bunz and Maes, 1998) or to different national contexts (see for example Heller, 2002).

Recognizing the trenchant nature of the academic and journalistic critiques visited upon the excellence project we have sought to provide an analytical account of *In Search of Excellence* which acknowledges its appeal. To this end we have attempted to explore the text's content within the context of its creation. Furthermore we have attempted to provide a critical assessment of this work while highlighting those moments when Peters' detractors offered commentaries on his work that were ill-informed.

Moving on to consider Peters' sequel to *In Search of Excellence*, we high-lighted the similarities that unite (a continuing focus upon leaders, cultures, cus-tomers and stories) and the differences (a disavowal of the normal conventions of academic modelling and theorizing) that divide these texts. Noting Peters' and Austin's (1985) rejection of academic theorizing in favour of an argument rooted in 'plain talk and common sense' we have attempted to re-examine the theoretical orientations that underpin (or should that be undermine?) this analysis.

Exploring Peters' and Austin's conviction that leadership is *the* difference between business failure and success we have argued that their text depends upon an under-theorized model of leadership. Furthermore we have suggested that this text remains persuasive and substantial only for so long as this model of leadership remains unnamed and beyond sustained academic scrutiny. In an attempt to reveal the moral economy of the excellence project as a whole, there-fore, we have attempted to demonstrate the existence of a range of implicit assumptions that give shape and substance to Peters' account of the business of management.

And yet . . . the controversy rages.

In 1984 *Business Week* ran a, now famous, cover story which argued that a significant proportion of Peters' excellent companies were suffering financial distress just two years after they had been trumpeted as exemplars of modern business practice. However 18 years later, on the occasion of the 20th anniver-sary of the publication of *In Search of Excellence*, Dan Ackman (2002), writing for *Forbes*, observed that:

> *In Search of Excellence* didn't name the biggest companies and ride with winners: In 1982 when the book was published, just three of the 43 com-panies ranked among the top 25 by sales on The Forbes 500s. And just 22 of the 32 public companies were among the 500 largest. Those 22 ranked, on average, 125th on The Forbes 500s by sales. Over the years the com-panies grew. By 2002, 24 of the firms were among the largest 500 public companies with an average Forbes 500s sales rank of 99.

Overall Ackman concludes that 'the companies Peters and Waterman called excellent [in 1982] have easily outperformed the market averages any way you slice it'.

In response to the question posed by *Business Week* in 1984, therefore, Ackman suggests that, with the exception of Atari and Wang (which went out of business altogether), the companies that are excellent 'now' are the companies identified by Peters and Waterman way back 'then' in 1982. Whether Peters can take any personal credit for this success and whether this success can be explained as a consequence of adhering to the eight attributes of excellence that were outlined by Peters and Waterman in 1982 remains, patently, the subject of on-going debate and conjecture.

In the chapter that follows we will move on to consider the remaining six texts that we have described as 'key' works in the Peters canon of management knowledge. Given our chronological format Chapter 2 will begin with an analysis of Peters' first single-authored, guru text entitled *Thriving on Chaos* (Peters, 1987).

2 The later works of Tom Peters
The guru years

Introduction

Chapter 1 offered a critical, analytical review of Tom Peters' early writings on the business of management. Accordingly we considered the context and content of *In Search of Excellence* (Peters and Waterman, 1982) and *A Passion for Excellence* (Peters and Austin, 1985). In addition we explored a range of criticisms that might be raised against the methods, orientations and aspirations of these works.

This chapter picks up where the preceding one concluded. Thus Chapter 2 offers a critical review of the context and content of the six key texts on business and management (see Chapter 1 for a complete listing of Peters' texts) that Peters has produced since 1987.

For ease of exposition our analysis in this chapter retains the chronological format employed in Chapter 1. Later chapters, as we shall see, adopt an alternative analytical approach that is based around a concern with stories, storytelling and with narrative form more generally. For the moment, however, we will persist with our chronological frame of reference. Accordingly, this chapter begins with an account of *Thriving on Chaos* (Peters, 1987) which was first published in 1987.

Thriving on Chaos

Thriving on Chaos, as you might properly expect, presents a picture of the world as 'chaotic'. In keeping with Peters' earlier analysis in *A Passion for Excellence* (Peters and Austin, 1985) this text of 1987 offers a starkly dualistic vision of organizations and management. This 'chaotic' metaphor divides the world of organizations into two camps: those who will thrive in an age of chaos and those who will fail. Building upon this stark and dualistic vision, *Thriving on Chaos* warns us that many contemporary organizations will fail because they are unaware of the revolution in management which the 'chaotic' nature of our times call forth. To save these organizations from failure, and so allow managers to 'thrive on chaos', Peters, now working as a sole author, offers a text with a different format to those that preceded it.

A chaotic format?

In Search of Excellence and *A Passion for Excellence* are utterly conventional books insofar as they are presented to readers on the understanding that they should be read from beginning to end in a sequential fashion (with the possible exception of the final 100 pages of *A Passion for Excellence*, which offers specialist advice to educators and which may, consequently, be skipped by the general reader without damaging the integrity or the narrative flow of the text as a whole). Compared with these earlier texts *Thriving on Chaos* is unconventional inasmuch as it does not oblige the reader to follow the linear sequence of an argument that grows as the text moves from its introduction towards its conclusion. Instead *Thriving on Chaos* might be regarded as a manual or as a handbook.

Outlining his reasons for departing from the conventional narrative form that characterized his earlier work and which, in truth, typifies most texts published in the arena of management and organization studies (this one included!), Peters tells us that his choice of format stems from a recognition of (a) the size of the task that he will outline and (b) the different problems and contingencies that each organization will face. Consequently he informs us that he has prepared a manual for managers; a 'handbook for a management revolution' that, like the handbooks prepared for the users of, say, complex technological equipment, will allow managers to select those portions of the text that apply most immediately to the current issues and problems they face.

Introducing the key arguments of *Thriving on Chaos*, Peters returns to a familiar theme. Echoing the concerns outlined in *A Passion for Excellence*, which called for a 'permanent revolution' in management, *Thriving on Chaos* warns us that we should not think that we can escape the chaos that threatens to envelope each one of us.

Carroll's (1983) critical review of *In Search of Excellence*, you will recall, suggested that a company that was excellent according to the eight attributes of excellence identified by Peters and Waterman would always struggle against an organization with more general factor and/or technology advantages. Responding to this criticism, *Thriving on Chaos* insists that current advantages of size and location, or advantages in technology or marketing, provide no long term security in an environment that is increasingly complex, competitive and interconnected.

In order to persuade his readers of the self-evidently truthful nature of his alarming account of our prospects in this (newly) chaotic world, Peters once again employs the rhetorical device, which he used to good effect in *A Passion for Excellence*. Thus he threatens us; he wounds our self-image (Clark and Salaman, 1996, 1998; Jackson, 1996) and then applies the balm of his common sense approach to management to salve the fear he has engendered. *Thriving on Chaos* begins, therefore, with a quotation from Barbara Tuchman, designed (a) to unsettle those who are complacent as regards the future and (b) to disarm those inclined to disagree with Peters' account of our impending futures which we reproduce below:

Three outstanding attitudes – obliviousness to the growing disaffection of constituents, primacy of self-aggrandizement, [and the] illusion of invulnerable status – are persistent aspects of folly.

(Peters, 1987: vii, parentheses in Peters' rendering of the quotation)

In the context of Peters' earlier discussions of excellence (see Chapter 1) the message that we are supposed to take from this inscription seems clear enough: it is folly to deny the scale of the changes facing business. Those inclined to disagree with Peters' analysis of our chaotic future are delusional for Peters knows best. Peters sees further. Peters sees clearly the ways in which the forces at work in our complex and fast-paced economies will impact on every business, every career and on every home and community. And to be fair Ackman's (2002) reappraisal of the enduring legacy of the excellence project does suggest (see Chapter 1) that, from a particular standpoint, this is not entirely an idle boast.

Let us consider this rhetorical appeal in the context of the text as a whole.

Context

Discussing the factors which underpin guru success, Huczynski (1993) observes that while those vaunted as gurus may be no more wise than their, less celebrated, colleagues these honoured commentators do tend to have a knack for communication.

Looking back on the work of commentators such as F. W. Taylor (1911), who offered consultancy services to managers in the early decades of the twentieth century, Huczynski reminds us that gurus are not peculiarly a phenomenon of the 1980s. Indeed he is adamant that Taylor qualifies as a guru because of the nature and scope of the advice he offered to managers and because his counsel is essentially immune to, and hence insulated from, any serious criticism (see Collins, 2000). Yet despite this insistence that management's gurus are a product of the early twentieth century rather than a peculiarity of the 1980s, Huczynski does concede that the guru phenomenon grew rapidly in the turbulent years of this decade.

Reflecting upon those factors which the management gurus of the early 1900s share in common with more modern gurus such as Tom Peters, Huczynski argues that authors become pundits when and where they successfully produce representations of managerial work that resonate with the fears and concerns of publishers, politicians and practising managers. Reviewing a variety of these popular texts, he argues that commentators become recognized as gurus when they succeed in the production of accounts of managerial work that are (amongst other things):

* memorable (hence the focus upon alliteration)
* individually focused
* composed of a number of steps
* supportive of the managerial role.

Commenting on the world of management's gurus, Kieser (1997) essentially reproduces Huczynski's analysis. However, he does add one small, but important, rider. In keeping with Napoleon Bonaparte's famous dictum, Kieser argues that gurus need to 'be lucky' if they are to succeed. In particular he suggests that successful gurus enjoy good fortune when it comes to timing.

In 1987 Peters got lucky with his timing. Very lucky indeed!

Black Monday

Thriving on Chaos was first published in America in October 1987. Commenting on the tone and structure of this work Crainer (1997) argues that this was Peters' 'first guru book – and the first he wrote without the tempering presence of a co-author' (1997: 205). And it shows!

Like *A Passion for Excellence, Thriving on Chaos* was conceived as a book which would offer advice on the thorny problems associated with the implementation of Peters' preferred approach to management. Suggesting that Peters had been stung by the criticism applied to his earlier works, Crainer argues that the 'the roots of *Thriving on Chaos* stretch back very clearly to *In Search of Excellence* – it is basically a lengthy riposte aimed at all those critics who suggested that Peters' theories could not be turned into reality' (1997: 206).

In other times reviewers might have dwelled on the chaotic nature of the text, since as Crainer notes '*Thriving on Chaos* is true to its title. It is badly organized with an ornate numbering system for the chapters which defies explanation' (1997: 206). But in 1987, in the middle of the month of October something happened that would make Peters' analysis of the nature of chaos, and its implications for the practice of management, a hot topic for debate.

Lewis's (1992) discussion of the literary depiction of the modern workplace (see Introduction) suggests that, for many of us, Monday is a 'black day'; a day overshadowed with gloom and foreboding because it signals the start of another tiring and tedious week devoted to the necessary evils of working and commuting. However, Monday 19 October 1987 was no ordinary start to the working week. This day, which soon became known world-wide as 'Black Monday', was for many an especially gloomy and dark start to the working week because, on this autumn day, the value of stock listed on New York's Wall Street stock exchange fell by 20 per cent. Other stockmarkets world-wide also suffered similar declines in the immediate aftermath of this New York collapse. Perhaps unsurprisingly newspapers spoke of 'meltdowns' as Editorials drew attention to the interconnected nature of modern economies and the global collapse in economic confidence. Suddenly the headline message of *Thriving on Chaos* seemed real and persuasive. Who could now reasonably deny that the world of business is complex and chaotic? *Context*, not for the first time, had stepped into the breach which the *content* of Peters' analysis had often struggled to fill.

Content

Peters, as we have seen, introduced *Thriving on Chaos* by rehearsing Tuchman's warnings as regards the dangers of self-deception. Given this concern over the folly of self-aggrandizement, it may come as a surprise to find that within the first few pages of *Thriving on Chaos*, Peters bestows upon himself the elusive qualities of leadership and vision, which in *A Passion for Excellence* he was happy to celebrate in others.

In *Thriving on Chaos*, therefore, Peters speaks of *his* knowledge, *his* practice and *his* vision for the future. Indeed he seems to elevate himself above the in-house managerial leader that he celebrated in *A Passion for Excellence* to become both 'hero' and 'narrator' for our chaotic times. In *Thriving on Chaos*, therefore, Peters is revealed not as 'the guide on the side' but as the 'sage on the stage'[1] and from this exalted position, as the paramount business leader, he conveys his stark message: that there are no longer any 'excellent' companies.

Harking back to the quotation from Tuchman, which prefaces his analysis, Peters implies that companies which consider themselves to be 'excellent' have embraced the three persistent aspects of folly, and so will surely fail. Other more aware organizations, he warns, will take advantage of what we might term the complacent folly of excellence, to undermine what, in less chaotic times, might have been a sustainable market advantage. In this regard the text of 1987 might be viewed as an extension of the logic of *A Passion for Excellence*. Thus, in different ways, Peters' texts of 1985 and 1987 warn us that organizations cannot *be* excellent because the chaotic nature of the business environment obliges companies and individuals to strive towards a goal that is constantly moving and hence unattainable as a state.

In an attempt to help organizations in this never-ending journey, Peters breaks from previous practice. In earlier texts he had discussed the necessity of business change. Furthermore, he had chosen to illustrate the problematic nature of organizational change with stories and vignettes and had attempted to use these narratives as a means of fostering wider debate and reflection. Thus *A Passion for Excellence* developed a whole raft of questions and topics for discussion designed to allow managers to embark on the processes of reflection that would lead organizations to develop appropriate responses to the issues that this reflection would throw up. Yet in *Thriving on Chaos*, Peters apparently now more confident in the role of guru is impatient with this gentler and more facilitative approach. The problems *and* the answers now seem clear to Peters. Consequently he disposes with the questions and instead adopts a more prescriptive tone.

In total *Thriving on Chaos* offers a basket of 45 prescriptions designed to ensure that managers commit to change being the only constant. Yet, as we shall see, there is something rather hollow about a prescription for chaos.

The nature of chaos

In the late 1980s a body of rather complex mathematical thinking known variously as 'complexity science' or 'chaos theory' became a 'hot topic' in many forms of academic and popular discourse. Chaos theory, if you will, became fashionable. In lecture theatres and in bars people discussed chaos theory. Chaos theory even found its way on to the 'silver screen'.

In the film *Jurassic Park* the actor Jeff Goldblum appears as a handsome, if philandering, mathematician schooled in the science of chaos and complexity (*if dinosaurs can be brought back to life by genetic engineering I suppose mathematicians can be sexy!*). Goldblum's role brings a degree of colour and an additional character dimension to this film. But, perhaps more importantly, this mathematician plays an important role in the film's plotting because Goldblum's character warns us – the audience – at the outset that the science of complexity demonstrates that any attempt to regulate the chaotic forces of nature will tend to conclude in catastrophic failure. The problem for the owners of *Jurassic Park*, and for the cast more generally, is that while the fact of this failure is broadly predictable, the nature, flow and consequences of the predicted breakdown are much more difficult to foresee.

Examining the implications of chaos thinking for management practice Letiche (2000) offers a critical appreciation of the science of complexity. He argues that theorizing on complexity and chaos is shaped by a concern with:

- process
- emergence
- self-organization.

In addition Letiche draws our attention to the diversity of thought, and by implication, practice which can be disguised by a tendency to assume that everyone understands and employs 'complexity theory' in the same way. Thus he notes that 'complexity theory can be conceptualized as a collection of new anti-mechanistic metaphors stressing process and *emergence*; it can also be conceptualized as the modelling via (mathematical) computational experiments of how events self-organize' (Letiche, 2000: 545, original emphasis). Reflecting upon the managerial implications of these, now potentially competitive and contestable, metaphors, Grint (1997b) offers a lucid introduction to some of the complexities which characterize this challenging field.

Grint argues that chaos theory and its broadly anti-mechanistic account of the manner in which our world adapts and changes implies six conditions that are critical to organizational analysis. Thus he tells us that the science of complexity insists that while (1) organization is both predictable and unpredictable it (2) mocks those models that would seek to forge a predictive relationship between a 'cause' and its 'effect'. This, essential unpredictability has, Grint suggests, clear implications for the practice of management. Indeed he argues that the science of chaos obliges managers to behave with caution because their actions have (3) irreversible consequences that tend to amplify in effect. Furthermore, Grint argues that chaos thinking implies that managers should allow a degree of (4) self-organization and (5) individual discretion because allowing the space for such local and adaptive responses should provide (6) the diversity of responses that are necessary to prevent the organization from suffering a complete and catastrophic collapse.

While broadly supportive of this analysis of chaos and complexity, Burnes (2005) is, nevertheless, keen to extend Grint's critique. Reviewing the body of literature concerned with 'complexity' and 'chaos', in the context of organization theory, he suggests that organizational commentators have, too often, applied this body of work in a fashion that either misunderstands or misrepresents the subtlety and diversity of this arena of scientific endeavour. For example, he observes that organizational commentators often render this body of literature in the singular – as complexity theory – whereas the truth of the matter is that this arena of scientific theorizing remains a contested terrain. Thus Burnes warns us that scientists have produced *theories* of complexity rather than a single theory of complexity that could be applied to the organizational arena with the blessing of all those who have expertise in this field of endeavour.

Letiche (2000) makes a similar point when he suggests that the field concerned with theorizing complexity is divided by a common language. Thus he argues that complexity theory 'can be interpreted to lead to both radical process thinking and to scientific realism. Complexity theorists can discuss *emergence* and self-organization . . . and actually be referring to very different universes of discourse' (Letiche, 2000: 545, original emphasis). However, Letiche warns us that organizational commentators who have sought to apply theorizing on complexity have, too often, failed to acknowledge the existence of these oppositional universes of discourse.

Pursuing the implications of this distortion, Burnes and Letiche warn us that organizational commentators have proceeded to apply their chosen theories of complexity *as if* this science offered only one model of our chaotic world when, in fact, it offers many 'different universes of discourse' (Letiche, 2000: 545). In addition they suggest that organizational theorists also tend to apply their preferred (and distorting) models of chaos in a very limited way. Thus Burnes (2005) suggests that organizational commentaries on chaos and complexity tend to invoke the science of complexity as a simple metaphor for disorder. However, both he and Grint (1997b) protest that scientists interested in the non-linear dynamic processes of complex systems actually have a concern with 'orderly disorder'.

Orderly disorder

It would be fair to say that the ambition of normal modes of scientific theorizing is to generate, through careful and detached observation, models of the world which can forge a predictive relationship between cause and effect. In this respect the prosecutors of normal science have an abiding concern with order.

Complexity theorists, however, reject this orderly account of the world because they argue that systems grow and change in unpredictable ways which cannot be apprehended by linear models of the world.

Yet complexity theorists also recognize that chaos has orderly elements. This recognition, they argue, makes our complex adaptive systems somewhat para-doxical insofar as they are both orderly and disorderly, predictable and unpre-dictable. For scientists of complexity, therefore, the world is chaotic insofar as complex adaptive systems outpace our attempts at purposeful intervention. That is to say that complex adaptive systems elude our attempts to predict, apprehend or, otherwise, control them. Yet at the same time complexity theorists argue that the chaos and turbulence we experience is patterned by a set of 'order generating rules', which are replicated as the overall system adapts.

Acknowledging this paradoxical element of complexity theorizing Letiche (2000), however, counsels caution. He protests that in the organizational arena, notions of self-organization have been applied in ways which neglect the funda-mental differences between, say, a weather system and our own healthcare system. Thus in common with Burnes (2005), Letiche argues that complexity theorizing tends to lose something in translation when it is transported from the natural to the social scientific world. Elaborating on this point Burnes observes that there is a need to acknowledge that, whereas the rules of self-organization which govern the underlying pattern of change in a chemical reaction reflect the laws of common chemistry, the order-generating rules that pattern change in human systems are, more properly, viewed as outcomes of human volition and interpretation, which defy our predictive ambitions.

More pithily Letiche complains that those who have sought to apply the science of complexity to organizational matters have failed to elaborate on the relationship between human consciousness and organizational complexity. Con-sequently Letiche warns us that while many organizational theorists speak confi-dently of self-organization, they have too often failed to reflect upon what such notions of self-organization might imply of and for our notion of self.

Mindful of the far-reaching consequences of such subtle distinctions, Burnes also warns us that chaos thinking has been further translated, and prematurely transformed, into a body of normative prescriptions which purport to explain exactly what managers must do to remain competitive in an arena that is said to be newly chaotic. The problem being, of course, that these normative prescriptions have a reductionist concern with and for prediction, which tends to undermine any attempt to appreciate the fundamental complexity of social organization.

Given these comments on both the nature and the limits of complexity theo-rizing, how does Peters' (1987) attempt to apply the science of chaos to the arena of management actually stack up?

An unsettling world

In our previous chapter we observed that critics of Peters have, too often, failed to acknowledge that this commentator has produced accounts of business and organization that, despite flaws in methodology and conceptualization, convey essential truths about the complex and contestable world of management. With this point in mind, therefore, it is important that we acknowledge that, at some level, all of Peters' key works on management prior to 1987 have had some flavour of chaos thinking as this has been elaborated by Grint (1997b). Peters' co-authored texts of 1982 and 1985, for example, each recognized elements of chaos thinking insofar as they suggested that the successful organizations of this period recognized (a) the limits of managerial control, (b) the inevitability of self-organization, (c) the vainglorious nature of 'hard' approaches to management, and so, (d) celebrated the virtues of local action, rule-breaking and individual discretion.

It is clear, then, that at some level all of Peters' texts on managing seem to recognize the managerial paradoxes which a chaotic view of the world throw up. And yet at the same time other aspects of Peters' work remain linear, mechanistic and, above all, stubbornly anti-chaotic in their orientations and suppositions. For example Peters:

1   seems to view chaos as a new development; a new epoch which is itself a product of social, economic and technological change. However, Letiche is adamant that chaos is an intrinsic feature of systems that is revealed when we apply non-mechanical metaphors to our attempts to appreciate the world. In this regard we might voice the suspicion that, for Peters, chaos remains a simple synonym for disorder *and* a marketing device designed to unfreeze managerial attitudes to change (Lewin, 1947), which has the additional benefit of excusing oversights and limitations in his analysis which may be written-off or excused as evidence of the paradoxes thrown up by our newly chaotic system.

2   tells us that systems are chaotic and are, hence, prone to wild fluctuations which are unpredictable and have irreversible effects. And yet he also assumes that these chaotic systems may be controlled culturally through the elusive qualities of some amorphous thing he places at the head of the organization and labels carelessly as leadership (see Chapter 1).

3   assumes that the organizations, which constitute this, our chaotic world, will react to his 45 prescriptions in a useful, orderly and predictable fashion.

Pulling this together we can see clear differences between Peters' account of 'chaos' and the analytical reviews of this complex area of scholarship discussed in this chapter. Thus Letiche (2000) and Burnes (2005) are clear that complexity thinking has useful implications for organizational analysis because its anti-mechanistic approach reveals the essential complexity that is denied by more conventional modes of thinking, which retain an ordering impulse. Yet, for Peters, chaos represents, not so much a mode of thinking, as a new epoch of organizing that has been ushered in by the processes of technological change and economic deregulation.

Furthermore, Letiche and Burnes also observe that complexity theorizing challenges our most basic and fundamental assumptions as regards the nature and practice of management. Yet in Peters' peculiar account of our newly chaotic system there persists a model of management that would be familiar to the architects of the 'Human Relations' school of management (see Roethlisberger and Dickson, 1964), which is represented with new metaphors as a viable response to the problems thrown up by our interconnected economies.

Overall then, Peters' analysis of the management of chaos might be said to be more contradictory than chaotic. His text of 1987 begins by announcing a new world of chaos but concludes with the assurance that such inherent complexity can be channelled, controlled and, ultimately, made to serve the will of skilful managerial leaders. Now what were the three persistent aspects of folly?

Liberation Management

Peters' next offering was published in 1992 soon after the Gulf War that was fought by a coalition of forces in order to secure the liberation of Kuwait from the occupying forces of the Iraqi military. In this book Peters, once again, promised a management revolution. To this end, and reflecting the book's production during a time of war (see Swofford, 2006 for one man's account of this war), Peters argued that practitioners of *Liberation Management* (Peters, 1992) should become 'corporate scud missiles'.

Metaphorical misadventures

Discussing the nature of science and the business of academic writing Latour (1987) argues that all writers – even the most reclusive of this breed – have to be skilled networkers and, to some degree, poets. Elaborating on the reasoning that underpins this claim, Latour tells us that authors have to acquire and develop the skills of the poet and the characteristics of the politician because readers are devious and obstinate 'contrarians' who are naturally disinclined to accept the perfectly reasonable statements as to the nature of the world, which scientists (of all types) toil to prepare.

In an attempt to overcome the objections of these 'contrary' readers Latour observes that academic authors of all disciplines – whether they be scientists or social scientists – must take steps to:

1   Forge alliances with other writers who can provide the evidential support that will demolish the fortress of 'the contrarians'. A few moments ago I took steps to build a network that would do just this. For example, I drew upon the support of Latour in my efforts to convince you, my readers, that we should pause to reflect on the essential nature of academic writing. In addition I allowed myself a few poetic flourishes: I conjured a collective noun – 'contrarians' – to label and thence to disarm my opponents. Furthermore I dragged these 'contrarians' from their normal places of business and placed them all in a fortress, which I then scheduled for demolition!

2   Convey their now, jointly authored arguments in a fashion that readers will
     find pleasing, and so worth repeating. To this end Latour notes that acade-
     mic authors regularly employ metaphorical forms of expression (such as the
     metaphor of chaos) and other more poetic flourishes in their analyses.

     In this regard it is worth observing that a few moments ago I took steps
     to bring a degree of pace and memorability to my analysis of the craft of
     writing. I gathered together all of those inclined to disagree with my work,
     labelled them as 'contrarians' and placed them in a fortress under siege. Ini-
     tially I had placed the 'contrarians' in *fortresses*, but I quickly changed this
     (rubbing the offending plurals from the page with my eraser) because I felt
     that it (a) strained the metaphor – in truth I doubt that my own network has
     the capacity to besiege many fortresses at once and (b) handed the
     metaphorical advantage back to my opponents inasmuch as the existence of
     many outposts of opposition to my ideas would, almost inevitably, lead to
     me being recast as '*the* contrarian', out of step with the majority who tend,
     naturally, to become identified with/as reasoned opinion.

In preparing his commentaries on the business of management Peters, like all
authors, has taken steps to forge networks and to construct metaphorical forms
of analysis as he attempts to convince us of the soundness of his case for change.
However, he often makes poor choices when it comes to the selection of
metaphorical devices – whether these be metaphors for chaos that turn out to be
profoundly unchaotic (see above) or metaphorical references to anal retentive-
ness that are linked to disturbing images of loosening (see Crainer, 1997).

These ill-advised metaphorical choices tend to undermine Peters' case (as
you would expect) *and* allow me opportunities for amusing, yet purposeful,
diversions. Thus it is worth observing that Peters' account of the manager as
'corporate scud missile', which features in *Liberation Management*, has always
troubled me.

On scud missiles

The scud missile, as you may recall, was a weapon deployed by Iraqi forces in
the first Gulf War. Originally developed by the Soviet Union in the 1960s the
scud missile was a direct descendant of the German V2 weapon that rained
down on London and the south east of England during the Second World War.
In common with the earlier 'V' weapon, the scud missile is inaccurate, often
unreliable and has a limited range. As a battlefield weapon it is, by and large, an
unsatisfactory means of delivering conventional weapons technology (the military and the suppliers of military ordnance have a preference for language forms
that turn the business of killing into a form of applied logistics). However, the
scud missile does have a use as a weapon of terror and was used by Iraqi forces
in 1991 to target (in the loosest possible sense of the term) civilian populations
in Israel and Saudi Arabia.

At one level, of course, Peters' support for what might be termed a scud missile approach to management is clearly a continuation of his support for ways of doing business, which celebrate energy, action and enthusiasm. But surely there must be a better metaphor for this than the metaphor of the corporate scud missile!

Does Peters really want us to think of the weapons of the oppressor as his preferred route to liberation? Does he really think that the future of management lies in the hands of those who – like the scud missile – lack direction, behave erratically and have limited capabilities? Let us see.

Context

Liberation Management was first published in America in 1992, a decade after the publication of *In Search of Excellence* in 1982. In common with this, the first of Peters' key texts on management, *Liberation Management*, surveyed an American economy in recession. At this time unemployment in the US was running at a rate of 7 per cent.

Fears concerning instability, dislocation and unemployment obviously play a major role in guru theorizing and we should not underestimate the extent to which gurus (and politicians more generally) seek to capitalize on our basic fears and insecurities. Nevertheless Crainer (1997) suggests that *Liberation Management* should be thought of as a product of Tom Peters' own, very personal, insecurities.

Commenting on the genesis of this text, Crainer argues that the origins of *Liberation Management* can be traced back to a televised debate between the author and Robert Reich (who would later become the United States Secretary of State for Labor) that was screened on CNN in 1985. Crainer tells us that Reich gave Peters a very public lesson on the history of trade and industrial policy in this debate. Indeed Crainer argues that Tom Peters was acutely embarrassed by his ignorance in these areas.

Being, like so many other top management consultants, both intellectually bright and psychologically insecure (see Crainer, 1997), Peters decided that he had to remedy the gap in his education which Robert Reich had so publicly exposed. Consequently he spent the summer of 1985 attempting to get to grips with economic history and, boldly as ever, began drafting a book on trade policy. This book on trade policy was later abandoned, but much of the preparatory reading later resurfaced in *Liberation Management*, which as we shall see made a return to the basic methods of *In Search of Excellence* despite abandoning much of the headline message of this earlier text.

Content

In Search of Excellence, you will recall, derived its authority from a programme of field research which sought to construct a model of business excellence by analysing the conduct of managers in a sample of high performance organizations. However, *A Passion for Excellence* and *Thriving on Chaos* both reject such an approach in favour of a line of argumentation that derives its authority from common sense and its content and energy from recounted conversations that had often taken place during Peters' seminars. In *Liberation Management,* however, Peters returned to the method of *In Search of Excellence* insofar as he made some attempt to gather primary data on management and organization in the period which he described with a metaphorical flourish (of course) as the 'nano-second nineties'.

To call this data-gathering exercise a programme of academic research, however, would be to give it false airs. Too often, what Peters passes off as an authoritative commentary on the actual management practices of a particular organization is, in truth, more properly represented as the outcome of a relatively brief interview with the founder or Chief Executive – that was, in any case, shaped by Peters' *a priori* concerns and personal convictions. Furthermore it is important to note that most of these interviews were contracted-out to freelance business journalists who would plainly have a vested interest in delivering field reports that reflected Peters' own concerns and preoccupations. Commenting on this process of data gathering Crainer observes:

> What is interesting about this approach is that Peters and his researchers often went into the companies with largely preconceived ideas of what they were looking for and wanted to find. The research was to some extent a self-fulfilling prophecy.
>
> (Crainer, 1997: 229)

What was it that Peters wanted and needed to find? Companies with energy and vitality; companies that were impatient with bureaucracy; companies that delivered in the absence of traditional organizational structures (and strictures); in brief the sort of companies that Peters had previously vaunted as 'excellent'. Given this, the core argument of *Liberation Management* is somewhat surprising inasmuch as it seeks to reverse the message of *In Search of Excellence.*

The structure of revolutions

Peters begins *Liberation Management* (Peters, 1992) by noting that his earlier books on management and organizing had been flawed. These earlier works, he tells us, had failed to comprehend, and so had failed to embrace, the forms of thinking required to engender a revolution in management. Notably Peters argues that each of his works prior to *Liberation Management* had a tendency to 'put the cart before the horse'. Thus he argues that while *In Search Of Excellence* and *A Passion for Excellence* urged managers to get close to the customer, the tendency to study action and to ignore structure, evident in both of these works, actually prevented managers from understanding that it tends to be organizational structures which obstruct the achievement of total customer satisfaction.

To remedy this oversight Peters, perhaps unsurprisingly, advocates a more structural form of analysis. Yet it might be countered that this renewed concern with structure amounts to a false dawn because Peters soon announces that it is a commitment to demolishing organizational structures, and a commitment to 'necessary disorganization', which holds the key to the revolution required. That Peters moves so quickly *from* recognizing the importance of 'structure' *to* announcing the need for the outright demolition of such organizational structures is disappointing because, in highlighting the limits of his previous 'action orientation', he actually stumbles over a key criticism that might be attached to most of management's gurus.

The limits to guru thinking

Discussing the nature of guru theorizing Huczynski (1993) observes that successful gurus devise and market accounts of managerial work which suggest, somewhat optimistically, that individual managers – when armed with the appropriate tools and technologies – can bring about positive and lasting change within their employing organizations (see also Kieser, 2003). Commenting on the validity of such advice Pettigrew (1985) has argued that it tends to be both flawed and misleading because it refuses to take account of the ways in which existing organizational structures might act to forestall, or to condition, managerial choices and managerial action. Thus Pettigrew argues that much of the advice on managing change that has been targeted at managers is unhelpful because it fails to understand that embedded structures and pre-existing institutional arrangements tend to set very definite limits as regards the viability of certain courses of action. Summarizing his concern with the advice targeted at managerial practitioners, therefore, Pettigrew suggests that guru advice on the problems of change management is flawed because it is acontextual, aprocessual and ahistorical in its analytical approach.

Reflecting on these issues Pettigrew does seem to concede that management's gurus may well have good reason to be impatient with the limitations of existing structures and policies. Nevertheless he argues that it would be folly to assume that pre-existing arrangements can be changed quickly and/or simply to accord with managerial aspirations.

Discussing the UK car maker, Austin-Rover, Williams and his co-authors (Williams *et al.*, 1987) echo this point and offer us a useful, concrete example of the ways in which previous decisions, embedded policies and institutional arrangements served to circumscribe managerial action in this organization. Indeed these authors demonstrate the ways in which particular assumptions concerning market expectations (that the Mini Metro, later renamed the Rover 100 would achieve volume sales) led Austin-Rover's management to make choices as regards production technology (they chose a dedicated as opposed to a flexible form of production technology on the understanding that the Metro car would enjoy a position in the market that would justify this dedicated form of production investment). Furthermore the authors observe that these misguided assumptions and choices as regards (a) the market potential of the car and (b) the most cost-effective means of producing this car set a context for future decisions which, effectively, prevented managers from exploring new options and new strategic directions within the company as a whole.

Surveying this sort of outcome Peters would probably protest that his account of organizational structures in *Liberation Management* has been designed to reveal the extent to which the maxim of traditional economic theorizing: that structure follows strategy is reversed by the experience of organization. Complaining that strategy tends to follow structure, therefore, *Liberation Management* argues that there is an urgent need for a remedy for this problematic state of affairs. Yet it is this focus upon change (in the absence of a feeling for continuity), and the suggestion that existing organizational structures require outright demolition, which prevents Peters from reaching a new and more developed appreciation of the realities of organizational practice.

Adding a little more detail to this critique, therefore, we might venture that Peters' (1992) account of 'necessary disorganization' fails to develop a proper appreciation of structures in context because:

1 While it would be fair to say that Peters does, indeed, acknowledge that strategy tends to follow structure, he tends to treat this outcome as an oversight and error, as a function of managerial ineptitude. Yet in the work of Pettigrew (1985) the links between context and action, and between strategy and structure, are explored in ways which suggest that these interesting dynamics constitute a fundamental element of organizational life that will not be wished away by the entrance of a new heroic leader. Thus Pettigrew's concern with structures in context produces an exploration of the limits and possibilities of action. However, Peters' concern to develop new structures for an altered context produces only exhortation. And this exhortation simply fails to recognize the limits of action and the obdurate nature of existing organizational arrangements.

2 By focusing attention on those organizations that scant research suggests enjoy the 'necessary disorganization' for future business success, Peters produces an aprocessual form of analysis insofar as he offers few insights into the transitionary process that other organizations, currently chained by their histories and bureaucracies, would be obliged to undertake *en route* to their supposed liberation.

3 Despite his claim to have rediscovered the importance of structures and the need to reconfigure structural arrangements for future success, Peters offers no meaningful account of the embedded processes and institutional mechanisms (such as trade union collective bargaining, the presence or absence of labour statutes, etc.) that shape, sustain or undermine the existing structures of business in their contemporary context.

Indeed it is ironic that a book which begins by rejecting both the method and the message of *In Search of Excellence* should culminate in a form of analysis that repeats and compounds the problems identified in Peters' earlier texts. Thus Peters uses an apparent concern with structure to generate headlines for his analysis, but actually ducks out of dealing with the most difficult and, according to his own analysis, the most pressing issues. So rather than offer a systematic analysis of structures in context, *Liberation Management* treats us to a collection of anecdotes, eulogies and reminiscences concerning the heroic qualities of those business leaders who, he tells us, have embraced 'necessary disorganization'.

Commenting on these anecdotes and reminiscences Byrne (1992b) highlights additional failings in *Liberation Management* which go beyond the academic concerns of our rather conventional critique. Thus Byrne makes two rather cutting observations on the content and style of Peters' (1992) work.

First, he argues that despite Peters' fieldwork activity, too much of the text has been derived from other publications. Consequently Byrne suggests that Peters' (1992) work lacks the power and appeal of earlier texts because too many of his observations are second-hand – clipped from magazines, books and newspapers – and formed at a distance from the real experience of managing.

Second, and more caustically, Byrne notes the size of Peters' *Liberation Management* and remarks that this guru offers good advice – if you can find it! *The Economist* (5/12/92) also offers a similarly acidic comment. Contrasting the energy and lucidity of Peters' seminars with the stamina-sapping nature of this text, this newspaper's reviewer noted that:

> A man who wants firms to 'think small' and to be accessible has ended up writing a book that is inaccessible.
>
> (96)

And concluded that no one would have the energy or desire to read more than the first 100 pages of this tangled thicket of text. Or as *The Economist* (24/9/94) later put it more pointedly:

> Mr Peters has not extended his passion for downsizing to his own prose.
>
> (73)

Crainer (1997), however, offers a more favourable review, which works hard to ignore such aesthetic limitations. *Liberation Management*, he argues, is an important path-breaking work; a text that set the scene for debates on management practice throughout the 1990s; a text that journalists still mine for quotes and examples. But is this enough?

Is it sufficient that we remember a book which promised a new structural mode of analysis and 'liberation' from the limits of existing practice as a resource for those who, like Peters, derive their key insights on business from magazine and newspaper clippings?

We now turn our attention to the two books which Peters produced in 1993 and 1994 and to the texts which followed in 1997 and 2003.

Fat work and lean years

Liberation Management is by the standards of modern business publishing a very big book (for an insider's account of this business see Hyatt, 1990; Anonymous, 1999). Peters claims to be proud of this work and claims to have enjoyed producing it. Yet the joy of writing is seldom unalloyed. In common with all long-term projects the process of writing a book has its highs and its lows, its hills and valleys. In truth it takes some fortitude to awake each morning knowing that the tyranny of the blank page awaits.

Authors tend to find different ways of expressing the difficulties they encounter as they attempt to record their thoughts and ideas. For example, I tend to speak of paper tyrants. George Orwell famously spoke of writing as an affliction. In the essay 'Why I write' (see Orwell, 1988) he observes:

> Writing a book is a horrible, exhausting struggle, like a long bout of some painful illness. One would never undertake such a thing if one were not driven by some demon whom one can neither resist nor understand.
>
> (187–188)

Some, more contemporary, writers have been heard to speak of 'thin' and 'fat work' as they discriminate between those projects which proceed at such a pace that they cause the writer to lose weight and other projects which cause the writer to gain weight.

'Thin work', as you might expect, progresses at a tremendous rate – so fast, in fact, that the author seems compelled to write at the expense of all other necessities. Consequently a 'thin work' may cause the author to suffer an alarming degree of weight loss.

'Fat work', in contrast, tends to proceed slowly and tends to enlarge its struggling progenitor as it refuses to grow. That is to say that a writer confronted by the slow pace of his/her progress may take comfort in/from food as s/he struggles to commit thoughts to print.

Viewed in these terms *Liberation Management* is properly viewed as a 'fat work', but not because it fills in excess of 850 pages (quite a contrast to the 850-word columns that had been Peters' main publication outlet between 1987 and 1992). No, *Liberation Management* is a 'fat work' in the sense that Peters gained 20 lb as he struggled to complete this text.

When we combine the fact of Peters' enlargement with the knowledge that the manuscript was delivered late to the publishers, and when we add to this Crainer's assertion that Peters developed a drink problem and chose to enter therapeutic counselling as he wrestled with his text, it seems reasonable to suggest that Peters' joy in penning *Liberation Management* was not unbounded. Indeed, given Peters' experience of writing *Liberation Management* it seems sensible to suggest that the production of this work may have exhausted Peters, draining him of the energy and inclination necessary to tackle another project in the form of his 1992 text. In this respect the struggle to produce *Liberation Management* may help to explain the character of Tom Peters' post-1992 offerings.

The Tom Peters Seminar and *The Pursuit of Wow*

In the years 1993 and 1994 Tom Peters released two texts on management and managing: *The Tom Peters Seminar* (Peters, 1993) and *The Pursuit of Wow* (Peters, 1994). The first of these texts, it would be fair to say, was dictated rather than written and emerged as an attempt to capitalize on the demand for copies of the slides which Peters uses to illustrate his seminars. In this regard *The Tom Peters Seminar* might be thought of as a Peters seminar, *circa* 1992, captured imperfectly in print and frozen in time.

The Pursuit of Wow also builds upon a stock of material that Peters had previously developed for another purpose. In this respect *The Pursuit of Wow*, like *The Tom Peters Seminar*, might be regarded as an attempt to supply market demand from inventory.

Context

Between 1987 and 1997 Peters produced a regular newspaper column that was widely syndicated. By 1994 he had produced 450 of his syndicated columns and had formed the opinion that these would make a successful book project. Commenting on this project of collation, however, Crainer suggests that *The Pursuit of Wow* failed as an attempt to meet market demand from inventory because only 20 per cent of its content actually derives from the Peters syndicated column – the remainder of the text being generated anew for the book. That the text produced in 1994 made so little use of the column archive is hardly surprising.

Good newspaper columnists produce insights into, and commentaries on, the sights, sounds and travails of everyday life. These columns if they are to attract and retain an audience must sprinkle wit, and where appropriate, anger and indignation over a canvas which captures the spirit of a particular place and time. Yet, because of this, individual columns seldom survive the process of reprinting. The witty asides and the knowing allusions that captured the spirit of the moment or the cupidity of some individual in, say, the springtime have often lost all reference come the autumn. The result being that newspaper columns, like physical comedy, seldom survive the process of retelling. The standard exclusion tends to apply to both – 'you really had to be there'. Given this it is unsurprising that readers and reviewers tend to be disappointed by the content and form of Peters' offerings of 1993 and 1994.

On content: the basic problem is that Peters' texts of 1993 and 1994 say little that – even then – was actually new because Peters had previously rehearsed many of the ideas that appeared in *Liberation Management* within his syndicated newspaper columns. Consequently *The Pursuit of Wow* – even at the time and place of its original production – seems unnecessary insofar as it often revisits or simply reproduces, in a much reduced form, ideas and arguments rehearsed in print before.

A similar argument applies to the content of Peters' seminar text. This book, you will recall, represents an attempt to capture both the ideas and the spirit of the seminars that Peters was delivering in the early 1990s. The difficulty being that in the early 1990s Peters' seminars were built largely around the arguments of *Liberation Management*. And by 1994 these ideas and arguments had gained a wider audience thanks to the 'data-mining' activities of the world's business journalists who seem to derive so much of their knowledge of Peters from libraries of press clippings.[2]

That is not to suggest, of course, that these texts of 1993 and 1994 are entirely without merit or have no interesting features. In truth the seminar text *is* intriguing because in this text Peters seems keen to introduce us, personally, to his redefined market and congregation.

A new parish?

In April 1989 Peters (1989) published a piece in *Inc* which offered a personal reflection on his career. In this article he observes that, in his early works on management, his heroes and role models for excellence had been the senior managers of *Fortune 500* companies. However, he confides that over time he has become pessimistic about the future prospects of these very large organizations. Looking back with hindsight to his second offering on 'excellence' (Peters and Austin, 1985) he tells us that on re-reading this work he can sense a growing disillusionment with America's giant corporations.

Only slowly, Peters tells us, did this changing focus and concern become apparent to him. However, by 1989 he was able to look back on his third text and observe that 'by the time I sat down to write *Thriving on Chaos* in the early winter of 1987 I had a whole new set of role models. The heroes of *In Search of Excellence* – IBM, Hewlett-Packard, 3M – had given way to the likes of Chapparral Steel and Weaver Popcorn'.

Viewed in these terms, the seminar text is interesting because in this book we see Peters seeking out, talking to and, to some extent, learning from those in the middle reaches of the occupational hierarchy, whereas in earlier texts he had reserved his time and his adulation for a small number of mavericks who sat atop their organizational trees plotting the mergers and acquisition policies, which Peters now seems to view with some suspicion (see Lorenz, 1986b for an account of Peters' ambivalence).

The Pursuit of Wow is, similarly, interesting for it too signals key changes in form and other, more minor movements in content, which have come to figure more prominently in Peters' later works.

Looking first at the shifts in content: *The Pursuit of Wow* is interesting because it introduces a key theme that has been a constant in Peters' work ever since. In this work Peters casts a critical eye over product (and service) design and rails against those organizations that, as he sees it, abuse their power. In this respect Peters' text of 1994 echoes many of the arguments put forward by Michael Hammer in his analysis of Business Process Reengineering (BPR) (Hammer, 1990). Thus Peters argues that America's largest organizations too often fail to place the customer at the heart of their business processes and, as a consequence, produce lacklustre service and shoddy products. Highlighting, as always, the competitive nature of the modern business arena, therefore, Peters (1994) argues that those businesses that wish to prosper in the future will have to rethink both their product designs and their organizational charts if they are to delight their customers. In short, Peters argues that 'the pursuit of wow' – the ability to surprise and delight customers through such things as design – is to be allowed to shape future managerial behaviour.

On the question of form there is perhaps less to say. Aside from its interesting cast list the seminar text is, in truth, scarcely worthy of further comment. It conforms to a fairly traditional narrative structure. It has, if you are prepared to persevere, 'a beginning', 'a middle' and 'an end'. Taken as a whole the seminar book is hardly compelling but it is, clearly, designed on the understanding that the reader will navigate the text in a traditional manner. That is not to say, of course, that *The Tom Peters Seminar* is just like Peters' earlier texts. The book is, in fact, distinctive in that the text is, thanks mainly to the input of the editorial firm, 'Word Works', an illuminated volume. Where earlier Peters books offered only densely packed text *The Tom Peters Seminar* is, like the texts produced in the medieval scriptorium, illustrated and illuminated by a collection of legends and inscriptions.

This illumination makes the text more welcoming and, at one level, more appealing. Yet ultimately the work fails to satisfy because, despite its decoration, it lacks the energy of the live seminar and the capacity either to build or to sustain the appropriate level of analysis.

The form of *The Pursuit of Wow* is more interesting and, I suppose, more shocking than that of the seminar text, principally because this text seems to dispense entirely with a traditional narrative structure. This work is composed of 210 related, yet distinct, elements that in different ways celebrate topics such as 'design', 'values', 'empowerment' and the skills of the managerial leader. Each of these elements is listed and discussed with just one aim in mind – to allow readers access to the tools and insights necessary to delight customers. Yet unlike *The Tom Peters Seminar* there is no 'beginning', 'middle' and 'end' to *The Pursuit of Wow*. Indeed no attempt is made to join the 210 elements of the text into a clear and consistent narrative.

Most books can be represented in linear terms as a journey, if you will, from ignorance to enlightenment, from passivity into action, from loneliness to love. Yet *The Pursuit of Wow* is different. It does not tell a story nor does it represent, in linear terms, a simple journey. Instead this book might be regarded as an exhibition, a spectacle. *Come in*, it says, *Look around. Move forwards, move backwards. Defy convention. Circulate!*

Putting this point in less florid terms we might suggest that *The Pursuit of Wow* offers a hypertextual (see Chapter 3) experience. In this respect *The Pursuit of Wow* appears to have been designed and constructed to precipitate the sort of 'yeasty responses' that will make readers and customers, more generally, shout *wow*. Yet as in the case of the scud missile, this brewing analogy represents an unfortunate choice of metaphor insofar as it provides us with the opportunity for another diversion that, as we shall see, tends to undermine Peters' preferred account of the business of management.

On yeasty responses

In suggesting the need for a 'yeasty response' to contemporary competitive dilemmas *The Pursuit of Wow* appears to demand a form of management practice that is lively, energetic and catalytic. In short Peters' text of 1994 seems to want managers to *fizz* with enthusiasm. Yet in pursuing the fuller implications of a typical yeasty response, Kurt Vonnegut (1973) warns us that such activity is inherently self-destructive.

Yeast, Vonnegut tells us, is fizzy and productive. However, he warns us that, beyond some level of activity, the activity of yeast becomes counterproductive. Indeed Vonnegut suggests that a yeasty response is inherently destructive because yeast is an organism which consumes its own environment until life in that environment (even for the yeast itself) becomes unsustainable!

Leaving such metaphorical misadventures to one side, however, it is worth pointing out that the year 1994 is significant in Peters' career as a writer and commentator on the business of management. Despite our earlier criticisms of this text, *The Pursuit of Wow* is worthy of note because in this text Peters signals a key change in his preferred form of presentation and in his preferred narrative format. This is a point that we will return to in Chapter 3. For the moment, however, we must continue with our chronological analysis of Peters' texts of 1997 and 2003.

In 1997 Peters published *The Circle of Innovation* (Peters, 1997). As we shall see this book continued with the narrative experimentation that has typified Peters' work since 1994.

The Circle of Innovation

In common with his texts of 1993 and 1994 *The Circle of Innovation* (Peters, 1997) is probably best thought of as another by-product of Peters' work as a management performance *artiste* on the lucrative seminar circuit that now allows commentators such as Peters to embark upon global lecturing tours. Introducing this text Peters tells us that *The Circle of Innovation* consists of his seminar slides, some additional explanatory text, and the combined knowledge acquired from the 400 seminars he has offered since the publication of *Liberation Management*. The sub-title of *The Circle of Innovation*, which like *The Pursuit of Wow* eschews a normal narrative structure in favour of a hypertextual format, is: 'You Can't Shrink Your Way to Greatness'. This, however, seems to contradict Peters' support in *Liberation Management* for those organizations that had pursued a strategy of downsizing their corporate staffs. Furthermore, this sub-title also seems to cause tensions with the support for radical decentralization that is evident in *The Circle of Innovation* itself. But we are not allowed to mention this.

In a typically grand and dismissive gesture, Peters tells us that all bets are off! His work *is* inconsistent, he tells us, because the world is! Only a cynic would ask for anything more. Only a cynic would venture that a tendency to reinvent the world, and to reverse your preferred pattern of thinking, is the product of the three persistent aspects of folly: the tendency to obliviousness, self-aggrandizement and the illusion of invulnerability. So at least Peters is not entirely inconsistent. These three aspects, at least, remain consistent within his pronouncements on management, even when 'excellence' is supplanted by 'innovation'.

Whither excellence?

In *The Circle of Innovation*, Peters' commitment to 'excellence' is finally and formally abandoned. Innovation, it seems, is the key to future success. However, we should note that while such pronouncements often generate useful headlines – principally because they excite the passions (and scissors) of the world's business journalists – they are seldom accurate as representations of Peters' texts. Thus we should note that, despite Peters' disavowal of excellence, it would probably be more appropriate to say that 'excellence' (striving to satisfy customers), becomes subsumed by 'innovation', since those factors previously regarded as being central to excellence – skunkworks, leadership, cultural management, change, leadership, leadership and leadership (see Collins, 2000) – now form the core of Peters' new and preferred buzzword: innovation. In this respect *The Circle of Innovation* should be read as a continuation of the key ideas and arguments that have shaped Peters' work since the 1980s. However, we should acknowledge that these continuities can be difficult to discern because this time around Peters' business beatitudes (Collins, 2000) are packaged differently. This time they are surrounded by photographs; by bold type; by bold phrasing (*yikes!*) and by what, apparently, is to be regarded as bold, profound and innovative thinking – to 'think revolution not evolution'; to work on your own ideal and not the ideal of someone else; to make mistakes; to bloody your nose; to innovate; I-N-N-O-V-A-T-E.

To convey the need for radical, business change Peters employs the eponymous 'circle of innovation'. This diagram presents an unbroken circle of innovation marked with 15 way-points. Through this device Peters seeks (a) to demonstrate the text's impatience with traditional narrative structures and (b) to highlight the core factors that, as he sees it, must underpin the process of innovation. Thus Peters' circle of innovation celebrates women as a market and as a business resource. In addition the text highlights the need for boldness as it waxes lyrical about the need for erasers and the power of mistakes. Furthermore *The Circle of Innovation* raises a rhapsody on the power of love.

But there are at least two problems with this account of innovation. The first is that Peter's praise for such things as love must be viewed with suspicion, since if inconsistency is the order of the day, then might it not be the case that management may well have to be faithless and loveless by design!

Like Peters' earlier discussion of leadership, therefore, this faith in innovation and his commitment to women and to bloody handkerchiefs seems to amount to little more than a contingent, expedient (and potentially a short-term) response to environmental 'needs'. And with this point in mind, we would do well to note that a contingent approach to management suggests that it may indeed be possible (and if we accept the logic of the market as our only metric, it may even be desirable) to shrink your way to business greatness.

The second problem with this account of innovation, in truth, is that we have heard all this before. Thus it is clear that Peters' newly found commitment to stained handkerchiefs is built upon a dualistic understanding of the world of business as a place where organizations are either conspicuously successful or conspicuous failures; where competition is, always and everywhere, 'red in tooth and claw'. And this model of the world of business was clear to see in his texts of 1982 and 1985 and was, furthermore, an element of the analytical approach which was criticized by those who reject that idea that business can be understood in such binary terms (see Van der Merwe and Pitt, 2003).

Re-imagine

Peters' 2003 offering entitled *Re-imagine* continues in much the same vein as the other texts produced since 1994, while amplifying many of the movements and trends that have been evident in this author's work since the publication of *The Pursuit of Wow*.

In common with Peters' seminar text (Peters, 1993), *Re-imagine* was 'dictated' rather than 'written'. Indeed Peters (2003) tells us that he filled around 37 audio-tapes with his thoughts on the business of management and then passed his words to a team of editors and designers who duly produced a first draft for his inspection. Given the primary role accorded to design (and designers) in the preparation of this text, it should come as no surprise that *Re-imagine* is a large and colourful text. It is much larger than any of Tom Peters' previous texts and is, in fact, about the size (and weight) of an elementary student textbook such as those prepared for students of management or economics. In common with these traditional textbooks *Re-imagine* offers a full colour presentation and is richly and vividly illuminated with photographs designed to illustrate or emphasize some aspect of Peters' text.

Yet this is no textbook. *Re-imagine* does not offer a full, rounded or balanced exegesis of the business of management as a textbook might aspire to do. It does not seek to provide readers with a coherent introduction to the complex and varied literature on management and managing. In fact reading may well be about the last thing you are supposed to do with this work, for this text is probably best thought of as a 'coffee table book'.

Coffee table books

The *Concise Oxford Dictionary* defines a coffee table book as 'a large, lavishly illustrated book'. When used in the context of everyday speech, however, these allusions to size and illustration take on particular connotations which question the essential nature and function of such books.

On my bookshelves I have a large and diverse collection of texts. I have, as you might expect, all of Tom Peters' books and pamphlets on management. I have read each of these texts on a number of occasions. However, I will confess that I do not really enjoy reading these works. I *do* enjoy the fiction of John Steinbeck and the non-fiction works of George Orwell. And when I get the chance to read a book, solely for my own enjoyment, I often select a book written by one of these authors from my shelves. On top of my bookshelves I have a number of the large and lavishly illustrated works that the *Concise Oxford* labels as 'coffee table books'.

My current favourite among these coffee table books is William Fotheringham's (2003a) *A Century of Cycling*. I was given this book as a Christmas present some time ago but I still look at it regularly, mainly because I derive a lot of enjoyment from its photographs of the legends of the world of professional cycling. And this, I suppose, is the thing that distinguishes my coffee table books from the other texts on my bookshelves which contain stories and essays. I *read* Steinbeck's fiction, I *study* Orwell's essays but I *look at* my coffee table books.

The fact that I employ these books in different ways does not, I think, reflect badly on me. I do not use Steinbeck's talents and abuse Fotheringham's because, the truth is, coffee table books are not actually meant to be read! Instead these texts are supposed to be held, admired and appreciated for their beauty as objects with an intrinsic artistic merit.[3]

Beauty, famously, is said to be in the eye of the beholder so I will not seek to impose my aesthetic sensibilities (or lack thereof) upon you the reader. You must judge for yourself the extent to which Peters' text provides a pleasing addition to the world of internal furnishing. For the moment, however, we will endeavour to maintain the symmetry of our chapter. Accordingly, we will proceed *as if* this text was meant for reading as we examine its (written) contents.

Content

Re-imagine, in common with all of Peters' texts produced since 1993, represents an attempt to capture the energy and excitement that those who attend Peters' seminars report as the defining feature of his stage performances. To this end the text is built around, and derives its energy from, the 'stories' and 'rants' – Peters' apparently bad-tempered complaints about the foibles and frailties of modern corporations and modern corporate thinking – that are used to introduce the various component parts of this work.

Of course *The Tom Peters Seminar* (Peters, 1993) was similarly built around the 'stories' and diatribes that Peters uses to convey his concerns to a live audience. Yet, as we have seen, this text fails to capture the essence of Peters' seminar performances because through the processes of transcription it has been channelled into a rather traditional and linear form of analysis that is quite unlike the creation that emerges when Peters interacts with his audience. This recognition of the difference between speaking to, and writing for, an audience, between living and recounting events in print, may help to explain another important feature of this text: its annotations and 'side bars'. Thus *Re-imagine* continually directs the reader's attention to 'marginal notes', designed, it seems, to expand or to explore an element of the main body of the text.

These 'marginal' features of the book work to reacquaint areas of the text divided by the normal conventions of typography *and*, as in everyday speech, provide the reader with digressions and diversions which s/he may choose to follow as preferences dictate.

And yet, for me, *Re-imagine* just does not work as an account of the problems of, and prospects for, management. It fails either to excite or to illuminate for despite its stylistic accomplishments, the actual text offers little that is new, memorable or surprising. Indeed Peters (2003: 83) concedes that the text of *Re-imagine* essentially replays the core elements of the speeches and seminars that he has offered his congregation since 1998. Consequently the text is familiar to those who know anything of Peters' pet concerns. Furthermore *Re-imagine* is often charmless and tedious despite its illumination and colourful setting.

Women, design, trust and imagination all make their entry exactly on cue as the author urges us to embrace good design and to make the most of women's potential – as a market to sell things to! Following the attack on New York in 2001 we are treated to a short account of the power and potential of the network organization. Yet all this is depressingly familiar, it's just that in earlier texts (Peters and Waterman, 1982; Peters and Austin, 1985) these networks were dubbed as 'skunk works'.

Reflecting the analysis first introduced in *In Search of Excellence* (Peters and Waterman, 1982) *Re-imagine* devotes a whole chapter to stories and storytelling. In this chapter Peters insists that the art of management and the arts of the storyteller are indivisible. Those with the best narratives, he tells us, have the most committed employees and the most ardent customers. Yet despite this, *Re-imagine* actually offers few real stories. And those few stories that Peters actually relays are, truthfully, seldom interesting, surprising or memorable in short, they are seldom worth retelling.

Perhaps the fact that Peters dictated this text explains the paucity of stories. Perhaps Peter's growing frustration with the corporate world (see Chapter 3) and his increasing willingness to season his prescriptions with bad-tempered ranting explains the absence of plotting and characterization in this, his most recent, narrative of management. Whatever the reason, one thing is clear: Peters' (2003) work lacks charm and wit. Too often narratives with the clear potential to become both entertaining and (from a managerial perspective) productive stories are either stripped of necessary motive and characterization or are cut short (Peters, 2003: 121), and so robbed of a satisfactory conclusion (see Chapter 4).

Despite the efforts of a whole design team, the format of the book is also familiar and yet somewhat perplexing. *Re-imagine*, in common with *The Circle of Innovation* and *The Pursuit of Wow*, it seems, has been designed to avoid the strictures of the traditional narrative – that is the need to tell a structured story that is ordered and coherent. The problem being that this impatience with the corporate world *and* with the normal traditions of narrative and narration means that the text, for all its illumination, seems to have been thrown up by the author and simply thrown at the reader!

Commenting on this *The Economist* (20/12/2003), eloquently as ever, noted:

> This is clearly not a book that is meant to be read – not at least by the traditional method of starting at the beginning and proceeding to the end. Its remorselessly shrill tone, alternating between the shocking and the motivational ... could easily cause a normal brain to explode after half an hour's continuous exposure. No, this is a book for dipping into for five minutes at a time in search of nuggets of wisdom, a sort of 'daily reader' for followers of Mr Peters' brand of management religion. It may well achieve its goal of taking management ideas to a new younger audience, aged around 30, being famous for their short attention span and need for instant impact and gratification.

Commenting on the consequences of this mode of analysis and presentation *The Economist* speculates on the real 'impact' of this text, and so produces a review that has something of the tone of an obituary. In a parting shot, therefore, the newspaper's reviewer notes:

> if the medium is the message, the message in this case is that business thinkers such as Mr Peters have become a lot less coherent than they were [25] years ago.

Given the criticism that rained down upon Peters' early works, and the controversies that have followed him ever since, this review of *Re-imagine* seems to suggest that this guru's estate is undercapitalized and rapidly diminishing. Surely a sad legacy for 25 years of work and international travel?

Summary

This chapter has offered a critical review of the key works on management produced by Tom Peters since 1987. In keeping with the format developed in Chapter 1 this account of Peters' work has been focused upon 3Cs, namely the *context* and *content* of this author's work and the *criticisms* – both accurate and inaccurate; justified and unjustified – which have been applied to his arguments and orientations. Yet in other ways these chapters differ.

Chapter 1, you will recall, spent a fair amount of time detailing the academic criticism that has been voiced in opposition to the excellence project. Discussion of the academic reaction to Peters' 'guru works', however, is more-or-less absent from Chapter 1, largely because the academic establishment has tended to ignore the more recent works of Peters. That is not to say, of course, that Chapter 2 is devoid of academic commentary. In fact we have sought to demonstrate the ways in which academic analysis of the controversies associated with such things as 'chaos' and 'structure' offer the insights necessary both to reveal and to pierce Peters' rhetoric on the nature of business and the conduct of management.

In the chapter that follows we will move on from the chronological method of analysis employed in Chapters 1 and 2 as we develop the concern with narrative, which was signalled in our discussions of *The Pursuit of Wow, The Circle of Innovation* and *Re-imagine* contained in this chapter.

3   Crazy days call for crazy ways?
Narrating Tom Peters[1]

Introduction

Let us begin this chapter by briefly revisiting our earlier discussions. The management commentator, Tom Peters rose to prominence in the early 1980s. He has been at the forefront of the billion-dollar industry that provides managers with advice and exhortation on organizational matters for some 25 years.

Yet despite this he remains a controversial character; a man who excites and polarizes opinion. He has been celebrated and vilified in turn. For some Tom Peters is a guru (see Kennedy, 1996, 1998; Crainer, 1998a). For others he is, if not a venerable guru, then at least a cause for celebration because, through his works and pronouncements, he has 'vivified, popularized and legitimized management' (Crainer, 1997: 275). To many in academia, however, he is a target for debunking. Indeed many academics have dismissed Peters as a purveyor of aphorisms and epigrams, which masquerade as sound analysis and sage advice (see for example Guest, 1992).

Much of this academic criticism is, of course, fully deserved. As we saw in the previous chapters commentators have observed that *In Search of Excellence* (Peters and Waterman, 1982) is the product of a suspect methodology and a flawed sampling mechanism (Carroll, 1983; Guest, 1992). Conversely Peters' follow-up work, *A Passion for Excellence* (Peters and Austin, 1985) has been criticized because it offers an inadequate theorization of the business of management in the absence of both a methodology and a sample population (Collins, 2000). Operating at a more aesthetic level of criticism, Crainer (1997) has also complained that later works such as *Liberation Management* (Peters, 1992) are confused, ill-structured and over-lengthy in their analyses and expositions. Yet despite these attacks Tom Peters has achieved a global, mass market for his books and seminars. Furthermore he has sustained this market for a quarter of a century.

In this chapter we will reflect upon the literary career of Tom Peters. Observing an oft-repeated Peters maxim: 'crazy days call for crazy ways', we will offer a distinctive analysis and reappraisal of this author's work as we suggest that Peters' narrative of organization and management has, itself, become increasingly crazed and fragmented. Analysing the changes evident in Peters' writings on management we will suggest that his narrative experimentation signals a growing frustration with orthodox forms of writing and a growing impatience with the elite of the corporate world. Furthermore, we will argue that the narrative changes evident in Peters' work reflect a desire to forge links with middle America and with the small and middle-sized business that, as Peters sees it, represents the way ahead for the US economy (Peters, 1989).

Accordingly, the chapter is structured as follows. In the next section we construct a stylistic as opposed to a chronological ordering of Peters' work. Having suggested this stylistic ordering, we will then attempt to rationalize the changes observed. To this end we will offer eight overlapping explanations for Peters' narrative experimentation. Finally we will reflect upon the ways in which this attempt to narrate Tom Peters might be used to inform future research. One branch of this research agenda will be explored in Chapter 4, where we subject this guru's storytelling to sustained academic scrutiny.

Another look at the work of Peters

By convention accounts of Tom Peters' canon have tended to offer chronological analyses of his texts (Crainer, 1997; Collins, 2000; Heller, 2000). Such chronological renderings are, of course, blessed by the twin virtues of simplicity and transparency. However, in this chapter we will argue that there is another means of structuring Peters' work, which sacrifices neither virtue. Indeed, we will argue that our alternative rendering of the literary career of Peters actually serves to improve our understanding of this commentator.

Discussing management's 'fads and buzzwords' I (Collins, 2000) note changes in the narrative structure of Peters' work. In making this observation I was treading a path previously worn by Stuart Crainer (1997), who has also highlighted key changes in Peters' mode of analysis and expression. Yet neither Crainer or I have sought to explain nor have we pursued the implications of the narrative changes observed. In this chapter we will seek to remedy this oversight. Accordingly, we will offer an account of Peters' texts, designed to explore and to explain the changes in the narrative structure of this pundit's works, which until now have evaded detailed academic scrutiny.

Reflecting our concern with the narrative form of this guru's texts we will review the key works of Tom Peters, which we listed in Chapters 1 and 2. On the strength of this review we will argue that this commentator has produced no fewer than four distinctive narratives of management since he burst on to the market for business books in 1982.

Yet, before we proceed further with this analysis we must first acknowledge that our narrative analysis of Tom Peters omits a number of this author's texts on management. Crucially this listing excludes the '50' series (Peters, 1999a, 1999b, 1999c) and the 'Essentials' collection (Peters and Barletta, 2005a, 2005b, 2005c, 2005d) on the understanding that these texts are either:

- 'signature' products; products written by others in the main but branded through the application of the Tom Peters label (the '50' series) or

- collections or summaries of ideas previously offered in the book *Re-imagine*, which have been repackaged to provide travel/airline-friendly editions (the 'Essentials' collection).

In addition we must also acknowledge that our narrative review of this commentator's work also omits the pamphlets published by the Tom Peters Group. These pamphlets (which omit the normal publisher's information such as date and place of publication) have titles such as:

- *Project 04: Snapshots of Excellence in Unstable Times*
- *Women Roar: The New Economy's Hidden Imperatives*
- *We Are in a Brawl with No Rules*
- *The Death Knell for 'Ordinary': Pursuing Difference*
- *Re-inventing Work: The Work Matters!*

The pamphlets listed above – which vary in length from just 11 pages to some 80 pages – are excluded from the current analysis because like the 'Essentials' collection they offer, in effect, summaries of ideas and arguments that may be found in a more developed form in the eight key texts discussed in Chapters 1 and 2.

In search of Tom Peters

Tom Peters is perhaps best known for his first management text, *In Search of Excellence*, which he published with Bob Waterman in 1982. That Peters is best known for this text is somewhat ironic since within the corpus of his work this book is anomalous. *In Search of Excellence* occupies this aberrant position within the Peters catalogue because, unlike all the other texts produced in the name of this author, it utilizes a continuous narrative structure to report the results of a rather traditional (if questionable) piece of business research. None of the texts produced in the name of Tom Peters since 1982 has sought to confirm a research hypothesis by means of sampling and/or statistical analysis. Given this it seems sensible to suggest that *In Search of Excellence* occupies a category on its own – a category of continuous narrative work – we will label as 'hypothesis-driven, sample-based research'.

In common with *In Search of Excellence*, Peters' follow-up text, *A Passion for Excellence*, which was produced in concert with Nancy Austin in 1985, retains a traditional narrative format whereby the argument of the text is constructed by means of a series of linked chapters which work, summatively, to produce a (more-or-less) cogent analysis. A similar narrative structure is also employed in two later texts: *Liberation Management* (Peters, 1992) and *The Tom Peters Seminar* (Peters, 1993). Yet unlike *In Search of Excellence* these three texts make no pretence to the norms of academic research: there is no sample population and no working hypothesis is exposed to the possibility of refutation in any of these later works. Instead these texts are driven by Peters' conviction and self-belief. Thus the works of 1985, 1992 and 1993 articulate:

- a belief in the virtues of common sense (see Collins, 1996, 2000),
- a belief that the practice of management has been hamstrung by the analytical tools and practices demanded by the academy and by the board (see Peters and Austin, 1985),
- a belief that good management is simple in purely cognitive terms, but problematic in socio-political terms – hence the focus upon 'the leadership difference' (Peters and Austin, 1985).

Given this focus upon common sense, we have labelled these three texts as 'belief-driven, continuous narratives' in distinction to the 'hypothesis-driven, sample-based research' narrative evident in our first categorization.

Thriving on Chaos produced in 1987 works within a narrative tradition that is unlike the categories so far delineated. Utilizing what might be termed a 'hub and spokes' approach (see Gabriel, Fineman and Sims, 1992, 2000; Collins, 2000 for other examples of this type of structure), this third type of text obliges readers to study a small number of introductory chapters in a pre-ordained, sequential fashion, but then encourages these individuals to browse the remaining chapters in an order that best reflects their own interests and concerns.

Introducing *Thriving on Chaos* Peters (1987) tells his readers that he has produced 45 prescriptions for management divided into five sections. However, he suggests that these sections are best read in a non-sequential fashion. Consequently he proposes that the reader should study his introductory commentary in the normal fashion but should, then, feel free to 'skim any of the five sections and pick the areas that appear most relevant to your competitive situation' (Peters, 1987: 40)

Extolling the virtues of this 'hubs and spokes' approach Peters tells us that his text has been designed to reacquaint those forms of thinking, and those areas of business, that traditional approaches to management have divided and compartmentalized. Thus he tells us that he has 'proposed a piecemeal reading of the book to deal with real-world implementation' (Peters, 1987: 44). From this it is clear that *Thriving on Chaos* represents an intermediate narrative form, which stands between the standard narrative, typical of the early Peters, and what might be termed the ante-narrative format (see Boje, 2001) that has become more pronounced since the publication of *The Pursuit of Wow* in 1994.

Since 1994 Peters has published three major texts which seem impatient with traditional, linear narrative forms. Given this impatience, we have chosen to label these texts as 'elliptical adventures in hypertext'.

On hypertext . . .

Hypertext is perhaps most commonly associated with computer-mediated sources of information such as the encyclopaedia, *Encarta*. In common with more traditionally formatted encyclopaedias such as the 'hard copy' version of *Encyclopaedia Britannica*, *Encarta* seeks to provide a browsing experience, which allows users (a) to search for general information on a specific topic and

(b) to pursue linkages within the *Encarta* database that will allow the browser to develop a more in-depth appreciation, tailored to their specific information needs. For example, a search on 'Loch Ness' will provide an initial entry on this, most famous of all Scottish lochs that might then allow the user to refine their search in relation to, say, topography, social geography, palaeontology, myth and legend or even tourism.

To facilitate this search capability each *Encarta* entry has been designed to provide a cogent response which is extremely concise and hence complete on its own terms. Thus each *Encarta* entry has been designed on the understanding that it could exhaust the curiosity of the user. And yet each entry must continue to allow the possibility of on-going inquiry. To this end, *Encarta* is based on hypertext: its many entries are designed to appear complete at the level of the paragraph. Yet each entry simultaneously suggests to the user the possibility and availability of more in-depth knowledge that is just a 'double-click' away. In this regard hypertext has an elliptical character.

In making use of this elliptical allusion to describe Peter's post-1994 works I am trying to suggest that this author's (hyper) texts have a circulating character which, in common with his 'hubs and spokes' narrative, works to (re)combine areas of business and areas of the text that are, more commonly, separated because hypertexts suggest unlimited possibilities for further/future inquiry. In this regard Peters' hypertextual narratives are quite unlike his more orthodox narratives: they do not conclude with a 'full stop', rather they tend to 'tail off' elliptically ... as they suggest the prospect of additional information and the possibility of future enlightenment.

Tom Peters has produced three texts – *The Pursuit of Wow, Re-imagine* and *The Circle of Innovation* – which have elliptical characteristics. Crainer (1997), however, would tend to disagree with this assessment. Following Weick, Crainer has suggested that *Liberation Management* should also be regarded as having a hypertext format. I cannot accept this judgement however. I do accept that *Liberation Management* is somewhat chaotic and I do agree that the text has, in Crainer's terms, many diversions and a mass of detritus. Yet, despite these features, it is clear that *Liberation Management* has been written on the understanding that the reader will follow the linear unfolding of Peters' argument and in this regard the book does not qualify as a hypertextual offering.

Of the three texts we have listed as being hypertextual in form and character – *The Pursuit of Wow, Re-imagine* and *The Circle of Innovation* – the earliest text is perhaps the most clearly hypertextual in form.

The Pursuit of Wow (Peters, 1994) consists of 210 numbered entries of varying length, which are loosely corralled under 13 headings. Each of these entries, whether 26 pages or two lines in length, is both complete according to its own terms of reference, and elliptical in the sense that each entry demands to be read – and re-read – according to its relation(s) to the remaining elements of the text. That said, *The Pursuit of Wow* is far from being fully, or properly, hypertextual since, aside from grouping the numbered features under 13 general headings, the text offers no useful means to construct a deliberate research strategy which might, for example, lead the inquiring reader from feature number 72 to, say, feature number 147. A similar lack of search/link capability, as we shall see, limits the hypertextuality of Peters' (1997) text *The Circle of Innovation*.

In some ways, *The Circle of Innovation* seems to straddle the division between the traditional, linear narrative formats identified in our first three categories, and the more radical, hypertextual approach to authoring described in this, our fourth category. Indeed, in one respect *The Circle of Innovation* appears to conform to the standard, linear narrative form that we expect from authors in the field of business management. It offers 15 chapters plus an introduction and afterword designed to explain to the reader the need for innovation, the limits of existing accounts of innovation and the need for a more creative and 'yeasty' response to the proccessual challenges posed by innovation. Yet, in other respects, the text demands to be read as an attempt to discourage linearity, for while the book does indeed offer a set of chapters, the graphical representation of these chapters that is used to illustrate the book throughout – the eponymous circle of innovation – is complete, unbroken and unnumbered (see Figure 3.1).

The necessary implication of this diagrammatic representation being that the text, like the circular processes of innovation, has in fact no beginning and no end. Reflecting this appreciation of the on-going and iterative nature of innovation, *The Circle of Innovation* allows the reader to choose any point on the circle

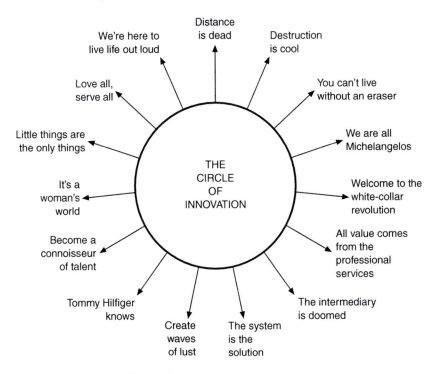

Figure 3.1 The circle of innovation.

as a starting place and, furthermore, facilitates a clockwise or anti-clockwise movement around the eponymous circle. Yet these two choices of movement do not exhaust the reading possibilities of this text – if they did the text would clearly belong to a linear narrative category. Thus it is worth observing that in the absence of any contrary injunction from Peters there is clearly nothing to prevent the reader from abandoning linearity altogether in favour of a strategy designed to cross the circle rather than simply navigating its circumference. Such a strategy is, in fact, clearly promoted by the character, style and lay-out of the text, which in common with Burrell's (1997) work seems to dare the reader to transgress the confines of a traditional narrative format (see Collins, 2000).

Aside from these hypertextual characteristics *The Circle of Innovation* has additional features which set it apart from Peters' earlier works. Unlike earlier texts such as *In Search of Excellence* (Peters and Waterman, 1982) and *A Passion for Excellence* (Peters and Austin, 1985), which offered the reader nothing but closely packed text rendered in a small font size, *The Circle of Innovation* has a number of distinctive elements. It offers:

* many figures and illustrations,
* distinct bodies of text rendered in a variety of font styles and sizes,
* acres of white paper, and
* a whole asparagus-field of exclamation marks.

This is a style and lay-out surely designed to encourage the reader – not to read in the traditional, linear sense – but to browse elliptically, around and between ideas and themes. Yet despite this, the text offers no means to construct a deliberate search strategy. Indeed aside from the 15 way-points indicated on 'the circle of innovation' there is, in truth, little to guide a search strategy beyond chance and good fortune.[2]

Peters' most recent work, entitled *Re-imagine* (Peters, 2003), is considerably larger than any other of Peters' offerings and is probably best regarded as a 'coffee table book' (see Chapter 2 for a discussion). This is a novel format for a book on the business of management. But it is not, it seems, a format that reflects the reading habits and preferences of this market niche. Thus it is worth noting that in 2005 Tom Peters and a co-author produced an 'Essentials' series of texts: four books which re-package *Re-imagine* in small format, 'plane friendly' editions (Peters and Barletta, 2005a, 2005b, 2005c, 2005d).

In its 'coffee table' format *Re-imagine* offers a full-colour as opposed to a black-and-white presentation. In addition it breaches the normal conventions of typography and book design by placing text over photographic images and on luridly coloured backgrounds – leading some to complain that this makes certain sections of the book virtually indecipherable.[3] Furthermore *Re-imagine* appears to transgress the normal conventions of authoring through the production of a text designed, it seems, to look like a developing notebook, or a 'work-in-progress'. Let us look more closely at this issue.

Work in progress

This chapter has been drafted on an A4 pad with an HB Pencil. Actually that is not a fully accurate portrayal. In fact it would be more accurate to suggest that this chapter has been *redrafted* thanks to the regular incursions of an eraser.

As I draft and redraft my chapters I often leave notes for myself in the margin and in the text. Some moments ago, for example, I inserted a short section of text on 'Loch Ness' into the margin. A few lines or so ago I inserted a sign in the text indicating, in retrospect, the need for a new paragraph. But you will have to take my word for this because respectable publishers do not generally accept such cluttered manuscripts and do not, knowingly at least, publish 'works-in-progress'. And with good reason! Writing, which flows from a 'stream of consciousness', generally turns out to be both meandering and heavily polluted!

So by the time you read this text the paragraph will not be new. Indeed from your perspective, as reader, the paragraph will seem always to have been where it stands now. And the margin will be empty once more – free to pursue its proper task as the drill-sergeant of the platoon of 21 consonants, five vowels and assorted punctuation marks which constitute the text.

To maintain this illusion of permanency authors often go to great lengths to avoid revealing their role in the production process. Thus authors will avoid addressing the reader directly – as I have just done – preferring, instead, to invoke a collective form of expression, as *we* do elsewhere in this work, to suggest that the author, text and audience are, quite literally, as one.

Recognizing the normal conventions of authoring and typesetting, therefore, it is worth observing that the reader of *Re-imagine* (Peters, 2003) confronts an unruly text; a text that has escaped the boot camp where the typographer drills his charges with an iron will. Indeed, in a number of ways, *Re-imagine* might be thought of as a text 'on the run'.

Unlike ordinary books (such as this) *Re-imagine* is a text with filled margins. It is a text pock-marked with underlinings, with dotted lines and with a variety of other annotations designed to reacquaint areas of the text, which the normal conventions of typography (and academic reviewing) would dragoon into separate regiments. These unusual features give *Re-imagine* a distinctive and somewhat organic feel.

Unlike most texts, which struggle to obtain and must struggle to maintain a fixed character (see Latour, 1987), *Re-imagine* seems to have a developing and emerging form – albeit one that the author, clearly, still seeks to control. In this regard *Re-imagine* is probably best thought of as a text which, like its author, seems to be out-growing the normal conventions of typography. Thus where *The Pursuit of Wow* and *The Circle of Innovation* seem merely to invite or to dare the reader to indulge in hypertextual browsing, the tone and lay-out of *Re-imagine* actually obliges the reader to move elliptically (see *The Economist*, 20/12/2003) . . . as both reader and author embark on a joint quest for inspiration.

In an attempt to summarize this narrative re-ordering of Peters' key texts, Table 3.1 offers both a brief reprise of the analysis offered above and a reminder

Table 3.1 A narrative ordering of Tom Peters' key texts.

Text	Date first published	Narrative type	Key themes	Total US sales	UK availability
In Search of Excellence	1982	Type I: Hypothesis-driven, sample-based, continuous narrative	Research reveals 'excellent' US organizations. US managers should learn from these and should adopt the 8 attributes of excellence.	4,200,000	In print
A Passion for Excellence	1985	Type II: Common sense or belief-driven continuous narrative	Attacks on failing 'excellent' companies miss the point. The legacy of the 1982 study demonstrates that excellence is a moving target. There is a consequent need to recognize that management is easy in cognitive terms but difficult in socio-political terms. Leadership is *the* difference and *the* route to corporate success. Some advice is offered for public sector managers.	1,065,000	In print
Liberation Management	1992	Type II	Here there is a focus upon structure rather than action as in 1982 and 1985. Where earlier texts focused upon eastern-based American corporations, the focus here is on the need for a revolution in management inspired by start-up organizations such as CNN and smaller, Californian firms.	216,000	Out of print

Title	Year	Type	Description		Status
The Tom Peters Seminar	1993	Type II	Approaches to management suggested by others – such as benchmarking – lack 'wow'. Wow is defined as the capacity to surprise and delight. Organizational supports for 'wow' are suggested.	186,000	In print
Thriving on Chaos	1987	Type III: Hubs and spokes	It is folly to think of 'excellence' as a state. The chaotic nature of the business environment necessitates an on-going revolution. The need for a broader, less American- centred analysis is expounded.	880,000	Out of print
The Circle of Innovation	1997	Type IV: Elliptical adventures in hypertext	Excellence is subsumed within a concern for innovation. Innovation and design are now said to be the key to future of business. A circular model of innovation is preferred.	186,000	In print
Re-imagine	2003	Type IV	The main focus is upon design and innovation. Persistent follies of management are outlined.	–	In print
The Pursuit of Wow	1994	Type IV	Wow – the capacity to surprise and delight is celebrated.	353,000	Out of print

Note
Type IV texts are listed according to their hypertextuality. *The Pursuit of Wow*, as the most hypertextual of these texts, is listed furthest from the preceding type.

of the core arguments (discussed in Chapters 1 and 2) which each of the texts seeks to convey.

How might we account for this changing narrative? Weighing up what we know of Tom Peters and what we have been able to ascertain about his project and his more general aspirations and orientations, the section which follows will enact a number of plausible explanations for Peters' narrative experimentation. In this endeavour we will be guided by Karl Weick's (1995) work on 'enactment', ambiguity and the flow of experience.

Since readers may be unfamiliar with Weick's work we will pause to consider this author's discussion of sensemaking and enactment.

Enactment, ambiguity and the flow of experience

It seems to me that all writers confront a dilemma. To write about life's labours, writers must take part in the labours of life. And yet it seems clear that writers must not take part too fully in life if they are to leave space for reflection and maintain the energy that is necessary for the craft of writing.

Discussing the life and works of the famous author Jack Kerouac, Ann Charters (1991) makes exactly this point. Indeed, she suggests that Kerouac lived a divided, almost schizophrenic, sort of existence as he penned his classic text *On the Road* (Kerouac, 1991).

On the Road

On the Road, as you are probably aware, recounts a number of trips which Kerouac undertook with friends. During these road trips Kerouac consumed vast quantities of alcohol and various types of narcotic. Indeed such was Kerouac's pace of life and such was his consumption of drugs – prescribed and proscribed – that his athletic frame soon succumbed to the serious, chronic ailment known as phlebitis.

Discussing the author's production of *On the Road*, Charters observes that Kerouac had to find some means of balancing his lifestyle with his life's work. She argues that Kerouac managed this balancing act by carving his life in two. Thus she notes that having spent time on drug- and alcohol-fuelled road trips of self-discovery, Kerouac would return exhausted to his mother's home and there would settle to the task of recording and recounting his 'beatific' experiences on paper, while his doting mother laboured to support them both.

Charter's account of Kerouac's life and life's work is obviously an extreme example of the writer's dilemma which I am trying to articulate. Nevertheless Charter's account of Kerouac's dual life – one part aesthetic and one part ascetic – does illustrate the tension between living a life and recounting life's events and adventures, which means that writers tend to lead a semi-detached sort of existence – viewing life both physically and figuratively through a window. Perhaps this is why so many biographies are 'ghost written'!

On hedgehogs and 'hedgehogging'

Reflecting upon the nature and processes of managing, Tony Watson (2001) picks up on a key element of this discussion. A scholar well known for his ethnographic studies of managers and managing, Watson draws inspiration from a hedgehog which, he informs us, he has been watching in his garden (through a window – of course) while writing at his desk.

Watson seems to envy this hedgehog. While he as an academic researcher is bound to his desk and is destined to agonize over everyday issues and larger concerns, the hedgehog is free to wander as it pleases and is blissfully unconcerned by the issues and problems which confront humanity, such as global warming, famine and war. The hedgehog, he tells us, simply 'hedgehogs' its way through life, from one garden to another.

Yet, like many writers (see also Grint, 1997b), Watson draws inspiration from this brush with nature. Indeed, Watson suggests that this brush with nature offers us insights into everyday life and its problems and dilemmas. With one eye still on the hedgehog, therefore, he argues that the course of human life is quite unlike the process of 'hedgehogging'. Thus Watson argues that, unlike hedgehogs, we can scarcely imagine, let alone hope to lead, 'simple lives'. Instead, as self-aware human adults, we are compelled to stumble through life, because we must navigate a passage through a world full of half-grasped issues and half-understood problems. In short, Watson argues that human life ('living' as opposed to 'hedgehogging', if you will) is full of ambiguities, which we must manage. This notion of life as being something that is both fluxing and ambiguous is central to the work of Weick (1995).

Reflecting upon the dilemmas of daily life Weick (1995), like Watson, argues that we are forced to find ways of managing ambiguity on a day-to-day basis. In seeking to cope with such ambiguity, he argues that we act upon the environments we inhabit in a distinctive way.

A land of grocers?

Shopkeepers periodically close their businesses in order to 'take stock'. They close their stores, sealing out the noise and bustle of the outside world, so that they might reflect upon the historic performance of their businesses. Yet, Weick protests that, as humans, we are inescapably part and parcel of the worlds we would make sense of. Unlike shopkeepers, therefore, we cannot simply close up and 'take stock' of our lives. Instead we must struggle on.

Consequently Weick insists that, because we are always 'in the middle' of something, we have to find a means of dealing with the ambiguities that would otherwise engulf us. Recognizing, therefore, that we cannot step off, step out or, otherwise, hope to exist separately from the complex and ambiguous world we inhabit, Weick argues that, in our attempts to make sense of our surroundings, *we must live out our lives by first, creating a world to live in.* In short, Weick argues that our sensemaking endeavours, our attempts to manage ambiguity on a day-to-day basis, turn upon 'enactment'.

Let us consider a concrete example of sensemaking and enactment.

The killing of Lauren Wright

In 2001 Tracey Wright was sentenced to a term of imprisonment for her role in the killing of her step-daughter, Lauren, who was by all accounts a sweet and delicate child of just six years of age (see the *Guardian*, 27/3/2002). Following the trial of Tracey Wright the managers of Norfolk social services mounted a press conference to explain their part in the events which had led to the death of Lauren. At this press conference it was acknowledged that the social services department which had been monitoring the family had failed in its duty to protect the child. In mitigation, however, Norfolk's social services protested that it had 'failed to make sense' of the injuries and ailments suffered by Lauren in the previous months.

Now while it would be correct to say that Norfolk's social services department (together with doctors, nurses and teachers) had somehow failed to realize that Lauren was being subject to a sustained and truly terrible programme of physical and mental abuse, a programme of abuse which would ultimately lead to her death, it would not be accurate to suggest that the social services department 'failed to make sense' of the evidence of this child's abuse. Lauren Wright did not die because Norfolk's social services department *failed* to make sense of her injuries. Instead it would be more accurate to suggest that Lauren died precisely because Norfolk's social services department was content to make sense of her injuries in a manner which ruled out child abuse as a plausible explanation. Contrary to the explanation offered at the press conference called by Norfolk's social services department, therefore, we should be clear that Norfolk's social service department had indeed 'made sense' of Lauren's injuries. Crucially (and tragically) they had accepted the stepmother's explanation that Lauren was an especially clumsy child, and so had accepted that this child would, in comparison with her peer group, suffer cuts, bruises and broken bones on a more regular basis. In this regard, and contrary to the alibi rehearsed by Norfolk's social services professionals, Lauren's death is at least in part due to the fact that the personnel of Norfolk's social services department *made sense of the child's injuries, in a particular way.*

Following Weick it is clear that Norfolk's social services had, in fact, 'enacted' a reality to *explain away* this child's injuries. Working together Lauren's social workers, teachers and doctors had, however unwittingly, created a world – a world where Lauren was well-loved and well-cared for, yet clumsy. Together these people had enacted or created a world where Lauren's injuries 'made sense' as the innocent results of a small child's clumsy play. Viewed in these terms, it is apparent that Lauren died not because of a failure to make sense but because of a willingness to enact – or to realize – a particular reality by reading into a situation a particular pattern of meaning. Had Norfolk's social services realized an alternative, abusive reality, by understanding Lauren's injuries as symptomatic of systematic abuse, she might have been alive today.

But what relevance has this tragic digression to our narrative exploration of the work of Tom Peters?

Making sense of Tom Peters

Weick suggests that sensemaking is a profoundly social process; a process driven more by reputation, plausibility and identity rather than by pure logic. In short Weick (1995) argues that, in sensemaking, people think as much socially as they do cognitively. In fact, he suggests that people think, *with* their belief systems rather than *about* their beliefs. Indeed, Weick's analysis of sensemaking suggests that people think backwards: they *see what they believe.* That is to say that they, retrospectively, construct accounts of events which accord with their own beliefs and orientations. Consequently Weick argues that what people believe is tied up with their own identities.

In attempting to construct plausible explanations for Peters' narrative experimentation I have had to make sense of the evidence I find around me. Yet my thinking in this regard has been perhaps just a little more reflexive than was previously the case because it has been geared to the production of a peer-reviewed monograph. Consequently I have been forced to (re)examine my earlier reflections on Tom Peters and, in so doing, I have been compelled to reflect upon Peters' identity as a pundit *and* my identity as an academic (and part-time manager).[4]

Indeed readers familiar with my testy response to the works of Tom Peters in earlier texts (Collins, 1998, 2000) might well accuse me of shifting identities! That charge is for others to judge and, truthfully, any such allegation would cause me little pain.[5] What is plain, however, is this: in forming judgements as to the nature and value of Peters' works, and in shaping hypotheses for the narrative experimentation observed in the work of this author, I have been extracting and responding to cues about:

- the character of Peters,
- the nature of his work and
- the overall significance of his ideas and orientations.

Furthermore in responding to these cues my thinking has been shaped by my identity as a 'critical', (but non-continental) European academic. Had I chosen a different path in life; had I, perhaps, chosen a managerial as opposed to an academic career; had I chosen an instrumental as opposed to a critical form of scholarship my reading of, and my reaction to, the works of Tom Peters would doubtless have been quite different. As an illustration of these processes and tendencies we can see, for example, clear differences between academic reactions to Peters (see Carroll, 1983; Guest, 1992) – *the sampling is skewed; the methodology is poor or absent; the conceptualization is poor* – and journalistic readings of Tom Peters (such as Heller's text of 2000), which focus upon more instrumental matters – *how might a manager actually apply this to make a difference to the 'bottom line'?*

In addition it is worth noting that my reading of Tom Peters, and my understanding of his orientations and intentions, reflects the particular identity that I have, over time, (re)constructed for this commentator.

Coming to terms with Peters

It would be fair to say that some years ago I was firmly encamped with those who viewed Peters with some mix of suspicion and derision. Viewing his work through a critical, academic lens I found myself annoyed and frustrated. And, in truth, some (probably a lot) of this frustration found its way into print as I derided his ideas. Yet over time I have shifted my position somewhat as regards Tom Peters – this is an admission that is inadvisable in my professional (and social) circles! So whereas I once regarded Peters simply as an opportunistic purveyor of myths and glib pseudo-solutions for life's complex problems, I now view him somewhat differently.

I still believe, of course, that the core of the academic criticism raised against this author remains valid, yet I have constructed in my own mind a new identity for Peters (and for myself – I suppose), which insists that this complex, thoughtful, stimulating – sometimes imaginative – path-breaking, broadly liberal man (Postrel, 1997) deserves a second look and merits a critical, yet a more even-handed, analytical review. Thus my review of Peters does not simply reduce this man to the sum of his analytical failings nor does it seek to define him in terms of his supposed inconsistency as an analyst and commentator. Instead my review recognizes explicitly his enduring appeal as a writer and speaker while seeking to make sense of the literary experimentation that, to date, has eluded academic scrutiny.

Reflecting this new rapprochement with Tom Peters the section that follows will consider a number of plausible explanations for Peters' narrative experimentation, which reflect, for better or worse, my background and shifting identity *and* the developing character I have reconstructed, in my own mind, for Tom Peters.

Accounting for narrative change

In this section we offer eight, potentially overlapping, explanations for the narrative change and experimentation identified above. Given the constraints of our own narrative format, however, we will simply enumerate, and so separate that which we have suggested may overlap.

Explanation one

Our first explanation for the narrative changes evident in Peters' works is based upon a reading of the context of *In Search of Excellence*. This explanation suggests that the format and the tone of *In Search of Excellence* should be regarded as products of a more conservative time. However our first explanation for the narrative changes observed in Peters' work also suggests that the initial success of this conservative text has emboldened Peters and has served to facilitate later, more radical, changes in his mode of expression.

Much of Peters' work on business and management might be read as a rejection of the training in business which he received from Stanford University (see Peters, 2001, 2003). At Stanford, Peters was trained in the tools and techniques of business analysis. He was taught that 'hard' data were the foundation of all good business decisions and that decision-making power must, therefore, rest with a skilled managerial elite. Yet since 1982 all of Peters' publications on management have rejected this tutelage in favour of a belief system which proclaims that 'soft' data provide an appropriate basis for decision-making and that the talent and skills necessary for the exercise of discretion exist at all levels of the organization (Peters and Austin, 1985; Peters, 2003).

Recognizing this radicalism our first explanation for Peters' narrative experimentation acknowledges, and seeks to explain, the anomalous nature of this text's narrative structure while noting the ways in which this author's subsequent texts depart from this narrative format. In this regard our first proposal suggests that the conservative format and design of *In Search of Excellence* should be read as a product of this text's intrinsic radicalism.

In short we suggest that *In Search of Excellence* has a conservative layout and design in part because this is how Peters and Waterman had learned to write at college and for clients. But perhaps more importantly *In Search of Excellence* has these distinctive characteristics because Peters and Waterman anticipated opposition to their radical message and, in the face of this anticipated opposition, the authors chose a traditional research design and a conventional format in the hope of minimizing their exposure to hostile criticism.

There are well known precedents for this. Discussing the work of the famous scientist Isaac Newton, Gribbin (1993) notes, for example, that when Newton set out to explore and to explain the nature of gravity he employed the notation of differential calculus. However, Gribbin observes that when this work was published Newton anticipated, and was most fearful of, the hostile reaction of his scientific peers. In an attempt to limit the severity of this expected adverse reaction Gribbin observes that Newton chose to express his ideas in a reworked geometrical format to reflect, it is suggested, the preferences (and the analytical limitations) of his contemporaries in the scientific academy.

Of course no scientist, today, would be lambasted for employing the notation of differential calculus as opposed to the geometrical approach to mathematics when discussing the strange world of physics. Similarly no management commentator would be attacked, today, for proffering an approach to management based around cultural management and empowerment. But in 1982 this message was novel and flew in the face of accepted codes of knowledge and practice.

Recognizing the genesis of the excellence project and its very public success as a publishing venture our first explanation for the changes observed in Peters' work runs something like this. In 1982 Peters and Waterman were preaching a radical message to a conservative elite. Accordingly, they set out to produce a narrative that would be acceptable to this elite. Yet, paradoxically, we suggest that the success of this text effectively transformed Peters into a 'brand' and changed the very basis of his knowledge claims. Thus our narrative re-ordering of Peters' texts demonstrates clearly that from 1985 onwards this author has been able to depend upon narratives that tap the wells of charisma and belief whereas, in 1982, he was compelled to call upon the authority of a scientific narrative to build his case for business change.

Explanation two

Our second explanation also recognizes the conservative nature of the elites of business and academia as it suggests that Peters' narrative experimentation reflects this author's growing frustration with America's (corporate) elite (see Crainer, 1997; Peters, 1989). In this explanation Peters' narrative experimentation is interpreted as signalling a desire to connect with a different population more inclined to accept *and* to act upon the excellence project.

In their 1982 text Peters and Waterman celebrated the wit, wisdom and energy of those Chief Executives who had controlled the helm of America's 'excellent' organizations. Yet in later texts Peters seems less taken with the behaviour of America's corporate elite. Indeed in subsequent texts such as *A Passion for Excellence* and *Thriving on Chaos* Peters is clearly impatient with the business elite of America. In *Thriving on Chaos*, for example, he suggests that in the face of changing technology, deregulating markets and shifting consumer preferences, America's boardrooms have simply run out of ideas. Addressing those who would seek a response to this increasingly chaotic world of business Peters warns:

> Don't look to GE [General Electric] for an answer. On the one hand, its former top strategic planner (now a line executive vice-president) is quoted by *Business Week* in early 1987 as saying that nine out of ten acquisitions 'are a waste of time and a destruction of shareholders' value.' The same article goes on to report that GE is thinking of acquiring United Technologies – a conglomerate with revenues of $16 billion.
>
> (Peters, 1987: 7)

Faced with such hubris Peters, we suggest, makes two important changes of direction. First his arguments in *Thriving on Chaos* become more prescriptive (and from 1987 progressively more abbreviated). Second he begins to redefine his heroes in order to celebrate the energy of smaller firms and the vision of middling entrepreneurs (Peters, 1989).

Recognizing this growing frustration with America's corporate elite our second explanation for Peters' narrative experimentation is based upon the suggestion that Peters' changing narrative structure reflects a willingness to by-pass the elite of corporate America (who demand hard data and short-term results) and denotes a desire to link up with the middling and marginal groups who, for the want of a Stanford MBA, are more inclined to accept the faith-based narratives that underpin his post-1982 texts.

Explanation three

Our third suggestion is also based upon a reading of the core credo that informs Peters' work. However, in this case we suggest that Peters has stopped offering densely packed argumentation and analysis because he has, however belatedly, begun to live up to his own preferred philosophy. Thus our third explanation observes a certain inconsistency in the format of Peters' early works. These texts, you will recall, celebrated instinct, soft data and 'managing by wandering around' while lambasting what had become codified as management. And yet, in *In Search of Excellence*, it took Peters more than 300 densely packed pages of argument and analysis to express the belief that business needs a simpler, less analytical approach. More ironically, *A Passion for Excellence* needed 400 pages of argument to explain that the message of *In Search of Excellence* had been overly complicated. Furthermore *Liberation Management* needed more than 700 pages to give this credo of simplification an international flavour.

In contrast later texts such as *The Circle of Innovation* offer readers what amounts to a 500-page 'flick book' of large type, pictures and blank spaces. This text picks up on earlier arguments made by Peters to the effect that innovation – the new by-word for excellence – is an intuitive and instinctual process. Yet in *The Circle of Innovation* this argument is offered in a form that better reflects Peters' preference for an imaginative, proactive or 'yeasty' approach to business. In this regard we suggest that Peters' emerging hypertextual approach to business writing may have developed as a reflection of his own distinctive feeling for managing as a process in which the vicissitudes of business are best addressed viscerally.

Explanation four

For more than a decade now Peters has argued that the arena of commerce is becoming increasingly capricious and unsettled. As a response to these 'crazy times' he has argued that managers must embrace 'crazy ways'. For example in *The Pursuit of Wow* (Peters, 1994), *The Circle of Innovation* (Peters, 1997) and *Re-imagine* (Peters, 2003) Peters warns managers that they must be prepared to change their recruitment practices in order to ensure that they hire 'mavericks' attuned to the chaos and craziness of the modern environment of business

Given this, our fourth explanation for Peters' changing narratives suggests that his preferred hypertextual format might be read as an attempt to mimic the craziness of the environment in the hope that 'zany' and energetic responses will be precipitated by a swirling or elliptical narrative. In this regard we suggest that Peters' hypertextual offerings have been designed (a) to demonstrate the complex and interconnected nature of the business world and (b) the fast pace of business, technological and societal change so that (c) he might precipitate new ways of thinking attuned to the essential character of global capitalism.

Explanation five

Our fifth explanation is concerned with design. In later texts Peters often complains (see for example his tirade on hotels – (Peters, 1994) that services as well as more tangible, or 'lumpy' products, are too often designed to reflect needs other than those of the user. In an attempt to persuade both producers and consumers of the virtues of good design, therefore, Peters has written much in recent years on what we might term 'the patterning of the organized world' (see Peters, 1994, 1997, 2003; Peters and Barletta, 2005c). Given this interest in design, and in the end-users of designs, it would surely be surprising (and to some extent disappointing) if Peters had not begun to experiment with narrative and had failed to question the traditional form and function of the management text?

Explanation six

Our sixth explanation reflects upon the limitations of Peters' skills as a writer and his preference for other forms of communication and interaction. In common with Crainer (1997, 1998b), Clark and Greatbatch (2003) have observed that many of those who have acquired a reputation as business gurus are in fact rather poor literary craftsmen. Discussing Peters' texts, Crainer (1997) notes that this commentator is, by his own admission (see Peters, 1993), a 'talker'. That is to say that Peters is a man more comfortable with the possibilities of talk than with the constraints of the written text. Given this, our sixth explanation for Peters' narrative experimentation is based upon the suggestion that Peters' hypertextual offerings have been designed self-consciously as attempts to capture the impact, energy and immediacy that he brings to his seminar performances, but which, it seems, he feels less able to bring to more traditional textual formats.

Explanation seven

Our seventh explanation for the narrative changes evident in Peters' work also reflects upon this author's capabilities as a writer and was in fact previewed in our previous chapter when we discussed *Liberation Management* (Peters, 1992). This text, you will recall, seems to infuriate reviewers who have complained that problems relating to the length, structure and layout of this work make it too easy to forget that this is an insightful work; a book which would set the terms of debate in managerial circles for the following decade.

Liberation Management began life as a treatise on trade theory and was conceived as Peters' attempt to manage the embarrassment he felt as a consequence of being bested by Robert Reich in a televised debate. Of course *Liberation Management* is no treatise on trade theory. It is, instead, an account of change management and 'necessary disorganization' in times of turbulence. However, the fact that this book drifted so far from its originally intended purpose is a testimony to the fact that the book's gestation was no less painful than its conception.

Discussing the pains and joys associated with the craft of writing we observed, in Chapter 2, that Peters seems to have had trouble completing this work. Indeed we noted that *Liberation Management* was delivered very late to the publishers and only then after Peters had called upon the services of a professional editor to tame what had become a large and unstructured manuscript. In addition we observed that, at this time, Peters' life itself had become the subject of a salvage operation as the author sought out the assistance of therapists and counsellors.

Reflecting upon these events we suggest that the experience of writing *Liberation Management* left Peters troubled and exhausted – lacking the will to attempt another literary project in the form of his text of 1992. Thus our seventh explanation for the narrative changes observed in Peters' work is based upon the suggestion that the pains Peters endured as he struggled, first, to prepare his treatise on 'trade theory' and, second, to complete his account of liberation in management were sufficiently intense to banish thoughts of similar future projects from his mind.

Explanation eight

Our eighth reflection on the changing narrative form of Peters' works is similarly based upon a calculation of the limits of the written text as opposed to the expansiveness of the staged seminar performance. Introducing *A Passion for Excellence*, Peters and Austin (1985) note:

> Perhaps five million people have bought copies of *In Search of Excellence* including its fifteen translations since its publication in mid-October 1982. If history is any guide, two or three million probably opened the book. Four or five hundred thousand read as much as four or five chapters. A hundred thousand or so read it from cover to cover. Twenty-five thousand took notes. Five thousand took detailed notes.
>
> (Peters and Austin, 1985: xi)

Given this sanguine analysis of his following (and market potential) we suggest that Peters' literary experimentation may be based upon the cold and rational calculation that there would be no, long-term, sustainable market for a traditional narrative on the business of management. Commenting on his 2003 text, for example, *The Economist* (20/12/2003) observed:

> This is a book for dipping into for five minutes at a time ... a sort of 'daily reader' for followers of Mr Peters' brand of management religion. It may

well achieve its goal of taking management ideas to a new younger audience, aged under 30, being famous for their short attention span and need for instant gratification.

Accordingly, our eighth and final explanation for Peters' narrative experimentation suggests that his adoption of a hypertextual narrative format represents an attempt at market renewal through the development of a product that has, it seems, been designed to reflect the reading preferences of an audience increasingly unwilling (or unable) to devote time and energy to the lengthy analyses developed through traditional narrative formats.

Concluding comments

Recognizing Peters' capacity to excite, and yet polarize, opinion this chapter has sought a middle way between the hagiology and the apoplexy that, so often, surrounds this author. To this end we have offered an analysis which recognizes the enduring appeal of Peters' commentaries. Looking more closely at the tone and format of these written works we have observed a number of changes and movements. On the strength of these observations we have developed a narrative account of the works of Tom Peters and we have, furthermore, proposed a new narrative typology for this guru's texts. We have suggested that Peters' experimentation has led to the production of no fewer than four distinctive narratives of the business of management. In an attempt to make sense of the narrative changes detailed in this typology, we have offered eight, variously overlapping, explanations for Peters' narrative experimentation.

Following Weick's (1995) analysis I have enacted a speculative (if informed) world that seeks to explain this author's changing narrative while accounting for movements in my own position as regards Tom Peters. On the strength of current research I have not been able, nor in truth have I sought, to gauge the relative weights of the eight suggestions put forward in this chapter. Instead I offer the following, more general, observations. Thus on the basis of the foregoing review of this notable guru, I suggest that Peters' narrative experimentation might usefully be regarded as the product of a successful career in business publishing/management consulting that has, nevertheless, been tempered by twin frustrations. These are, namely, a frustration with the structures and strictures of narrative orthodoxy and a related frustration with the short-term orientations and innate conservatism of the US business elite.

In anticipation of further reviews, reanalyses and hagiologies that will doubtless emerge to mark the 25th anniversary of the publication of *In Search of Excellence*, this review of Tom Peters' narrative experimentation suggests and (I hope) precipitates new avenues for critical, yet constructive, research into Tom Peters and the gurus of management more generally. Thus the reappraisal of Peters' literary career developed in this chapter suggests that future research on this author might do well to:

1   Reflect upon Dr Peters' appeal within particular demographics.

- Has Tom Peters truly turned his back on the old elites of corporate America?
- Has he formed, successfully, a common purpose with middle management and business entrepreneurs?
- Is he now attracting a following among the under-30s?

2   Reflect upon the longer-term consequences of Peters' narrative experimentation.

- Each of us can remember key tales and vignettes from the early works of Peters, yet as his texts become more terse and abbreviated, there is perhaps a danger that the works of this author will become less attractive, less memorable and so less portable. So a key question that surely merits further analysis is this: will Peters' narrative experimentation impact negatively upon the longevity of his arguments and analyses?

3   Consider the future of business publishing.

- Given the (apparent) limitations of the under-30 demographic and Peters' frustration with the limitations of the printed word, does Peters' recent narrative experimentation signal the demise of the management guru text as we know it? Is the next logical step in this process of narrative experimentation and development the dawn of, what might come to be known as, the 'Downloadable Doctor'; the 'Guru in an IPod'?

In the chapter that follows we will travel down one of the avenues suggested for future research on this guru as we analyse the stories which Peters has crafted and relayed in his various accounts of managing.

4   Stories and storytelling in the work of Tom Peters

Introduction

Over the course of the last 100 pages, or so, we have examined the career of a man named not as a guru of management, but as *the* guru of management. Noting that many readers will know perhaps very little of this man's life and works we have produced a potted biography and a brief curriculum vitae for this author. Through the production of these materials we have attempted to signal the enduring significance of Tom Peters' commentaries. Indeed we have attempted to signal the ways in which this guru's accounts of the business of management have entered and altered both the language of organization and the business of publishing.

Yet because this account of Peters' work and career is no simple exercise in hagiography we have sought to probe the oversights, omissions and misapprehensions that tend to undermine his mission to revolutionize business thinking and practice. Observing that Peters' particular brand of revolutionary foment has (a) altered over time and (b) been set out in a variety of narrative formats, we have attempted to make sense of the changes observed. To this end Chapters 1 and 2 offered critical, chronological analyses of this author's key works. In contrast Chapter 3 focused upon the format of this guru's texts. It proposed a new narrative typology for Peters' work and suggested a number of plausible explanations for the changes in narrative form observed.

Throughout all this, and despite our concern with the changing format of Peters' work, we have attempted to avoid detailed consideration of the literature concerned with organizational narrative (see for example Grant, Keenoy and Oswick, 1998; Boje 1991, 2001; Gabriel, 2000, 2004; Grant *et al.*, 2004). At key points, of course, issues and concerns germane to this body of literature *have* surfaced in our analysis. For example, in our introductory chapter we insisted that Peters' provision of a new language of (and for) managing represents a significant and enduring achievement because it has made space for new modes of organizing. Similarly, in our analyses of *In Search of Excellence* and *A Passion for Excellence*, we drew attention to the ways in which organizational stories and 'vignettes of implementation' served to make these texts readable, memorable and portable. Yet we have shunned the academic literature on organizational narrative and storytelling. We have, in truth, treated it like a silent fart at a polite dinner party. That is to say that we have ignored it – studiously – overlooking the many ways in which it has insinuated itself into our company.

Yet we can continue with this pretence no longer. In order to move forward with our reanalysis of the work of Tom Peters we must now acknowledge and embrace the literature on narrative and storytelling. Recognizing this, our current chapter is structured as follows. We begin by noting the development of a narrative perspective in organization studies and by acknowledging the ways in which this perspective has, to employ a phrase used elsewhere in this text, *entered and altered* this domain of academic inquiry. Having accomplished this we will then move on to examine a sub-set of the literature concerned with narrative and organization as we look in more detail at storytelling in organizations. Recognizing the existence of an on-going debate as regards the essential character and capacity of organizational stories, we will attempt to outline the terms of this dispute and our preferred means of navigating within these troubled waters. From here we will turn our attention to the key works of Tom Peters that we discussed throughout Chapters 1, 2 and 3. Building upon Gabriel's (1995, 1998, 2000, 2004) attempts to delineate the essential/minimally qualifying characteristics of (organizational) stories we will attempt:

1   to signal the importance of storytelling in Peters' commentaries,
2   to chart the presence of organizational stories in each of Peters' key works published between 1982 and 2003,
3   to explore both the changes and the stabilities evident in Peters' storytelling endeavours in a manner that might provide insights on this guru's project and career.

Given our concern with narrative and storytelling we will seek to illustrate our analysis and argument, wherever possible, with examples that either draw upon or reflect the arts of the storyteller.

Narratives of organization

'Our eyes met across a crowded room – corny I know.'
'She moved into the house next door with her student friends. I remember saying to my flat-mate, "That's the girl I'll marry" '.
'The cinema was in darkness and I just, well, sat on his lap'.

The scene:
A polite dinner party. No discernible flatulence – but it's early yet! Three stories about how six individuals came to be three couples. Three opening lines for three tales of love by accident. Three different stories with quite different opening gambits.

Yet not all narratives exhibit such diversity. Some narratives are rigidly stylized; some indeed are, quite literally, conventional.

My elder son, Jack – named after my mum's favourite brother and my favourite uncle (but that's another story) – has always enjoyed having stories read to him. But recently he has taken to adjusting the dynamics of our relationship. Now at bed-time he insists that he should tell me a story.

Such childish things...

Modern children's books are truly wonderful. They are beautifully crafted, richly illustrated, playful, imaginative and brilliantly diverse. Despite this Jack's tales all tend to begin with the same words. Fixing me with the widening eyes that he now uses in his attempts to communicate a sense of joy and excitement, therefore, Jack announces his newest tale with the words, *Once upon a time...*

In fairness, I feel I should point out that, as I draft this, Jack is aged four. In addition I think we should also concede that the first lines of a narrative – whether this be a tale of epic triumph involving dragons or a story of love by accident – can be very hard to 'get down'.

Academic authors are not immune to such problems. They, too, can struggle to get the opening lines of their text 'down'. Given these struggles many academic authors opt for an expedient – if slightly inelegant – solution. That is to say that academics often resolve the difficulties associated with introducing their texts by adopting an opening gambit that turns upon two hinges – chronology and controversy. For example, introducing their *Sage Handbook of Organizational Discourse*, David Grant and his co-authors offer the following opening line:

> A growing disillusionment with many of the mainstream theories – and methodologies that underpin organisational studies has encouraged scholars to seek alternative ways in which to describe, analyse and theorise the increasingly complex processes and practices that constitute 'organization'.
>
> (Grant *et al.*, 2004: 1)

This now fairly conventional method of introducing an academic discourse has a number of obvious merits:

1   It is economical. In common with other authors, academics seldom have space for an elaborate prefacing statement – or as Cliff Oswick terms it: throat-clearing. Academic authors, in fact, need to 'pitch' their ideas quickly and economically in order to ensure that the bulk of their budget (generally some 5,000 to 7,000 words) is devoted to articulating the ideas, developments and/or interactions that they really need to elaborate in order to acquire and retain an audience that is, primarily, interested in *current* controversies.

2   It signals its currency insofar as it alludes to a concern that is still 'growing'. An example from the 'popular' (as opposed to the academic) press should serve to illustrate this growing concern with narrative. In addition this illustration should help to signal the core concerns of a narrative

form of analysis, while demonstrating the extent to which this 'growing' concern has seeped into the day-to-day discussion of organized processes and events – despite the scepticism of some.

Writing for *The Times* (18/05/2004) Daniel Finkelstein, a former Tory apparatchik, offers a critical review of Tony Blair's political future that is couched in narrative terms. However, he confesses that he was initially hostile to reading such political movements and processes in narrative terms. Thus he confides:

> Now, when Blair's advisers started to talk about needing a 'narrative' your reaction was probably like mine – that it was another of those dreadful, meaningless, management consultant-style phrases that Downing Street seems to love.

But now Finkelstein is a convert. Indeed he is convinced that the New Labour project must be understood in narrative terms.

Looking back on Labour's electoral success in 1997, Finkelstein argues that the Labour manifesto, which launched the 1997 campaign, demands to be read as a narrative of 'modernization'. Furthermore he protests that this story of modernization was attractive to the British electorate precisely because the narrative of the incumbent Conservative Party (which Finkelstein argues focused upon the need to cure the 'British disease') had reached its natural conclusion. Thus Finkelstein observes:

> Once the British disease had been vanquished, the story was complete. After that, the public lost an understanding of what the Tories were doing and why. They saw them as tired, pointless, sleazy.

Taking his inspiration from the screenwriter, Robert McKee, who has observed that film-makers tend to resort to dialogue that is clichéd 'when they do not know the world of their story', Finkelstein argues that recent changes in Blair's narrative reveal that he 'no longer understands what his story is'. Indeed he argues that Blair's retreat into cliché demonstrates that: 'New Labour has literally lost the plot'. Thus Finkelstein confides:

> When I heard Tony Blair make that cheesy conference statement that he had 'no reverse gear' [it] was so obviously not true to his character and equally obviously pinched from Margaret Thatcher. It didn't even have the merit of being commendable.

Despite his initial reservations, therefore, Finkelstein is now convinced that the field of politics can usefully be explained in narrative terms. Indeed he tells us that his analysis of the words, written and spoken, by our politicians provides a powerful means of exploring the changing face of British politics *and* the growing insecurity of the New Labour project.

3   It gives the casual browser a reason to continue reading in as much as it is
    (a) highlights the existence of a dramatic contest between an orthodox
    mainstream and an alternative future and (b) suggests the prospect of rich
    rewards in terms of new descriptions, practices and theories.

For our purposes today, however, a little more prefacing is called for. In a
book such as this we do not need to enter the scene quite as late as those with
more limited (word) budgets.[1] Indeed we can 'cut away' to an earlier scene in
order to acknowledge that the chronology of the disillusionment, to which Grant
and his colleagues allude, dates back at least to the birth of the excellence
project.

Once upon a time...

In the 1980s three influential texts on the business of management were published. Deal and Kennedy (1982) produced a book on 'the rites and rituals of
corporate culture'; Pascale and Athos (1986) produced a text that celebrated the
managerial virtues of key Japanese corporations and Peters and Waterman
(1982) produced their now famous account of the practices and processes
adopted by, they claimed, the very best American corporations. In slightly different ways each of these texts proposed a narrative account of managing insofar
as they (a) questioned the 'hard', scientific orthodoxy of mainstream management studies and (b) suggested the need to consider the function of rhetoric,
symbolism and corporate myth-making in the pursuit of competitive success.

It is within the context of the publication of these three narrative accounts of
the business of management that the academic 'disillusionment' which Grant
and his co-authors signal must be understood. Thus the 'alternative', narrative
perspective which Grant and his colleagues note has been growing in influence
represents both a reaction to the hard, scientific orthodoxy of the academy *and* a
reaction to the 'softer', yet nonetheless, instrumental concern with narrative,
myth and rhetoric articulated by the likes of Tom Peters.

In short Grant and his collaborators suggest that contemporary, critical academic interests in narrative reflect a disillusionment with:

* the orthodox patterns of thought associated with the academic mainstream,
  which focus upon 'cause and effect', and so tend either to ignore, or to denigrate, organizational narratives,
* the cultural readings of organization produced in the early 1980s, which
  promote a narrative understanding of organizational life, yet tend to assume
  that managers will simply be able to secure control over organizational life
  through the skilful manipulation of narratives and stories.

Narratives are not optional

Barbara Czarniawska (1997, 1999) has done much to promote a critical narrative appreciation of the business of managing. Making a robust case for a critical narrative perspective on organization, she displays none of Finkelstein's hesitancy. Indeed, Czarniawska argues that narratives have always been central to the business of management. We organize our lives, she tells us, linguistically; in and through discourse. Recognizing this, she protests that life in the absence of narrative is, quite literally, unthinkable (see also Gabriel, 1995). In this regard Czarniawska's case for a narrative perspective makes it clear that the emergence of an explicitly narrative perspective in business and management studies reflects not so much the development of organizational narratives, as the formal acknowledgement of their pervasiveness.

Pursuing these organizing narratives, Czarniawska focuses her attention primarily on the academy rather than on the gurus of management. She observes that the mainstream, or conventional, account of business and management studies leads to the production of narratives which tend to mimic the conventions of scientific texts. For Czarniawska, therefore, the narratives of organization produced by the mainstream in management studies tend to be pre-occupied with 'cause and effect'. She complains, however, that such narratives limit and distort our appreciation of the complexities of organizing because they begin by assuming that which requires fuller explanation and elaboration. Thus she argues that mainstream narratives of organization and management tend to view organizations as *settings* where interesting things transpire. Yet Czarniawska protests that organizations are not to be regarded as stable entities and institutions. Organizations are not the backdrops for action. Organizing *is* the action. And the action takes place in and through language (see also Chia and King, 1998; Tsoukas and Chia, 2002; Tsoukas, 2005).

Putting language in its place

We tend to think of language as a means of representing – clearly, faithfully and in a factually accurate way – a world which is external to us. Those adopting a narrative approach to the study of management and organization dispute this however. Language, these commentators protest, constitutes rather than reflects reality. Words matter, therefore, because they have a capacity to make particular representations of our realities real. This is why influential actors such as the politicians discussed by Finkelstein and the Chief Executives vaunted by the likes of Tom Peters hire press secretaries and speech-writers; this is why social actors who would exercise influence over us struggle to attach themselves to words such as 'empowerment' (Keenoy and Anthony, 1992), 'values' and 'responsibility' (see Fairclough, 2000).

Orwell provides perhaps a seminal appreciation of the power of language in his novel *Nineteen Eighty-Four* (Orwell, 1968). This novel, as you are probably aware, offers a dystopian vision of a totalitarian future.

The language of Newspeak

Winston Smith, the hero of Orwell's tale, lives in a world where his movements are under constant surveillance and his very thoughts are criminalized. Resistance in this regime is apparently futile. Those who transgress, it seems, are invariably apprehended and punished. Yet this is insufficient for the rules of 'Oceania'. To make opposition to 'Ingsoc', the official doctrine of English Socialism, literally unthinkable, a new form of English known as 'Newspeak' is under preparation (see Taylor, 2003).[2]

In the often overlooked appendix, which documents the nature and purpose of Newspeak, Orwell tells us that this refinement of the English language had been conceived as an attempt to limit what could be said, thought and, in the final analysis, achieved in Oceania. Concepts deemed to be superfluous to Ingsoc such as 'freedom', therefore, would have no place in the vocabulary of Newspeak. Thus Orwell tells us:

> The purpose of Newspeak was not only to provide a medium of expression for the world-view and mental habits proper to the devotees of Ingsoc, but to make all other modes of thought impossible. It was intended that when Newspeak had been adopted once and for all and Oldspeak forgotten, a heretical thought – that is a thought diverging from the principles of Ingsoc – should be literally unthinkable.
>
> (Orwell, 1968: 241)

It is this understanding of the power and potential of language that underscores Grant *et al.*'s (2004) narrative perspective. Thus the 'alternative' appreciation of organization and management suggested by Grant and his colleagues reflects an understanding that such narrative appreciations of organization can:

1   reveal the limiting nature of 'scientific' narratives of management,
2   demonstrate the complex and dynamic nature of social organization,
3   generate distinctive renderings of the dynamic complexities of organizing that transgress the confining boundaries of both orthodox scholarship and the hyperbolic imaginings of the gurus.

As we shall see the pursuit of such alternative realizations of the processes of organizing has generated a broad array of work that is often surprising and imaginative.

Transgressive texts

What might be termed 'the critical, narrative turn' in organization studies has produced a rich variety of texts. Yet, at root, each of these texts share something in common. Each shares a desire to cross, or to breach, the laminations that might otherwise limit our orbits (Wright-Mills, 1978) and confine our understandings (Fine, 1994).

Knights and Willmott (1999), for example, have produced an alternative text-book that calls upon narrative forms that are either excluded from or marginal-ized within orthodox (or modernist) academic texts (see Gabriel, 1998, 2000) to generate a richer and more intimate appreciation of the nature and processes of managerial work. Thus Knights and Wilmott use novels and films to explore the business of management. Of course, these authors are neither the first nor are they the only authors to employ such texts to illustrate the nature of managerial toil. For example, Brawer (1998) has produced a text which suggests that 'insights on management' may be gleaned from 'great literature'. Similarly Read (2001) has suggested that each of us could learn a lot about managing our-selves and others from the children's television character 'Mr Benn'. Yet it is what Knights and Willmott do with their fictional texts which (a) sets their work apart from the works of Brawer and Read and which (b) makes their text trans-gressive in the sense that Czarniawska (1999) has advocated.

Brawer and Read call upon a variety of literary works (whether Mr Benn counts as great literature I leave up to you) to illustrate and to improve the conduct of management. Yet Knights and Willmott would tend to reject this instrumental application of 'fiction' as unhelpful. Examining the academic text-books that are produced ostensibly to educate students in the ways and means of management, Knights and Willmott find themselves troubled. The textbooks, they complain, do not in fact provide an education in management. Instead these texts provide students with access to a limited number of ideas, tools and tech-niques that they will only ever be called upon to demonstrate in their written and oral examinations. In an attempt to generate a richer and fuller appreciation of those processes and practices of managerial work that orthodox textbooks have excluded from the curriculum, therefore, Knights and Willmott (1999) employ fictional narratives. Yet these narratives are invoked, not to improve manage-ment in the limited and rather instrumental terms that Brawer and Reed seem to aspire to, but to explore larger issues which shape relationships beyond the classroom. Thus Knights and Willmott use the work of novelists and film-makers to reveal and to explore the hidden realm of organizing (Burrell, 1997) where power, identity and subjectivity may be viewed in and at work.

Czarniawska (1999) also employs the work of novelists in an attempt to produce a similarly transgressive account of organization in narrative terms. In common with writers such as Knights and Willmott and Wright-Mills (1978), Czarniawska observes that the work of novelists has often acted as an inspiration for those who aspire to create accounts of the business of management that remain more firmly grounded in the mundane complexities of managing and organizing.

Discussing the relationship between the novelist's representation of the world(s) of work and the scientific texts produced by mainstream scholars of management, Czarniawska insists that both communities produce narratives. However, she argues that these communities produce narratives that depict the scenes of ordinary life in rather different ways. Thus Czarniawska tells us that the novelist's narrative and the organizational scientist's narrative represent different genres of work. Commenting on the differences between the narrative genres of 'science' and 'literature' she argues that 'a work is ascribed to a certain genre according to the frequency with which it uses certain rhetorical devices' (Czarniawska, 1999: 30).

Storywork, Czarniawska tells us, is metonymic and depends upon the fabrication of associations whereas the narrative of science is paradigmatic and turns upon substitution. The craft of the scientist and the art of the novelist differ, therefore, not because one speaks to the truth and the other speaks in riddles and allusions. No, the scientist and the novelist differ only insofar as they are expected to invoke different rhetorical devices as they narrate their concerns and experiences.

Nonetheless Czarniawska does concede that, when used as a category, the concept of 'the novel' is simply too broad to allow a balanced comparison to be made between 'the novel' on one hand and 'organization theory' on the other. In an attempt to introduce some balance to proceedings, therefore, Czarniawska argues that we should compare 'organization theory', a sub-genre of social scientific theorizing, with a similar sub-genre of the 'the novel'. To this end she suggests a comparison between 'organization theory' and 'the detective story'. On the strength of this comparison she argues that detective stories and orthodox narratives of organization theory are analogous. Both genres, she tells us, are 'built around problem-solving in a social context' (1999: 77). Furthermore, they both share a preference for a realist style and exhibit a common narrative structure. Outlining this realist approach Czarniawska notes that, at the outset, each text describes a situation in which

> there is something amiss, it is neither clear nor obvious what it is (there are many false clues), this 'something' must be explained (the problem must be diagnosed) and – although this is optional in both detective story and organisation studies – the way of solving the problem ought to be prescribed.
>
> (1999: 79)

Andrew Brown (2000, 2003) provides a similarly challenging and transgressive reading of two key organizational texts. In common with the analysis offered by Czarniawska (1999), the texts analysed by Brown are both concerned with situations in which something went awry. But these are not detective novels. These are not strictly-speaking imagined or otherwise fictionalized accounts of organizational life. On the contrary, Brown's texts are accounts of death in (and by) organizations which seek, in the words of the oath, 'the truth, the whole truth and nothing but the truth'.

Analysing the reports of the Allit Inquiry (which was concerned with attacks on children by the nurse Beverly Allit) (Brown, 2000) and the Cullen Inquiry (which was concerned with the events that culminated in the Piper Alpha oil rig disaster) (Brown, 2003), Brown suggests that the products of these public inquiries might usefully be subject to a narrative analysis. Indeed he argues that a narrative review of these reports reveals that they must be structured and indeed plotted in conventional ways if they are to enjoy the faith of the general public. Moreover he insists that, in revealing the ways in which such reports are staged and framed, his narrative reviews of the workings of these public inquiries have a capacity to generate alternative renderings of events that call upon the voices of those who are variously silent throughout or silenced by such proceedings. A similar concern with absence and silence defines Carter's and Jackson's (2000) account of the aesthetics of death and memorial. Yet the 'texts' analysed by these authors are quite unlike those considered by Brown.

Analysing the cemeteries which contain the remains of British and Commonwealth soldiers, sailors and airman who died overseas while serving their monarch, Carter and Jackson argue that the layout, architecture and inscriptions of these monuments should be read as an attempt to deny or to disguise the monstrous realities of combat. Thus Jackson and Carter suggest that Britain's war graves might be read as texts which confirm the fact of death-in-war, while concealing the, utterly horrifying, processes of killing and dying.

In contrast to the study of Carter and Jackson, Nanette and John Monin (2003) offer a narrative analysis of four texts that most would accept as being centrally concerned with management and organization. Studying sections of text written by F. W. Taylor (1911), Mary Follett (1987), Peter Drucker (1955) and Rosabeth Moss Kanter (1984), Monin and Monin argue that one of these four texts has been ignored by both the scholarly and practitioner communities. Follett's work, they warn us, has been overlooked by successive generations of management scholars, and is in danger of being lost altogether because its narrative structure departs from the normal conventions of the managerial text.

Monin and Monin argue that contemporary narratives of management generally portray managers as glamorous individuals who achieve mastery over their organizations because their skills, knowledge and/or personal characteristics allow them to 'lead from outside, beyond, or above the group' (2003: 71). Follett's narrative of management is different however. Follett's manager, the Monins argue, does not stand above the organization and does not stand aloof from his/her colleagues. Follett's manager is not served, rather s/he services. Her managers do not lead, they converse!

Looking to the other, more popular, narratives of management and managing in their sample, the Monins are struck by the contrast with Follett's. Taylor's managers are born to rule. Drucker's managers form a modern Praetorian Guard. Kanter's managers are both heroic and paternalistic; working to secure the future of America's polity and economy. Each is in their own way obviously special – attractive, necessary, heroic. Follett's managers, however, lack such special characteristics. They represent an everyman not a superman and this, the Monins claim, provides 'a possible reason for the discard of Follett's text through much of the twentieth century: it is a narrative without a hero' (Monin and Monin, 2003: 73).

In common with the Monins, Czarniawska's (1997, 1999) work on narratives of organization demonstrates a similar concern with the everyday processes of exchange. Indeed Czarniawska complains that too many narratives of organization are constructed in a fashion which places writing at some remove from the realities of organizing practices. Thus she argues that those who would inscribe management need to develop transgressive texts that in departing from the conventions of the scientific narrative have a capacity to reflect and to maintain the essential complexity of managing. Thus Czarniawska suggests that academics should seek to construct narratives of managing that celebrate the polyphonous and polysemous nature of social organization.

A structure for narrative?

In an attempt to bring some structure to what might otherwise constitute a bewildering array of perspectives, practices and voices Grant *et al.* (2004) suggest that the field concerned with the ways in which language constitutes and reconstitutes organization (see, for example Gioia and Chittipeddi, 1991; Dunford and Jones, 2000 for accounts of the importance of language in strategic change efforts) might usefully be regarded as comprising four overlapping domains, variously concerned with:

- conversation and dialogue
- narratives and stories
- rhetoric
- tropes.

Grant and his co-authors tells us that the domain concerned with conversation and dialogue views action in consequential terms as a product of on-going linguistic and textual exchange. In this arena of inquiry, conversation and dialogue are analysed temporally and rhetorically. Such conversational exchanges, they tell us, are worthy of academic study for it is through conversation rhetorics that such things as 'the customer', 'the organization' and the 'need to' engage in certain practices are constituted. Furthermore they warn us that the effects of these conversations are persistent and potentially pernicious. Thus Grant and his colleagues argue that conversation rhetorics, once constituted, may be deployed as a resource to facilitate or indeed to constrain future forms of action and organizing.

The domain concerned with narratives and stories is similarly concerned with the processes and practices of organizing. Writers active in this arena suggest that organizations should be regarded as arenas where narratives and stories 'animate and orientate' (De Cock and Hipkin, 1997) individuals in the pursuit of global (Boyce, 1995) and/or more local projects and concerns (Gabriel, 1995; Collins and Rainwater, 2005).

The domain concerned with rhetoric, as you might expect, is concerned with the more strategic elements of discourse. Typically studies in this area set out to reveal the existence of particular rhetorics and, in so doing, attempt to make readers aware of the ways in which such rhetorics constitute understanding and organization (see Keenoy and Anthony, 1992; Fairclough, 2000).

Grant *et al.* suggest that the fourth domain of discourse, concerned with tropes, is often obscured by or subsumed within the third domain that is concerned with rhetoric. However, Grant and his colleagues suggest that a more detailed consideration of the four master tropes of metaphor, synecdoche, metonymy and irony can provide both crucial insights into the processes and practices of organization (see Hamilton, 2003a, 2003b) *and* alternative readings of such organizing practices. In pursuit of such alternative renderings of the practices and processes of social organization, the authors encourage their academic colleagues to essay more ironic encounters with the business of management since, they tell us, the trope of irony is centrally concerned with key features of our organized lives such as dissonance and paradox.

Having highlighted the range of practices and perspectives which characterize the field concerned with language and organization and having mapped the four domains that make up this terrain, we will now look in more detail at the sector concerned with stories and storytelling as we prepare to re-examine the works of Tom Peters.

In the section that follows, therefore, we will consider the debate which has grown up around organizational stories and storytelling. As we reflect upon this debate we will attempt to develop a consensus on the distinction between stories and other related narrative forms. Turning our attention to the key works of Tom Peters, outlined in Chapter 1, we will discuss the ways in which this literature on narrative and storytelling has shaped our attempts to identify, extract and analyse the stories that Peters' uses to inscribe his key concerns.

Organizational stories and storytelling

A confession: despite our earlier comment on the opening gambit employed by Grant *et al.* (2004) it is, nevertheless, true that *in recent years much has been written on narratives, storytelling and organization* (Boje, 1991; Czarniawska, 1997; Clark and Salaman, 1998; Boje *et al.*, 2001; Gabriel, 1995, 1998, 2000, 2004; Jackson, 2001; Watson, 2001). While it would be fair to say that much of this work calls on and is, in part, derived from earlier analyses of folk-tales and folklore, it would be more accurate, perhaps, to suggest that the current interest in storytelling and organization represents a significant departure from those accounts of folklore which sought simply to harvest and catalogue stories. Thus contemporary academic interest in storytelling is predicated on an understanding that organizational stories have meaning and significance only when they are analysed in context as organic and vital constituents of social organization. Recent interest in organizational storytelling, therefore, has been driven by an understanding that organizational stories can provide important insights into the complexities of management and the essential plurality of social organization (Boje, 1991, 2001; Gabriel, 1995, 1998, 2000).

Gabriel's (2000) attempt to rehabilitate the study of organizational storytelling begins by observing that a discontent with modernist scholarship has redeemed the 'story' from its position as a quaint subordinate to the facts of 'history' such that stories are now widely acknowledged to be not reflections of organizational reality, but creators of organizational meaning and organizational realities. Thus Gabriel suggests that the increasing interest in stories and in storytelling has been facilitated by postmodern scholarship and its tendency to see stories (as generators and creators of meaning) everywhere. However, Gabriel disputes this tendency to 'see stories everywhere' – as the creators and generators of meaning – on two counts. First, as we shall see below, he argues that not all narratives qualify as stories. Second, he insists that stories do not always and everywhere generate meaning because, while stories are portable and travel well, they are often modified as they travel. Thus Gabriel suggests that stories have a fragile and 'polysemic' quality, which makes them susceptible to translation (Latour, 1987).

Boje's analysis of narratives and 'narratology' also demonstrates a concern with polysemy as it attempts to uncover worlds and experiences which are otherwise denied in official corporate (hi)stories. Reflecting upon the corporate successes and excesses of the *Nike* corporation, for example, Boje (1998) argues that the stories of the oppressed (who produce *Nike* apparel) may help to break down the fantasies (Gabriel, 2000, 2004) which have grown up around the consumption of *Nike*.

Contrasting the stories which *Nike* likes to tell about its policies and endeavours in the Third World (*Nike* as the handmaiden of economic development and social improvement), with the tales which *Nike's* employees in these lesser developed countries tell of their experiences (*Nike* as violent corporate predator), Boje has sought to 're-story' (Boje, Alvarez and Schooling, 2001) *Nike*, in the hope of generating an alternative understanding of the life and work of this corporation. Comparing *Nike's* official history with grass-roots stories which narrate the reality of working for *Nike* in the Third World, Boje argues that his 're-storying' endeavours should help to ensure that *Nike* will have difficulty in producing and sustaining the carefully crafted tales of corporate benevolence and munificence which it has been keen to share with the general public. It is worth noting, however, that this attempt to 're-story' *Nike* seems to show only a limited commitment to plurality insofar as it produces but one alternative to *Nike's* attempt to explain (away) their activities in the Third World. Thus we might suggest that Boje's (1998) 're-storying' falls short of a full commitment to the pursuit of the worlds and experiences of *Nike's* workers because Boje has been too keen to speak (out) on behalf of the workers and their common complaints.

Writing alone Boje (2001) offers a more nuanced and more challenging account of organizational storytelling as he attempts to tease out the deeper implications of his 're-storying' endeavours. Following Weick's (1995) account of sensemaking, he begins by noting that, on a day-to-day basis, people confront a key problem: how to make sense of a 'complex soup' of ambiguous and half-understood problems, events and experiences. Reflecting upon this problem of ambiguity, Boje suggests that people construct and retrace their lives retrospectively through stories. For Boje (2001), therefore, stories have a particular significance and a distinctive meaning. Indeed Boje warns us that we must distinguish 'stories' from 'narratives' (which for ease of exposition we will reproduce as 'Narratives') if we are to understand the richness of organizational sensemaking. Demonstrating a now keener interest in the plural nature of organization, therefore, Boje warns us that Narratives are not to be confused with stories. Narratives, he argues stand aloof from the flow of experience. Narratives are plotted, directed and staged to produce a linear, coherent and monological rendering of events, while 'stories are self-deconstructing, flowing, emerging and networking, not at all static' (Boje, 2001: 1).

Reflecting upon the Narrative understanding of organization, which comes to us from such august sources as the *Harvard Business Review* (see also Collins and Rainwater, 2005), Boje argues that academic analysis has, too often, confused stories with Narrative. Thus he complains that 'so much of what passes for academic narrative analysis in organization studies seems to rely upon sequential, single-voiced stories' (Boje, 2001: 9).

In an attempt to provide an alternative to these monologues of business endeavour, Boje introduces the concept of the 'antenarrative' which, he argues, resituates the concerns of the field of organization – directing inquiry towards a concern with flux and emergence. This focus upon flow and fragmentation, as we shall see, has a profound affect on Boje's antenarrative conceptualization of stories.

Antenarratives

For Boje (2001), 'antenarrative' has two faces. On one face, Boje's focus upon 'antenarrative' is based upon the understanding that 'stories' precede Narrative. For Boje, then, stories are 'antenarrative' in that they come before the processes of staging and directing, which, as he sees it, lead to the development of 'sequential, single-voiced', top-down Narratives.

On the obverse face, Boje calls upon the rules of poker. Thus he suggests that an 'antenarrative' represents 'a bet' (or 'an ante') that retrospective sensemaking may emerge in the future from 'the fragmented, non-linear, incoherent, collective and unplotted' (2001: 1) stories, which come before Narrative accounts.

This account of stories and Narratives overlaps to some degree with the account offered by Gabriel (2000). In common with Boje, Gabriel agrees that stories offer local and intimate accounts of situations, events and predicaments. Indeed, reflecting upon the complexities associated with the analysis of stories and storytelling, Gabriel argues that storywork – literally the art of constructing meaningful stories – is a delicately woven product of intimate knowledge. In addition Gabriel (1998, 2000) seems to agree with Boje that a story represents a speculative bet on the shape of the future. Thus Gabriel tells us that when a storyteller announces a tale s/he covenants with the audience. Furthermore, he agrees with Boje that it is vitally important to distinguish 'stories' from other 'narrative' forms. At this point, however, the accounts of storytelling prepared by these authors begin to diverge. Yet, somewhat ironically, the differences that tend to divide the analytical approaches of these scholars actually flow from a common concern with the intensification of work and with the narrative impoverishment that is consequent upon the increasing intensity of labour.

Narrative impoverishment and work intensification

Both Boje and Gabriel have complained that it can be difficult to unearth good stories and talented storytellers in organizations. Indeed each has suggested that it is becoming increasingly difficult to witness organizational storytelling in its natural surroundings. Pondering the cause of this narrative deskilling Gabriel suggests that contemporary developments such as kaizen, Total Quality Management (TQM) and Just-in-time (JIT) production may be a root cause of this decline in organizational storytelling since these initiatives intensify the pace of working, and so reduce the opportunity for spontaneous interaction at work. This shared recognition of poetic decline at work, however, takes Boje and Gabriel in opposite analytical directions.

Lamenting the perceived decline in organizational stories, Gabriel simply renews his commitment to the understanding that stories are (increasingly rare and) special forms of narrative with definite characteristics. Boje, however, adopts a different and more radical tack: he moves 'upstream' (Latour, 1987) and begins to redefine the very nature of organizational stories. In an initial move Boje (1991) suggests that the terse narrative which announces 'you know the story' might itself be considered a story in its own right. Later in a more radical move (Boje, 2001) he suggests, as we have seen, that stories should be regarded as those special forms of narrative that exist *prior* to the crystallizing processes of casting and plotting. Thus in a reaction to the top-down and monological Narratives relayed by organs such as the *Harvard Business Review*, David Boje insists that stories are to be found within the flowing soup that is organization and exist prior to the rigidities of plotting.

Gabriel, however, disputes these moves and I tend to agree with his reasoning. For Gabriel stories – despite literary deskilling – represent a rich and, in any sense, a vital resource for organizational theorists. And on this matter he and Boje are in perfect agreement: stories are interesting because they offer a means to tap the ambiguous and polysemous nature of organization. But for Gabriel plots, staging and direction remain the central characteristics of stories. Taking issue with Boje's first move, therefore, Gabriel protests that while the 'terse stories' observed by Boje represent invitations to recall either a pattern of events or a particular rendering of a tale, they are not, properly-speaking, stories. These 'terse tales', Gabriel warns us, lack 'performativity, memorableness, ingenuity and symbolism' (Gabriel, 2000: 20). Thus Gabriel argues that Boje's terse stories 'amount to little more than delicate fragments of sense, communicating metonymically, as if they were product brands' (Gabriel, 2000: 20–21).

Regarding Boje's second move, Gabriel concedes that the moments of narrative expression captured in Boje's unscripted and unplotted *ante*narratives might reveal something to us about organizational ambiguity and about the complexities of sensemaking in organizations. Yet he protests that these antenarratives cannot be regarded as poetic tales. Thus Gabriel insists that Boje's antenarratives are more properly described as prototypical stories; narratives which, in time, may come to acquire the attributes of a good tale.

The novelist John Steinbeck, I think, offers a good illustration of Gabriel's reservations concerning Boje's attempts to swim upstream within the narrative flow of organization. In a key scene from *Of Mice and Men* Steinbeck shows both the importance of performance in storytelling and the joy that flows from the anticipation of a familiar tale, well-told. Thus Steinbeck's dialogue confirms that:

1   stories can work to craft a shared understanding of the present and an agreement as regards the preferred shape of the future,
2   storytellers have to work to deal with, or to incorporate, interruptions.

Yet, perhaps more importantly, our reproduction of Steinbeck's words illustrates the ways in which:

1   Boje's terse stories would tend to break the covenant between storyteller and audience,
2   Boje's unstructured and unplotted antenarratives would drive a wedge of disappointment between audience and storyteller.

Of stories and audiences

John Steinbeck's (1974) *Of Mice and Men*[3] tells the tragic story of an unlikely friendship between two ranch-hands, George and Lennie. George is small and quick-witted. Lennie, in contrast, is large and slow-witted with a child-like innocence. George and Lennie are unrelated. Yet, despite this, George loves Lennie like a brother and Lennie returns the affection with all of his kind heart.

George's love for Lennie, however, must be regarded as a real achievement, for Lennie is a continuing source of trouble and upheaval. Thus George complains:

> God a'mighty, if I was alone I could live easy. I could get a job an' work an' no trouble. No mess at all.
>
> (1974: 15)

But, thanks to a combination of Lennie's slow wits and the cruelty and misunderstanding of others, George cannot live easily. He continues with his complaint:

> You can't keep a job and you lose me ever' job I get. Jus' keep me shovin' all over the country all the time. An' that ain't the worst. You get in trouble. You do bad things and I got to get you out.
>
> (1974: 15)

Despite these trials, however, George will never abandon Lennie. George and Lennie have a plan. And at every opportunity Lennie makes George recount the story of the future life they plan together.

Reacting to George's tirade against his many obvious failings Lennie takes shelter in a tried and tested response: he announces his intention to 'go off in the hills an' find a cave' (1974: 17). And when George retreats, assuring Lennie that they will stick together, the big man seizes his opportunity to make George tell him, once more, how things will be:

'Lennie pleaded: 'Come on, George. Tell me. Please, George. Like you done before.'

'You get a kick outta that, don't you. A'right, I'll tell you, and then we'll eat our supper...'

George's voice became deeper. He repeated his words rhythmically as though he had said them many times before. 'Guys like us, that work on ranches, are the loneliest guys in the world. They got no family. They don't belong no place. They come to a range an' work up a stake and then they go inta town and blow their stake, and the first thing you know they're poundin' their tail on some other ranch. They ain't got nothing to look ahead to.'

Lennie was delighted. 'That's it – that's it. Now tell how it is with us.'

George went on. 'With us it ain't like that. We got a future. We got somebody to talk to that gives a damn about us. We don't have to sit in no barroom blowin' in our jack jus' because we got no place else to go. If them other guys gets in jail they can rot for all anybody gives a damn. But not us.'

Lennie broke in. '*But not us! An' why? Because ... because I got you to look after me, an you got me to look after you, and that's why.*' He laughed delightedly. 'Go on now, George.'

'You got it by heart. You can do it yourself.'

'No, you. I forget some a' the things. Tell about how it's gonna be.'

'O.K. Some day – we're gonna get the jack together and we're gonna have a little house and a couple of acres an' a cow and some pigs and...'

'*An' live off the fatta the lan*',' Lennie shouted. 'An' have *rabbits*. Go on, George! Tell about what we're gonna have in the garden and about the rabbits in the cages and about the rain in the winter and the stove, and how thick the cream is on the milk like you can hardly cut it. Tell about that George'.

'Why'n't you do it yourself. You know all of it.'

'No ... you tell it. It ain't the same if I tell it. Go on ... George. How I get to tend the rabbits.'

'Well,' said George. 'We'll have a big vegetable patch and a rabbit-hutch and chickens. And when it rains in the winter, we'll just say the hell with goin' to work, and we'll build up a fire in the stove and set around it an' listen to the rain comin' down on the roof – Nuts!' He took out his pocket-knife. 'I ain't got time for no more.' He drove his knife through the top of one of the bean-cans, sawed out the top, and passed the can to Lennie. Then he opened a second can. From his side pocket he brought out two spoons and passed one of them to Lennie.

(Steinbeck, 1974: 17–18, original emphasis)

Proto-stories, opinions and reports

Noting the importance of plotting and performance in the art of storytelling, Gabriel has attempted to forge a categorical distinction between organizational stories and the other, related, narrative forms commonly found in organized settings. Thus Gabriel argues that there is a need to distinguish:

- 'opinions' (which may contain factual or symbolic materials but tend to lack both a plot and characters),
- 'proto-stories' (which, while they may have a rudimentary plot, remain incomplete insofar as they offer, say, a beginning and a middle but no satisfactory ending) and
- 'reports' (which offer an historic rather than a poetic rendering of events, and so produce stubbornly factual and causative, as opposed to symbolic, accounts) from 'proper', or 'poetic', stories.

Disputing Boje's reservations regarding plotting and performance, therefore, Gabriel insists that (properly so-called) stories build on 'poetic' qualities, and so depend upon plots as well as embroidery and embellishment.

Yet, despite their dispute over terminology, Gabriel and Boje seem to concur that the analysis of storytelling offers a means to resituate and recapture the flow and the plurality of social organization. Thus Gabriel seems to agree with Boje's suspicion of Narratives when he argues that 'stories' are quite unlike histories and 'reports'. Reports, he warns us are monological, invite factual verification and so seek to crystallize events, whereas stories are local, organic and polyphonic and depend upon poetic licence for the generation of meaning.

Pursuing this concern with poetic licence Gabriel (2004) argues that those who would entertain us with embroidered plots and embellished events must call upon the '6Fs' of poetic narration.

The '6Fs' of Narratives

Gabriel (2000, 2004) tells us that stories allow poetic licence and indulge embellishment. This necessarily implies that storytellers must be allowed to arrange and, where necessary, rearrange characters, situations and events in order to secure the attention and affiliation of their audiences. Acknowledging this, Gabriel (2004) tells us that the poetics of storytelling call upon '6F' factors. Namely:

- Framing – whereby characters are arranged as being, variously, central for or marginal to the tale.

- Focusing – where special emphasis is placed upon a particular cluster of events and/or characters at the expense of other characters and/or events.
- Filtering – where certain events or characters are removed from a tale in order to secure the integrity of the plot-line or to maintain the pace of the story.
- Fading – whereby specific events or characters are introduced or/then removed from the tale to reflect the needs of the plot.
- Fusing – where multiple events and/or characters are merged into singularities to collapse, for example, temporal distinctions.
- Fitting – where characters or events are re-interpreted or represented in line with the overall requirements of the story as opposed to, say, the actual historical record of events.

In an attempt to illustrate the operation of these '6F' factors we will consider three stories that, as we shall see, turn upon particular coalitions of these narrative tools. Our first two examples are drawn from the works of the novelist John Steinbeck (1970) and the sociologist Barbara Ehrenreich (2006) respectively. Each of these examples offers powerful demonstrations of the importance of 'framing', 'filtering' and 'fitting' processes, in part because they deal with stories that breach the covenant between storyteller and audience. Our third example comes from William Goldman's (2001) reflections on the filtering processes that are central to cinematic storytelling. This third example is interesting because it deals with a story whose success, in narrative terms, depends upon a very radical process of 'filtering'.

The Pearl

The Pearl is a famous short story normally credited to the imagination of the Nobel laureate John Steinbeck (1970). However, Jay Parini (1994) argues that this story has its origins in a folk-tale which Steinbeck heard on a trip to the 'sea of cortez' with his friend Ed Ricketts (see Steinbeck, 1990).

The folk-tale tells of a poor young fisherman who, one day, finds a massive pearl. Taking up the story Parini tells us:

> The pearl is worth so much that the boy's future seems, to him, assured: he will now have the opportunity to be drunk as long as he wishes, 'to marry any one of a number of girls, and to make many more a little happy too'. If he gets into trouble, he can buy sufficient masses at church to squeeze him [self] out of purgatory. When he takes the pearl to a broker in town, he is offered far less than it is worth. Offended he tries another, then another; all try to cheat him.
>
> (Parini, 1994: 383–384)

Chastened by his experiences the fisherman hides the pearl. However, he is soon seized by a group of avaricious men who demand to know the whereabouts of his treasure. When he refuses to divulge the location of the pearl the fisherman is severely beaten. Troubled by the turn his life has taken since he happened upon the pearl, the fisherman retrieves his treasure, curses it and hurls it back into the sea so that he may return to his former life.

This, in a nutshell, is the tale that inspired John Steinbeck. However, Parini (1994) and French (1975) argue that Steinbeck makes crucial changes to the story, reframing it and filtering it, to make it suitable for the readers of *Woman's Home Companion* where it was first published. Thus French notes that Steinbeck re-casts the 'ingratiating rascal' (1975: 128) of the folk-tale giving him a name, a wife and an ailing infant son such that, in Steinbeck's rendering of the tale, the pearl is especially precious because its sale will allow the fisherman to purchase medicine for the boy.

In keeping with the original folk-tale Steinbeck's fisherman, now named Kino, also attempts to sell the pearl but he, too, finds himself surrounded by cheats. When these tricksters fail in their attempts to swindle Kino they decide that they will take the pearl by force.

To evade these would-be thieves, Kino flees with his wife and child into the mountains. However, the family, is pursued and the infant son is shot and killed. Enraged Kino, in turn, kills three of the men who have chased him into the mountains before returning to the coast. At this point and with his life in ruins Steinbeck allows the fisherman to return the pearl to the sea.

Commenting upon the poetic licence that Steinbeck exercises over this story French argues that Steinbeck has taken a bawdy folk-tale and transformed it into a simple-minded and sentimental story. Furthermore he complains that these changes – in the name of morals and morality – are (a) unnecessary and (b) cause Steinbeck to fail the tale. Thus French (1975) notes that to reflect the moral sensitivities of his readers and publisher, Steinbeck converts the central character from an 'ingratiating rascal' into a man with all 'the makings of a stubborn middle-class bore with a fretful American Suburbanite wife' (128). Yet French argues that this is unnecessary because in the original folk-tale the rascally fisherman actually spurns the pearl, and so chooses a life of hard work and intermittent hunger over the trials of riches and avarice.

In addition French complains that Steinbeck's rendering of *The Pearl* is incomplete. In the original folk-tale the fisherman, as you will recall, casts the pearl back into the sea and, in so doing, is freed from the problems that have recently beset him. Yet this option is not open to Steinbeck's fisherman. Kino cannot simply shrug off what has happened and return to his previous life. His flight into the mountains has cost him his boat and the life of his infant son. Furthermore his rage has caused him to murder his pursuers. Thus French and Parini warn us that Steinbeck's narrative frames and focuses the tale of *The Pearl* in a particular way. However, they complain that Steinbeck's focus and his framing device actually fail the tale because his new, and bowdlerized, rendering of Kino's trials generates too many questions and too many loose ends to allow a satisfactory conclusion: Will Kino be tried for murder? How will he deal with the loss of his infant son? Can his marriage survive this tragedy?

Talking turkey

Investigating reports of increasing insecurity, poverty and despair within America's white-collar corporate workforce Ehrenreich (2006) also provides a very good example of a story that fails (and disappoints) due to deficiencies in plotting.

While attending a 'corporate boot camp' – a meeting designed, ostensibly, to allow those currently unemployed or fearful of impending lay-offs to acquire the skills, energy and contacts that will allow them to secure alternative employment – Ehrenreich recounts a galvanizing story (see Hamper, 1992) which singularly failed to improve her attitude.

Patrick, the self-styled counsellor, who has the task of leading his despairing charges through their corporate boot-camp experience, recounts an apparently autobiographical tale concerning his friend Mitch and himself. According to this tale Patrick had been at Mitch's house some years ago for a Thanksgiving celebration. Before the dinner, that forms the centrepiece of such celebrations, it seems that he and Mitch had been hungry and had decided to sneak into the kitchen to make themselves turkey sandwiches. They had been tucking into their illicit snacks when Mitch abruptly fell to the floor and began to thrash around.

Thinking that Mitch was playing one of his famous pranks Patrick, it transpires, ignored his antics and did nothing until his friend began to turn blue-in-the-face. It was only later, Patrick confides, that he discovered that Mitch had suffered a stroke.

Reflecting on this tale Ehrenreich finds it unsatisfactory for a number of reasons. First she complains that Mitch is unable to manufacture a suitable moral that would justify the inclusion of this tale in a corporate boot-camp. Just what is the lesson of this story? Does it warn us to seize the moment because we cannot be sure of our futures? Is it an entreaty to pay closer attention to the needs of our loved ones? It is a warning against the theft of turkey?

Beyond this listing of questions, however, Ehrenreich raises a second, and more serious, objection to Patrick's story. She seems to concede that Patrick's inability to articulate a moral for his tale would be a relatively minor concern if the story were simply a good one. After all each of the questions listed above *could* form the foundation of a sensible reading of the events recounted by Patrick. Yet Patrick's story jars with Ehrenreich's experience of the Thanksgiving celebrations enjoyed by Americans and, for this reason, the story fails. Thus Ehrenreich objects:

- No matter how hungry Patrick and Mitch were they would not despoil the turkey prior to the meal since this fowl is, by tradition, carved at the table by a senior member of the family.
- Noting that Patrick's tale locates the two key characters alone in the kitchen on Thanksgiving Day, Ehrenreich protests that this place tends to be a hub of activity just prior to the meal as the family co-operates in a frenzy of potato-mashing and gravy-making. A plot, which places two men alone in a

kitchen as a Thanksgiving meal approaches its crescendo, she tells us, just does not add up.

From Ehrenreich's perspective, therefore, Patrick has reneged on the promise that, Gabriel (1998) observes, is made whenever a story is announced. And so she worries about the ways the tale has been fused and fitted together: Is the time-line messed up? Did the events take place some time after the meal? Did the basic events actually occur but Patrick added the element of Thanksgiving Day to give the tale extra poignancy? Is the story a complete fabrication?

Through such musing Ehrenreich, again, gives us reason to doubt Boje's antenarrative conceptualization of storytelling. Thus she makes us aware of (a) the virtues of rehearsal, (b) the importance of plotting and (c) the importance of trust in storytelling because she reveals the manner in which a hastily assembled tale that was intended to challenge her own self-image and understanding actually causes her to question the identity and capability of the storyteller. Somewhat ironically, therefore, Ehrenreich's account of her boot-camp experience reveals the ways in which a story designed to reduce the objections of a fee-paying audience actually served to diminish the presence of its narrator.

A Bridge too Far?

William Goldman (2001) offers an insider's account of the filtering processes that are part-and-parcel of effective storytelling. Discussing the development of the screenplay for the film *A Bridge too Far* Goldman, the screen-writer for this tale, notes the ways in which the selection of a particular over-arching theme led to the events that constituted this great project to be filtered and condensed for the cinema.

A Bridge too Far is concerned with the military operation which commenced on 17 September 1944. The objective of this mission was to capture a number of key bridges in Holland in order to cripple German resistance and bring the Second World War to a speedy conclusion. Operation Market Garden, as the plan was codenamed, called for 35,000 troops to be airlifted into enemy territory. These paratroopers were ordered to seize and hold a number of key bridges until relieved by an armoured corps of some 30,000 military vehicles, which had been ordered to punch a route through to those who had taken part in the airborne assault.

History records that Operation Market Garden failed to secure all its objectives (see Ryan, 1975). But Goldman's task is not to chronicle this military operation. This, he tells us, is simply impossible within the restrictions of his cinematic format:

> There were simply too many incidents that cried out for inclusion – *five* Victoria Crosses were awarded for heroism at Arnhem [the last of the bridges].
>
> (Goldman, 2001: 281, original emphasis)

Instead Goldman's task is to tell an entertaining story that can account for the organizational failures and human heroics associated with this strategic endeavour in a manner that, nevertheless, captures the suffering and waste that is modern warfare. So Goldman confronts a key problem: his need for narrative integrity means that he must reduce and filter his material. Yet his material is uncommonly rich and his stage vast.

Eventually, he tells us, he happened upon his story – almost by accident. While writing the speech that General Horrocks, the Commander of the armoured corps, would offer as a briefing to his men, Goldman stumbled across his unifying theme.

In this speech Horrocks portrays the US and British paratroopers as the besieged homesteaders of the old American west and suggests that the advancing armoured column might be thought of as the cavalry speeding to their rescue. Writing that speech Goldman argues:

> was the light bulb at last going on. Because I realized for all its size and complexity, *Bridge* was a cavalry-to-the-rescue story – one in which the cavalry fails to arrive, ending, sadly, one mile short.
>
> That was my spine, and everything that wouldn't cling I couldn't use. *All five* Victoria Cross stories fell out of the picture. Super material went by the board. But it had to.
>
> (Goldman, 2001: 282, original emphasis)

The essence of stories

Acknowledging the importance of the framing and filtering processes that served Goldman so well, a number of authors have attempted to codify the essence of stories (see Czarniawska, 1997; Søderberg, 2003). Gabriel (2000, 2004) offers perhaps the most comprehensive of these codifications. He argues that stories – properly so-called – exhibit a number of key characteristics. Thus he tells us that stories:

- involve characters in a predicament,
- unfold according to a chain of events that, in turn, reflects the structure of the plot and the essential traits of the characters involved,
- call upon symbolism/symbolic factors,
- indulge poetic embellishment and embroidery,
- have a beginning, middle and an ending,
- seek to convey not simple facts but more general and enduring truths.

Elaborating on this final, discriminating factor, in particular, Gabriel tells us that:

> stories purport to relate to facts that happened, but also discover in these facts a plot or meaning, by claiming that facts do not merely happen but that

they happen in accordance with the requirements of a plot. In short, stories are not 'just fictions' (although they may be fictions), nor are they mere chronologies of events as they happened. Instead, they represent poetic elaborations of narrative material, aiming to communicate *facts as experience*, not facts as information.

(Gabriel, 2004: 64, original emphasis)

Crick (1982) makes a similar point as he surveys the works of George Orwell. Discussing Orwell's apparently autobiographical accounts of his public school days and his later tramping adventures (see the essays entitled 'Such, such were the joys' and 'The Spike' in Orwell, 2000), Crick observes that Orwell's stories of his school days and other adventures are far from being simply factual accounts of his early years. Indeed, in his biography of Orwell, Crick argues that this celebrated writer embellishes his school experiences. Furthermore he notes that Orwell's 'biographical' reminiscences fuse characters and embroider events.

Yet Crick is understanding in the face of these poetic liberties. Orwell does not really deceive us, for he was not, Crick tells us, simply trying to document his own youth. He was, instead, attempting to highlight more general movements, concerns and social processes. Thus Crick protests that Orwell's embellishments and exaggerations have been manufactured in the name of a more general and more enduring truth that reveals the manners and insecurity of a particular strata of the English middle-classes *and* the hardships, poverty and desperation endured by the various elements of England's working-classes.

The poetic tropes

Reflecting upon the poetic qualities of such unique but generalizable stories (see Tietze *et al.*, 2003), Gabriel (2000) argues that 'proper' stories will call upon a number of eight 'poetic tropes' or generic attributions as they attempt to make events meaningful. Outlining these poetic tropes, Gabriel suggests that poetic tropes are the attributes which breathe life into stories and give them the capacity to communicate experience. Poetic stories, therefore tend to attribute:

1 Motive – which might variously define events to be accidental or incidental.
2 Causal connections – which outline the cause and effects of actions.
3 Responsibility – where blame and credit are allocated to actors and actions.
4 Unity – such that a group comes to be defined as such.
5 Fixed qualities – such that heroes are heroic and villains, villainous.
6 Emotion – to describe the emotional characteristics of actions.
7 Agency – whereby volition is variously raised or diminished.
8 Providential significance – which is important in certain tales, where higher forms may seem to intervene to restore justice and order to the characters and events which constitute the tale.

The careful organization of these tropes, Gabriel notes, allows for the construction of many different plots and characters. Thus he observes that authors can structure the poetic tropes to produce a number of different 'poetic modes', designed variously to inculcate pride in, or to bring laughter forth from, the enraptured listener. Documenting the main poetic modes, Gabriel notes that a tale may be (a) comic, (b) tragic, (c) epic or (d) romantic depending upon the construction and organization of characters and events. For example 'epic' tales have particular attributes which, as we have seen, cause Boje discomfort.

'Epic' tales concern the lives and endeavours of heroic figures. Consequently they often have simple and rather linear plot-lines. Indeed epic tales tend to devote little time to the intricacies and complexities of character development. Instead they focus upon action, movement, achievement and closure. In contrast, comic tales are designed to produce laughter. Indeed in the case of the comic tale it is worth noting that the laugher of the audience is often achieved at the expense of the main protagonist. Thus while the qualities of the epic hero lead inevitably to triumph, the character flaws of the main protagonist in the comic tale lead inexorably to failure because (for example) the protagonist has had the vanity to interfere in events and processes which exceed human understanding (see Collins and Rainwater, 2005).

In the section that follows we will attempt to apply this appreciation of the nature, purpose and key characteristics of stories to our critical review and reanalysis of the works of Tom Peters.

Putting stories to work

Tom Peters is generally regarded as an engaging and entertaining speaker. Even those who are otherwise sceptical of his ideas and orientations generally concede that his seminars are popular. Furthermore, reviewers also tend to concede that his books sell well because they are littered with amusing stories and engaging characters (Maidique, 1983). Yet, as we have seen, Peters has experimented with the narrative form of his work and, in recent years, this has culminated in a form of writing that has all but abandoned the conventions of a traditional and continuous narrative in favour of a more disjointed non-linear, or hypertextual, format. Regarding these developments observers could be forgiven for wondering if Peters has both literally and figuratively 'lost the plot'. Here we will attempt to address this concern as we examine the stories that Peters employs in his attempts to secure the consent and affiliation of his readers.

But before we turn to this issue we must pause to consider why this matters. Why should we focus upon the stories that Tom Peters recounts in his texts? And mindful of the twin hinges of currency and controversy that shape academic discourse: Will this account of Peters' plotting (or lack thereof) actually tell us something new about this author?

Do stories matter?

Noting the recent growth of academic interest in organizational storytelling Gabriel, as we have seen, has argued that stories – when studied *in situ* – are an important resource for academic inquiry because they provide insight on and access to elements of organized life, which have been obscured by those forms of scholarship that have pursued *facts* in a search for *the* objective truth (Gabriel, 1998, 2000). Yet he also acknowledges that this academic interest in stories has spawned an array of texts that views stories variously as: 'vehicles for organizational communication and learning ... as expressions of political domination ... as dramatic performances ... as occasions for emotional discharge ... or as narrative structures' (Gabriel, 1998: 84–85).

The guru literature concerned with stories and storytelling is, by comparison, unvariegated. Indeed an instrumental concern with narrative, which views myths and stories as the primary tool for organizational change and development, is characteristic of modern guru texts (see Huczynski, 1993). Thus the works of authors such as Deal and Kennedy (1982) and Peters and Waterman (1982) are united by a common conviction that managers can and, indeed, should learn how to manage and change their organizations *through* stories.

In Search of Excellence, for example, produced a large number of organizational stories that were designed (a) to reveal the characteristics of business excellence and (b) to galvanize (Hamper, 1992) or to reanimate and reorientate (De Cock and Hipkin, 1997) those who would, after reading the text, devote themselves to the search for excellence. Similarly *A Passion for Excellence* reproduced a large number of 'implementation vignettes' designed to reveal the common leadership practices of those who had the necessary passion for business change.

To some extent this guru concern with storytelling as a mechanism of/for management control has been confirmed in academic work. For example Gioia and Chittepeddi (1991), Boyce (1995) and Søderberg (2003) have explored the managerial problems of organizational change endeavours and have provided some support for the gurus' conviction that organizations can be reshaped by skilful storytellers. Thus Gioia and Chittepeddi have suggested that managers achieve change in organizations by, first, creating narratives that establish and engender 'the need' for such change. In an earlier account of the politics and processes of change management Pettigrew (1985) makes a similar point when he draws attention to the ways in which the managers of *ICI* sought to provide organizational members with particular readings of events in the wider context that suggested an imminent crisis in (and for) the internal workings of the organization. Echoing this account of 'sensemaking and sensegiving', Salzer-Mörling (1998) points out that the Chinese character for 'boss' depicts a man with two mouths and suggests that this reveals the ways in which managers must orchestrate events and must speak sense to and for others.

Yet where the gurus of management simply seek to capitalize on such orchestration, more critical, academic scholars take one step back. Gabriel, for example, acknowledges that humans do use stories to make sense of day-to-day problems and ambiguities. Furthermore he also acknowledges that social elites use stories in their attempts to (re)orientate the sensemaking activities of their peers and subalterns. Yet he is also keenly aware that stories have limitations as sensegiving devices. Stories, he warns us, do not always and everywhere generate and carry the meanings intended by their various storytellers because organizational tales are fragile and open to translation. Thus, in opposition to Peters, Gabriel finds that local understandings and improvisations often out-pace or, worse, tend to object to the managerial orchestration of stories. Similarly Sims (2003) suggests that the orchestrators of organizational sensemaking can find it very difficult to 'get their stories straight' (Buchanan, 2003) because those who must speak metaphorically from two mouths find themselves before three distinct audiences.

Discussing the peculiarities of middle-management, Sims argues that this group at the front-line of organizational attempts to animate and orientate the thinking and actions of others finds itself in an unenviable position. Middle-managers, he argues, must create narratives that are acceptable to three distinct constituencies – their superiors, their subordinates and themselves! Sims suggests that 'the most critical of these audiences is the internal one' (Sims, 2003: 1199). Yet, despite this, he argues that the middle-manager's need to impress his/her bosses *and* the associated need to manage the orientations of subordinates causes the incumbents of mid-level organizational positions to construct and relay, key narratives that either undermine or ignore their own problems and concerns.

Does our story matter?

Turning our face to Peters once more it should be clear from the foregoing analysis that stories *do* matter to this pundit. For Tom Peters stories are not just a tool for change and development. Instead stories are to be regarded as *the* tool of choice for modern organizations. Thus Peters has suggested that, for organizations, stories may matter more than products (Peters, 2003). Those organizations with the best stories, he tells us, will have committed employees and faithful customers.

In an attempt to elaborate on this point *and* to convince us that it provides a faithful account of the business of management Peters has, of course, called upon the craft of the storyteller. He has gathered and crafted stories in a self-conscious attempt to intervene in the day-to-day flow of narrative sensemaking.

The account of Peters' storytelling, developed in the following section, acknowledges this fact. Indeed it reflects and builds upon this guru's commitment to the power of stories. Yet we do not come to praise Caesar. Having constructed a comprehensive catalogue of Peters' storywork we will, for the first time, subject this guru's storytelling to sustained academic scrutiny as we question his sensemaking and sensegiving endeavours. This attempt to examine the nature, meaning and effects of Peters' storytelling makes our critical review of

Tom Peters' storywork novel and productive because it locates this guru's work within the critical academic literature on organizational storytelling *and yet* tests his attempt to orchestrate organizational sensemaking within its own terms of reference.

Thus our construction and subsequent analysis of Tom Peters' storywork catalogue seeks to:

- confirm the sensegiving potential of Peters' stories while acknowledging the limitations of such sensegiving endeavours,
- generate explanations for the changes observed in Peters' storywork catalogue,
- capitalize on the debates which surround organizational storytelling to explore the nature and limitations of Peters' attempts at narrative sensegiving,
- raise questions concerning Peters legacy and future as a guru, while signalling areas for future research.

Method

In an attempt to chart, describe and analyse the stories that Peters constructs for his readers, the eight works previously identified as key elements of Tom Peters' canon of management have been subjected to a detailed analysis which might usefully be termed a 'forensic reading'. Following Gabriel, this review of Peters' texts sought to identify those narratives which because they:

- place characters in a predicament,
- unfold in a manner that reflects the structure of the plot and the essential traits of the characters involved,
- depend upon symbolic resources,
- proceed to a satisfactory conclusion,
- seek a relationship with a deeper and more enduring truth than is achieved through mere factual verification,

might properly be characterized as poetic stories.

To assist with the process of charting these tales, and to facilitate subsequent verification of this charting process, a cataloguing form similar to that employed by Gabriel (1995) was developed. This form collected information detailing:

- The locations and opening words of each tale identified.
- The main characters and dominant theme of the tale.
- The underlying emotional qualities of the tale – whether pride, sadness, etc.
- The dominant narrative type – whether tragic, comic, etc.

Readers may well protest that this attempt to signal the dominant narrative type of the tale under study tends to downplay the ways in which stories might be subject to alternative readings or reviews (see for example, Boje *et al.* 2001; Collins and Rainwater, 2005). Yet in response to this (anticipated) objection we might counter that it is possible to recognize, simultaneously, the feasibility of alternative readings *and* the intention of the original storyteller. Thus our attempt to chart the dominant narrative type of each tale encountered is not intended as an absolute judgement as to *the* nature of the narrative under review, rather it should be read as an attempt to name the author's intention and is based upon an analysis of the story in its context. That said, the cataloguing exercise did reveal a few instances when Peters failed in his storytelling endeavours. Thus a very few stories have been catalogued as 'ambiguous' because in these instances Peters, like Patrick the boot-camp counsellor (Ehrenreich, 2006), has proved unable to *give* a clear sense of his intentions and orientations. Thus the nature and moral of these 'ambiguous' tales remains opaque and open to question – perhaps even for Peters himself! (see Table 4.2, below).

On average it took some five days of labour to catalogue and to chart the stories contained in each of Tom Peters' key works. This work was undertaken during the late summer and early autumn of 2004 (during a period of study leave granted by the University of Essex). Subsequent reanalysis and verification of this initial cataloguing took a further 15 days. In total, then, it took some 10 weeks of labour to create the catalogue of Peters' storytelling endeavours that will be reported in this section.

This 'forensic reading' of Peters' key works has facilitated the analysis laid out in the sections that follow.

Losing the plot?

Our attempt to catalogue Peters' work from a storytelling perspective (see Table 4.1) provides support for our primary charge against Tom Peters – that this celebrated guru has lost the plot. Indeed our data suggest that Peters, once the parable-telling apostle of business change, may now be close to 'poetical apostasy' when it comes to writing about the business of management.

Table 4.1 A count of stories in the key works of Tom Peters

Text	Total number of stories	Page count
In Search of Excellence	137	322 + 36
A Passion for Excellence	165	422 + 25
Thriving on Chaos	118	523 + 02
Liberation Management	112	763 + 34
The Tom Peters Seminar	41	291 + 03
The Pursuit of Wow	57	326 + 08
The Circle of Innovation	38	499 + 21
Re-imagine	44	352

Cataloguing Peters

Peters' earliest works are comparatively rich in storytelling resources. *In Search of Excellence* and *A Passion for Excellence*, for example, contain 137 and 165 narratives, respectively, that qualify as stories in our interpretation of these matters. However, later texts such as *The Pursuit of Wow* and *The Circle of Innovation*, which are similar in size to Peters' earlier, co-authored works offer the reader far fewer tales and, jointly, exhibit far fewer stories (57 and 38) than *In Search of Excellence* alone. Indeed in comparison with this, Peters' first key text, later works such as *The Tom Peters Seminar* and *Re-imagine* are poetic deserts offering just 41 and 44 stories each.

Given the importance which Peters attaches to organizational storytelling this diminishing catalogue surely merits an explanation! Recognizing both the limits of our current inquiry and the power and potential of local narratives I offer not one, but six narratives which variously overlap and yet vie to account for the 'headline' changes we have observed in Peters' catalogue of stories.

The first two of these six explanations reflect on the changing nature of organization, whereas the final three reflect Peters' own changing concerns and orientations. The third explanation tendered, as we shall see, is of a hybrid form. It reflects, to some extent, the intersection between the worlds of management and the celebrity world of the management guru inhabited by Tom Peters.

Explanation one

Both Gabriel (1998, 2004) and Boje (1991), as we have seen, have complained that good stories can be hard to find within organizations and have suggested that organizations are becoming 'narratively deskilled'. If we accept and pursue this logic then we happen upon our first explanation. Thus our first explanation suggests that Peters' later texts contain fewer stories because the increasing pace of work has caused the well of organizational stories to begin to run dry. Or, more plainly, the relative absence of stories in Peters' later works may reflect and correspond with a simple decline in storytelling within organizations.

Explanation two

Our second explanation, like the first noted above, also suggests that Peters' texts contain fewer stories simply because, as time has passed, there have been fewer stories told in organized settings. Yet, where our first explanation portrayed this as a more-or-less organic outcome of work intensification, our second proposal draws attention to the role of managerial actors as follows: the managerial texts written in the early 1980s, as we have seen, argued that managers should take steps to craft, and to share, organizational stories that would inculcate appropriate behaviours and attitudes at work. However, our second explanation suggests that the decline in organizational storytelling that is evident in Peters' work may be the result of managers failing to pay proper attention to the need to cultivate and disseminate stories in and at work. This explanation, if at all accurate, would be ironic given Peters' insistence on the power of stories *and* the now mainstream concern with all things 'narrative'.

Explanation three

Tom Peters is now in his 60s. He has been in and around organizations for some 40-or-more years. Indeed he was at the forefront of a movement which saw organizational stories move to the centre of the manager's agenda.

Commenting on this managerial interest in storytelling both Boje and Gabriel have observed that gurus and consultants (such as Peters) tend to study stories from a particular vantage-point. In short, Peters' tales have, in Boje's (2001) terms, a Narrative character. That is to say that his organizational stories tend to be top-down, monological and heroic.

When first encountered these managerial Narratives can be both engaging and entertaining. Yet their appeal fades quickly and, before long, these tales of corporate endeavour tend to look hackneyed and tend to sound clichéd. Recognizing this our third explanation for the decline in organizational storytelling observed in Peters' work is based upon the suggestion that 'the corporate culture rage' (Thackray, 1993) has led to the overproduction of, what might be termed, 'monologues of monotony' that even Peters – once the high-priest of this movement – now finds boring, clichéd and scarcely worthy of reproduction. In an echo of Finkelstein's (2004) analysis, therefore, our third explanation for the changes observed in Peters' storywork catalogue suggests that this guru may now prefer poetical silence to a headlong retreat into cliché.

Explanation four

Our fourth explanation for the decline in Peters' storytelling reflects more directly on the habits and practices of this celebrated guru.

Gabriel (2004) argues that storytelling is a craft that requires and rewards patience. Good stories, he tells us, require careful plotting, sound characterization and thoughtful embellishment. Stories crafted in haste invariably break the covenant between storyteller and audience.

Peters' early works are, at one level, a testament to his listening skills. As he travelled in search of the secrets of organizational excellence (see Chapter 1) Peters became an assiduous collector of organizational stories and corporate mythology (see Gabriel, 1998). Consequently his early works were rich in poetic resources. Yet Peters *and* his approach to studying organizational matters have, it seems, aged poorly. He has become a guru, of course, but his celebrity has not brought contentment. In fact he has become grumpy and increasingly impatient with his flock (see Peters, 1989, 2003).

Reflecting upon this impatience our fourth explanation for the changes observed in Peters' catalogue of stories is rooted in Peters' own observation that those at the apex of their particular industries can easily lose sight of the factors that nourished their earlier successes (Peters and Austin, 1985). Thus our fourth explanation for the changes observed in Peters' storywork suggests that this pundit's own market success and celebrity may have blinded him to:

- the limits of his own appeal and authority,
- the seductive potential of storytelling.

Explanation five

In the early years of his guru career Peters was able to tap into the knowledge and insights of those at the very heart of corporate America as he elaborated his vision(s) of the future of management. Yet as his career has developed he seems to have become increasingly distanced from the realities of organizational life, in part because a hectic schedule of speaking engagements has simply denied him the opportunity to (re)immerse himself in the daily trials of managing and organizing. In addition it is clear (see Chapter 3) that, in the past 15 years, Peters has also become increasingly estranged from the elites who once furnished him with his epic tales of corporate endeavour (see Chapter 3).

This coalition of absence and estrangement provides us with our fifth explanation for Peters' decline as a storyteller and an echo of our fourth explanation. Thus our fifth explanation for the decline in Peters' storytelling is based on the suggestion that key changes in this commentator's life-style and working patterns mean that this celebrity no longer enjoys the intimate connection to the daily rhythms and routines of organizing that Gabriel (2000) insists is central to effective storywork.

Explanation six

Our sixth explanation, again, carries echoes of our fourth suggestion for the declining number of stories in Peters' texts, yet takes this one step further. In common with explanations four and five this suggestion also recognizes Peters' increasing impatience with corporate America and acknowledges that his more recent texts tend (a) to report the cold facts of the competitive situation and (b) to prescribe what managers should do in the light of these facts (see Peters, 2003). Yet, where our fourth explanation saw the decline in Peters' storytelling as an outcome of a privilege abused, our sixth explanation suggests that the relative absence of stories in this author's texts amounts to a loss of faith in the Peters' credo. In short our sixth explanation suggests that the decline we have observed in Peters' catalogue of storywork is, in fact, symptomatic of this guru's 'poetical apostasy'.

Digging deeper

These six attempts to provide an explanation for Peters' growing poetic impoverishment are fair enough, I suppose. They may or may not account for the changes observed in Peters' 'storying': future research may add clarity to the situation. But, for the moment, we need to move on.

Plainly a narrative account of Tom Peters must do more than simply harvest this author's organizational tales and count the bushels gathered. Stories need to be understood dynamically as the essence of organization. They are not just objects to be counted, for they have subjects and themes which both bear and reward closer scrutiny.

Further, and more detailed, scrutiny of Peters' story catalogue, as we shall see, has generated interesting speculations on this guru's works *and* promising avenues for future inquiry.

Tales and propaganda

Gabriel (2000, 2004) and Boje (1991, 2001) have observed that written accounts of the business of management such as those that appear in the *Harvard Business Review*, represent either fabrications of reality or partisan projections of a top management world-view that jar with the everyday stories which people tell one another at, or about, work. Both Boje and Gabriel, of course, do complain that, in their fieldwork activity, they often struggle to unearth good stories and talented storytellers. Nonetheless they protest that when organizational actors choose to relate tales of working, certain story types tend to dominate. Thus Boje and Gabriel suggest that employees tend to favour tales that highlight the laughable and/or paradoxical elements of their working experiences and would seldom, if ever, choose to relay an heroic or epic story to a colleague.

In this respect the analyses offered by Boje and Gabriel make it clear that, despite Maidique's (1983) celebration of Peters' storytelling, all of this gurus' narratives of organization – even those richest in poetic resources – tend to be distorted to some degree because epic tales of heroic endeavour predominate.

Epic tales

As Table 4.2 shows Peters tends to favour particular types of tale when he relates his case for business change. Within *In Search of Excellence*, for example, 97 of the 137 tales recounted (71 per cent) qualify as epic or heroic

Table 4.2 An analysis of the stories recounted by Peters in his key works sorted by narrative type (relative percentage weightings appear in brackets)

Text	Epic tales (%)	Comic tales (%)	Tragic tales (%)	Romantic tales (%)	Tragi-comic tales (%)	Ambiguous tales (%)
In Search...	97 (71)	21 (15)	9 (6.5)	0 (0)	8 (6)	2 (2)
A Passion...	132 (80)	9 (5)	12 (7)	0 (0)	5 (3)	7 (4)
Thriving...	111 (94)	0 (0)	6 (5)	0 (0)	0 (0)	1 (1)
Liberation...	92 (82)	1 (1)	17 (15)	0 (0)	2 (2)	0 (0)
Seminar	33 (81)	2 (5)	3 (7)	0 (0)	2 (5)	1 (2)
Wow	53 (93)	0 (0)	3 (5)	0 (0)	1 (2)	0 (0)
Circle	29 (76)	3 (8)	2 (5)	0 (0)	1 (3)	0 (0)
Re-imagine	30 (68)	2 (5)	7 (16)	0 (0)	5 (11)	0 (0)

narratives insofar as they deal with the exploits of special individuals who merit our admiration because their courage or tenacity has led them to overcome obstacles or difficulties. Peters' later texts are perhaps his least heroic, but even in these books the epic narrative is still predominant. Thus in *The Circle of Innovation* 29 of the 38 tales relayed (76 per cent) are of the epic or heroic form and in *Re-imagine* no fewer than 30 of the 44 tales recounted (68 per cent) qualify as heroic tales of endeavour.

Comic tales

The comic tales that Boje and Gabriel suggest are more typical of the stories that people tell of/at work never amount to more than a tiny minority of the tales recounted by Peters. Combining the comic with the tragically, or darkly, comic form identified by Gabriel as an important hybrid narrative type it is clear that comic tales are not a particular feature of Peters' repertoire: for example none of the 118 tales relayed by Peters in *Thriving on Chaos* have a comical thread and only three of the 112 tales relayed in *Liberation Management* have a comical element.

Comical tales *do* feature a little more prominently in those works that derive most directly from Peters' speaking engagements (see Chapter 2). Thus it is worth pointing out that 10 per cent of the tales relayed in the *Tom Peters Seminar* and 16 per cent of the stories recounted in *Re-imagine* are of a comic or darkly comic form. Yet having made this observation we must also note that these are texts that remain impoverished in poetic terms such that, in the seminar text, this figure of 10 per cent represents just four of the 41 tales relayed and in *Re-imagine* the figure of 16 per cent accounts for just seven of the 44 stories exhibited.

Tragic tales

Tragic tales are similarly underrepresented in Peters' accounts of the business of management. These tales, which encourage readers to empathize with, or take pity on, characters who find themselves in unenviable predicaments, typically account for somewhere between 6 and 8 per cent of the stories recounted by Peters. However there are exceptions. *Liberation Management* which, as you will recall, was written at a time when Peters experienced a number of personal and professional difficulties (see Chapter 2) has a total of 17 (15 per cent) tragic tales. Similarly *Re-imagine*, perhaps Peters' grumpiest and most disaffected text, has 7 (16 per cent) tragic tales.

Romantic tales

The fourth story type discussed by Gabriel (2000) is the romance. Gabriel (1995) has observed that 'romantic' tales seldom accounted for more than 10 per cent of the stories he and his colleagues collected throughout their research.

Furthermore he seems to imply that such romantic tales are products of maturity and organizational immersion insofar as he observes that none of his students ever recounted a romantic organizational tale on their return from their work placements.

Romancing the Stone?

Romantic tales, as you might expect, deal with matters of the heart. They relate stories of love. Peters professes a love of business (see for example, Peters, 2003). Indeed he protests that business excellence is a product of passion and obsession (Peters and Austin, 1985). Yet despite this talk of love, lust, passion and obsession, Peters' storytelling repertoire is devoid of romance. Had Peters not been, so clearly, a man of conviction and strong belief, had he perhaps just one fewer ex-wife, it might have been tempting to put this lack of romance down to a certain coldness of character. But since Peters is so clearly warm-blooded we must look for another means to account for the absence of romance in his tales of corporate endeavour.

Peters between the mill-stones?

Gabriel's (2000) analysis of organizational storytelling provides perhaps the most direct (and the most cutting) means of rationalizing the absence of romantic tales in Peters' narratives of business. Gabriel's analysis, as we have seen, suggests that romantic tales become available to organizational researchers who succeed in associating with mature respondents and/or successfully immerse themselves in the day-to-day processes of organization. Given this, there is surely room for the suggestion that the paucity of romantic tales in our catalogue of Peters' work demonstrates one or a number of the following problems:

* that Peters' research lacks depth,
* that Peters' researchers failed to develop a rapport with their respondents,
* that Peters' respondents lack maturity and/or self-confidence.

David Sims (2003) provides an interesting account of organizational story-telling, which may offer us an alternative (and less cutting) means to rationalize the nature of Peters' storytelling endeavours and the omissions we have observed in this catalogue. Sims argues that middle-managers are under pressure to narrate their experiences of working in ways that will make sense to three distinct constituencies – their superiors, their subordinates and themselves! However, he suggests that the middle-manager's need (a) to impress his/her bosses and (b) the associated need to organize and orientate his/her juniors causes these individuals to relay tales that undermine their own sense of self.

If we stretch Sims's analysis only slightly, we have a potential explanation for the absence of romantic tales in Peters' story catalogue. Thus Sims's analysis of managerial narratives suggests that Peters' awareness of the (rational) expectations of senior management (see Peters, 1989) may have caused him to ignore stories that deal with love and romantic passion at work, despite the pain and discomfiture that this may cause him at a personal level.

Viewed in these terms the absence of romantic tales in the Peters' catalogue of storytelling may represent evidence of Peters' own organizational liminality (Czarniawska and Mazza, 2003) insofar as it suggests that this, the most famous of the business gurus still feels the need to pander to the 'hard' approach to management that he claims to defy.

Of course we cannot be sure that in choosing not to speak of romantic matters Peters causes himself pain. But one thing *is* clear. Our cataloguing of Peters' storytelling demonstrates that, nowadays, he is either less willing or less able to relay stories of managing. Furthermore, our more detailed analysis of Peters' story types suggests that this author's attempts at organizational sensegiving produce (a) a bogus account of managing because (b) his storywork lacks an intimate connection with the world of work, and so, (c) tends either to ignore or to downplay the complex realities of organized life *and* the peculiarities of managerial work. But we should not get carried away!

In truth Peters' declining story tally might matter comparatively little if a reduction in the number of stories relayed by this author were to be compensated, say, by the development of tales which, despite being fewer in number, were more elaborate, more surprising, richer in their characterization or better able to precipitate a deeper emotional response from their audience. After all Peters (Peters and Waterman, 1982; Peters and Austin, 1985; Peters, 2003) is clear that it is the individual with the best *not* the most stories who will triumph in the organizational and market arenas.

Yet, countering this observation, it is worth making two points. The first of these is relatively prosaic as far as analytical observations go. The second, however, is potentially more serious for Peters.

- While Peters is correct to point out that quality not quantity matters in the court of public opinion it is, nevertheless, undeniably true that a good story counts for nothing if the audience is absent or asleep. Indeed, if we accept Peters' claim that stories are essential to managerial sensegiving, it seems obvious that the reader who encounters 137 stories over 350 pages (as is the case with *In Search of Excellence*) or 165 stories over 450 pages (as is the case with *A Passion for Excellence*) is more likely to be engaged by, and attuned to, the author's message than the reader who must struggle through some 500 pages of 'opinion' and 'reports' in order to enjoy just 38 galvanizing tales of business (Hamper, 1992).
- Peters' tales do not just decline in number. They also change form. Over time his narratives become more shrill (*The Economist*, 20/12/2003); his characters become less agreeable; and those few stories that remain are too brief and too hastily rendered to act as sensegiving devices.

Let us explore this further.

On moral tales

It would be fair to say that the stories which Peters relates in his many texts on management are, at root, 'moral tales'. No matter whether their poetic thrust is comic, tragic or epic, at root, all Peters' tales carry a strong moral message concerning the merits of hard work, good manners and honest competition. Given Peters' explicit focus upon the importance of 'values' and 'beliefs' in the pursuit of business excellence this should come as little surprise. What should, perhaps, surprise us is that:

1   Peters' dominant narrative has remained unchanged despite wider changes in American business and society.

In 1982 (see Chapter 1) America was clearly ready for some 'good news' (Huczynski, 1993) and was clearly only too keen to celebrate the maverick individuals who, Peters and Waterman (1982) argued, would lead the turn-around of American Society. But 25 years on, do such heroic narratives still make sense? Do they still have a capacity to resonate (Grint, 1994) with the concerns of the working population?

Commenting on the 'corrosion of character' which he regards as one of the necessary consequences of market liberalization, Sennett (1998) argues that American workers have lost their narrative thread. In the 'good old days', he suggests, the life narrative of the aspiring American was built upon a promise of job security, a rising standard of living and a comfortable retirement. However, Sennett complains that key changes in the economy and polity of America (and elsewhere) suggest that today's employees will suffer insecurity at work and are threatened by a diminishing standard of living when in work and in (a delayed) retirement.

In the face of such changes Sennett, like so many other commentators, takes a narrative turn. He suggests, for example, that America's growing band of evangelistic and fundamentalist Christians might be interpreted as the product of a search for a new and meaningful narrative that can locate and explain these changes, while providing succour to those who must cope with this new age of uncertainty.

Looking down on such changes – he is old enough and rich enough to be insulated from them – Peters, too, has questioned the old narrative of the American Dream. In the context of a volatile and capricious labour market he protests that employees must now think of themselves as 'brands' and must develop a portfolio of skills that will make them a unique sales proposition (Peters, 1999c, 2003). Yet, despite his faith in the power of branding, he has become increasingly angry and disaffected. Corporate America, Peters complains, suffers from hubris. It won't listen (to him) and it won't learn. Furthermore, he complains that corporate criminality as in the Enron case, for example, is a betrayal of all those mavericks who love business but choose to play within the rules set by statute (and common) law. Yet despite this, his core narrative theme remains essentially unchanging. Americans may have become cynical, depressed and disaffected but Tom Peters, it seems, remains a true believer. Others may seek narratives that mine the organization for dissonance, paradox and irony (see Grant *et al.* 2004) but Peters continues to produce heroic narratives which protest that all will be well, that 'branded' individuals will prosper.

In the face of obvious signs of change, decay and betrayal, therefore, Peters takes his cue from George Orwell (1983) and *Animal Farm*. Despite his protestations of disaffection, therefore, Peters appears as an ingratiating supplicant before the twin titans of liberalisation and globalization. In an echo of Boxer, the tragically naïve, old work-horse, Peters announces 'I will work harder' (Orwell, 1983: 64 and 100) to become indispensable (see Peters, 1999c, 2003).

2   Peters' most recent text (Peters, 2003) waxes lyrical on the power of stories and yet this work contains almost no poetic tales. Thus *Re-imagine*:

- bombards the reader with fact and opinion,
- introduces proto-stories, which soon collapse for the want of a convincing motive or satisfactory ending

In short, *Re-imagine* hectors where it should woo. It preaches when it should perform.

Twenty-five years on from the publication of *In Search of Excellence*, Peters, so often vaunted as the master of the moral tale, now offers 'terse narratives' of business. But like Boje's terse stories, these tales self-destruct because they lack 'performativity, memorableness, ingenuity and symbolism' (Gabriel, 2000: 20). They are all moral and no tale! And worse still – Peters, now, wants us to see him as the hero of the hour!

Narrator and hero

In Chapter 3 we observed that during the past 25 years Peters has redefined his heroes. Indeed we observed that Peters' exemplars of managerial excellence have shifted from the east coast boardrooms of the largest American public corporations and are now to be found in smaller, entrepreneurial and 'start up' organizations in a variety of locations – including American's west coast, Britain and Europe. Yet Peters' changing definition of his model business hero is not properly reflected in the cast list of his stories of organizational endeavour. Indeed it is apparent that, as time passes, Peters moves from being the narrator of his organizational stories to become both narrator and hero!

Tables 4.3 and 4.4 analyse the stories told by Peters in each of his key texts and attempt to identify the key actors of the tales relayed. These tables reveal certain stabilities *and* key movements in Peters' narrative of business.

Dealing first with the stabilities: it is evident that throughout his guru career Peters has often chosen to conceal the identities of the heroes/protagonists of the tales he has related in print. Indeed many of the tales recounted by Peters, as Tables 4.3 and 4.4 show, concern 'mystery' individuals. That Peters should

Table 4.3 Main actors ranked 1 to 6 featuring in stories appearing in key works of Tom Peters

Text and story count	Key actors 1–6 (story count in brackets)
In Search of Excellence (137)	1. Anonymous (31) 2. IBM (17) 3=. Dana (8)/ Hewlett Packard (8) 5. 3M (7) 6. Authors (5)
A Passion for Excellence (165)	1. Anonymous (30) 2. Authors (19) 3. IBM (6) 4=. GE (5)/HP (5) 6. Domino's (4)
Thriving on Chaos (118)	1. Anonymous (32) 2. Author (11) 3. Tenant (5) 4=. Domino's (4)/'The Japanese' (4) 6=. 'Imagined You' (3)/Worthington (3)/SAS (3)
Liberation Management (112)	1. Anonymous (45) 2. Author (26) 3. Ingersoll-Rand (6) 4=. Union Pacific Rail Road (5)/Titeflex (5) 6. Imagination (4)
The Tom Peters Seminar (41)	1. Author (14) 2. Anonymous (12) 3. Union Pacific Rail Road (2) 4=. Remaining stories each feature different actors
The Pursuit of Wow (57)	1=. Author (22)/Anonymous (22) 3. Fed Ex (4) 4=. Bank of Boston (3)/Verifone (3) 6=. De-mar (2)/ Imagined You (2)
The Circle of Innovation (38)	1. Author (27) 2. Anonymous (22) 3=. Bob Waterman (2)/Southwest Airlines (2) 5. No other actor features more than once
Re-imagine (44)	1=. Author (19)/Anonymous (19) 3. No other actor features more than once

Table 4.4 An analysis of the growing prominence of the author as a key character appearing in stories relayed by Tom Peters in his key works since 1982

Text and story count	Author(s) as key character – number of stories and rank ordering	% of total stories where author appears as key character
In Search of Excellence (137)	5 stories – 6th in total story count	4
A Passion for Excellence (165)	19 stories – 2nd	12
Thriving on Chaos (118)	11 stories – 2nd	9
Liberation Management (112)	26 stories – 2nd	23
The Tom Peters Seminar (41)	14 stories – 1st	34
The Pursuit of Wow (57)	22 stories – 1st=	39
The Circle of Innovation (38)	27 stories – 1st	71
Re-imagine (44)	19 stories – 1st=	43

choose to conceal the identity of these actors is unsurprising. Indeed three lines of explanation come to mind.

(1) Deep background

Journalists and researchers of all kinds often find that some individuals will agree to be interviewed for a project, or programme of work, only on the understanding that their identity should not be revealed to others. Furthermore, researchers often have to give their respondents an undertaking that their words and ideas will be couched in ways which prevent others from tracing their original source. Thus Peters' preference for 'anonymous heroes' may simply reflect the normal dynamics of academic and journalistic inquiry.

Yet there are additional means of rationalizing Peters' taste for the anonymous which take us beyond the generalities of research and into the specifics of the business of consulting.

(2) The business of consulting

Discussing the origins of the excellence project, Crainer (1997) offers an additional explanation for Peters' preference for mystery and anonymity in his storywork. Discussing the origins of the excellence project Crainer notes that, within McKinsey, the title of Peters' and Waterman's (1982) book was the subject of much debate. Indeed he tells us that an earlier 'working title' for this text (which suggested that the 'secrets' of excellence would be found within) was vetoed by 'the Partners', who reasoned that a professional organization such as McKinsey should neither betray client confidence nor divulge proprietarial knowledge that has a clear market potential. Thus a concern with client privilege may help to explain Peters' preference for anonymity. But there is one final suggestion that bears analysis.

(3) Audience affiliation

Clark and Greatbatch (2002) offer us a third rationale for Peters' preference for anonymized heroes. Studying the live performances of management's gurus, Clark and Greatbatch argue that speakers must work carefully to secure and to maintain the affiliation of their audiences. Analysing the stratagems and ploys employed by a variety of notable public speakers – Peters included – they argue that orators will often choose to anonymize the identities of the heroes (and villains) of their tales because this:

- prevents members of the audience from being exposed to a potentially critical or hostile analysis,
- prevents audience members from undermining the orator's tale, for example, by interrupting to clarify or correct a point of fact – *actually that's not how it was at IBM, during my time with the company we never . . .*

On the changes evident in Peters' cast-list of heroes: we should acknowledge that, at one level, Peters' changing cast of heroes does seems to confirm his own admission that his exemplars of modern managerial excellence have shifted position and location (Peters, 1989) – at least in a negative sense. Thus the key companies vaunted and celebrated in Peters' texts of 1982 and 1985 – IBM, Dana International, Hewlett Packard and 3M – simply drop out of sight after 1985 and never again feature prominently in Peters' texts. The problem being that Peters tells few tales of his new business exemplars. In fact he chooses instead to make himself a leading figure in his tales of organization. Thus Peters moves from being sixth on the cast list of *In Search of Excellence* (appearing in 4 per cent of the text's tales) to second place on the cast list of *A Passion for Excellence*, *Thriving on Chaos* and *Liberation Management*, appearing as a key actor or hero in 12 per cent, 9 per cent and 23 per cent of the tales recounted in these texts respectively. Thereafter Peters is always the lead actor in his dramas of management and in *The Circle of Innovation* he is the hero of more than 71 per cent of the tales recounted.

Peters' elevation to lead actor in his tales of business practice is, I think, a double-edged sword. His early tales of business excellence often detailed the obsessional behaviour and other, more quirky, habits of America's top business-men. In the early 1980s these tales were surprising and memorable – in part due to the extreme behaviours of their heroes. Now, apparently estranged from these actors, Peters' few remaining tales relate mostly to his own, very personal, experiences of poor design, dingy hotels, surly receptionists and thoughtless bar-tenders. Thus Peters' texts of 1982 and 1985 tell tales of 'high society'. However, from 1993 onwards Peters' stories have more in common with 'kitchen sink dramas'.

At one level, of course, these tales of everyday trials and torments probably reflect, more adequately, the day-to-day experiences of Peters' readership. Consequently these stories should have some potential as sensegiving devices. Yet, for me at least, this guru's 'kitchen sink dramas' fail as endeavours in sensegiving because Peters consistently narrates from the wrong side of the fence.

On the dark side of the road...

Discussing the changing experience of work, Sennett (1998), Ehrenreich (2002, 2006) and Abrams (2002) tell tales of organizational cupidity and obstruction that, at one level, are similar to those relayed in Peters' recent works. In these texts the authors, like Peters, regularly find themselves on the receiving end of a very bad deal. But these authors narrate their experiences differently. Ehrenreich and Abrams may well feel that they are, albeit temporarily, victims of 'the system', but they do not feel themselves to be unique or special in this. Instead their tales of corporate insensitivity demonstrate, above all, an empathy with, and a certain degree of sympathy for, those poor individuals who – for want of a better option in an economic regime that could scarcely care less – must continue to work for minimum wage in a system of work that, while thoughtless from the outside, is nothing less than heartless on the inside!

Compared with these accounts of work and organization Peters' most recent attempts to secure the affiliation of his audience must be looked upon as failures. These 'kitchen sink dramas' of organized stupidity seek to portray Peters as an ordinary everyman in touch with the day-to-day problems of normal folk. Yet his sensegiving endeavours either implode or backfire. Consequently he appears neither homely, nor comely, as he rails against the daily trials of organizational life because his tirades are, in effect, little more than the grumblings of a rich old man; a man who has lived a life free from dirty work, heavy-lifting and bread-line wages that so many must endure.

As the saying goes: beauty may be just skin deep, but ugly goes all the way to the bone!

Not happily ever after

Twenty-five years ago Peters clearly understood something about the business of management. He recognized that business is a moral economy (even when it breaches society's norms) and he correctly perceived that managers are in the business of providing (and sustaining) meaning for those who toil each day. But all that was some time ago. Somewhere along the way Peters either forgot or lost faith in the power of stories such that, in his silver jubilee year, this celebrated guru has simply lost the plot.

In total, then, our analysis of Peters' shifting narrative (see Chapter 3) and changing storywork suggests that this guru – if indeed he is still deserving of this accolade – is out of step with his own philosophy; out of touch with the realities of modern working; *and* out of ideas.

Conclusions

This chapter has analysed Tom Peters' key texts on management from a story-telling perspective. Recognizing that the academic concern with stories and storytelling is a sub-set of a more general concern with narrative, we have sought to outline the key elements of a narrative concern with organization and we have attempted to explore its key insights. Moving on to examine the academic literature concerned with organizational storytelling we have explored the debate, which persists, as to the essential nature and form of the story. Taking our lead from Gabriel (1995, 2000, 2004) we have outlined the defining characteristics of the poetic story and on the strength of this device we have produced a catalogue of Peters' key texts on management, which counts the stories he tells, while seeking to account for the declining number of tales exhibited in his work. To this end we have produced six, overlapping explanations for Peters' declining 'storywork'.

Looking in more depth at the nature of the tales relayed by Peters we have highlighted both the predominance of the epic form and the absence of the romantic form from this catalogue. In addition we have also analysed the changing cast list of Peters' tales. This attempt to identify the key actors in Peters' dramas of business seems to confirm our earlier suggestion (see Chapter 3) that Peters has indeed turned his back on the corporate elite of America's east coast.

Yet our analysis has also revealed that these founding heroes of the excellence project have been displaced, not by other businessmen (and women), but by Peters himself. Examining the tone and content of these tales, which give Peters a star billing, our analysis of this author's storywork questions both Peters' legacy as a guru and his future as a commentator. Thus our analysis of Peters' storytelling practices and preferences, we suggest, demonstrates that:

- Peters seems doubtful of his own espoused credo,
- this guru is increasingly insensitive towards the wider movements, trajectories and problems which employees today must face.

This widening gap between the world-as-it-is and Peters' own (increasingly impoverished) storyworld suggests that work, workers, the unemployed, under-employed, laid-off and 'pensioned-off' need a voice; a new narrative *and* new narrators.

5 Doubting Thomas

Introduction

This text has focused upon the work and career of the celebrated business guru Tom Peters. It has been produced to coincide with the 25th anniversary of the publication of his first book on managing, entitled *In Search of Excellence* (Peters and Waterman, 1982). This anniversary, we have argued, is particularly worthy of note because, for the past 25 years, Tom Peters has been at the leading edge of a movement which has acted to (re)shape our appreciation of the very nature of managerial work. However, we have acknowledged that, for some, this anniversary is no cause for celebration. Consequently we have attempted to offer a fresh look at the work of Tom Peters that can acknowledge the extent to which this author and commentator tends to excite and yet polarize opinion.

Most commentaries on the gurus of management can be placed somewhere on a spectrum of responses that range from 'the hagiologic' through 'the apologetic' to the downright 'apoplectic' (see Collins, 2003). This text seeks to avoid the social and intellectual traps associated with both hagiologic and apoplectic responses to Tom Peters. Yet this account of Tom Peters also seeks to avoid the simple compromise positions offered by the apologists for the gurus of management (see Collins, 2000). Tip-toeing between these positions on the spectrum that typifies the responses of the 'guru industry' (Collins, 2000, 2005), this text retains its own voice and uses this to articulate a distinctive point-of-view.

A reprise

In our introductory chapter we sought to outline Peters' rise as a business guru and attempted to signal his continuing presence at the head of the management advice industry. Chapters 1 and 2 built upon this analysis and together offered a chronological analysis of the key texts produced by this author between 1982 and 2003.

Basing our critical review of Tom Peters around a concern with the '3Cs' of context, content and critique, we sought to establish that the appeal of this guru's various commentaries on management needs to be understood, in context, as a product of the particular issues, crises and opportunities facing business at particular points in time. Yet having conceded this point we, nevertheless, argued that a number of rather serious and damaging criticisms might be raised in the face of Tom Peters' various manifestos for business change.

In Chapter 3 we moved on from this chronological analysis. Thus Chapter 3 sought to explore and to account for the narrative changes in Peters' texts. These narrative movements, we observed, had previously been commented upon but had not been subjected to sustained and critical inquiry. In an attempt to remedy this oversight we proposed a fourfold narrative typology for Peters' texts and tendered a number of plausible explanations for the changes observed.

In Chapter 4 we continued with this narrative review and reanalysis of Peters' key texts. Observing a growing concern with 'narrative' in the field of business and management studies we examined, in outline, the aims and orientations of such a narrative perspective. Noting that there is within this general narrative approach to the study of management and organization a sub-set of academic literature focused upon stories and storytelling, we proceeded to offer a more developed account of the controversies that shape academic accounts of story-telling in organizations. Concentrating on the contest between David Boje (1991, 2001) and Yiannis Gabriel (1995, 2000, 2004) we have attempted to reveal the ideas that unite *and* the perspectives that divide the commentaries prepared by these formidable authors.

Following Gabriel's (2004) delineation of the essence of the poetic story we mapped Peters' key texts from a storytelling perspective. On the strength of this mapping exercise we observed:

- a general decline in the number of stories relayed by Peters in his key texts,
- Peters' preference for certain story-types that tend to lionize key actors while downplaying the role and significance of other actors and wider organizational processes,
- that Peters moves from being the simple narrator of business change to become the hero of his organizational stories.

In addition Chapter 4 offered a number of suggestions that might be used either to explain or to explore further the changes observed in Peters' story-telling endeavours. Noting Peters' decline as a storyteller *and* the increasing dis-tance between his narratives of change and the more general experience of modern working, we concluded by suggesting the need for a new narrative and, by implication, new narrators of business and change.

In the remainder of this brief, and concluding, chapter I propose to signal areas for future inquiry, beyond those already suggested or otherwise alluded to in Chapters 3 and 4. This listing of areas and topics for future inquiry is not meant to provide an exhaustive list of topics and questions for research in this area – the terrain is simply too big for me even to consider making such a claim. Instead I wish to raise a number of questions and to make a number of proposi-tions for research, in the light of the foregoing analysis, which in various ways reflect upon Peters' current capacity and future capability as a management commentator.

In total I will tender five sets of questions and propositions that signal areas for future inquiry and reflection. The first two of these five might be regarded as generalized reflections on the gurus of management and the market for their wares, while the final two of these five reflect, more directly, on Tom Peters and his personal capability in this marketplace. The middle set of our series of reflections, as you might expect, offers questions and propositions that straddle the general concerns of sets one and two and the more local issues raised in sets four and five. Taken together these five sets of questions and propositions constitute, I hope, a useful outline of an agenda for future analyses of Tom Peters and for further inquiry into the gurus of management more generally.

(1) Is the time of the gurus passing?

In earlier chapters we observed that in the years prior to the early 1980s the best seller lists had been dominated by biographies of the Hollywood stars, by sex and diet manuals, and by chronicles of political malefaction. However, we observed that in the past 25 years the public has chosen to supplement its reading on sexual positions and dietary technique (or should that be the other way around?) with the studies of business technique and management practice that have been prepared by the gurus.

The segment of the publishing industry concerned with the production and proselytization of the gurus' message has done very well. But the popularity of recent, more critical, accounts of the business of management, such as those offered by Monbiot (2001) and Bakan (2005), may signal a growing disaffection with the simplistic readings of the business of management prepared by the gurus.

Our first proposition, therefore, is as follows:

> The time of the gurus is passing. Recent, high profile scandals, such as those associated with *Enron* and *Tyco*, combined with corporate changes which continue to demand employee loyalty in a non-reciprocal way have (a) made fertile ground for more critical texts *and* (b) suggest a return to earlier reading habits and preferences.

A number of questions follow from this:

- Is the overall market for guru texts in decline? If so is this a sustained decline and are there variations in this pattern?
- Has a mass-market for more critical accounts of the business of management been established and, if so, is it (a) generally established at an international level and (b) sustainable?
- If there is, indeed, a more general market for books on the seamier side of corporate life, has this grown at the expense of the gurus?

•   How might the appeal of these more critical readings of corporate life be accounted for? Are they a product of bitter experience or are they a youthful rebellion?

(2) Do wider geo-political movements make this a bad time for guru publications?

Our first proposition speculated that changing experiences and orientations have made space for 'counter-guru' texts that, in many ways, reflect a return to earlier reading habits and preferences. This, our second proposition, has similarities to the first concern raised above. Yet where our first proposition suggested a crisis for the gurus that is borne of movements in, say, the business and educational worlds, our second proposition notes the importance of the US market and suggests that recent, and larger, geo-political developments such as the invasions of Afghanistan, Iraq and Lebanon, and the 'war on terror' might (a) promote a new market segment concerned with such geo-political movements that (b) simultaneously depresses the market for business guru texts.

Thus our second proposition suggests that:

> The daily broadcasts, which signal the military and corporate might of America act (a) to forestall further public inspection of the business of management, in part because such introspection would (b) tend to look trivial in comparison with these wider movements and events.

A number of questions follow from this:

•   Has the American market for guru texts actually declined in the past 5–6 years? If so, can this decline be linked to the various 'wars' announced since this time?
•   Has a more general market for books designed to explain/explore recent geo-political movements been established? If so, is there any reason to suggest that this market segment has grown at the expense of the gurus of management?
•   Is the publishing industry now disinclined to publish guru texts? And somewhat more prosaically: To what extent has the market for military and political biographies concerned with the west's current wars simply crowded-out guru texts by filling the diaries of the various 'ghost writers' who service these segments of the publishing industry?

(3) Is the market for guru texts facing a crisis of renewal?

This proposition straddles the general reflections on management's gurus offered above and the local questions that reflect more directly upon Tom Peters that we will review below.

Discussing Peters' most recent key text, *The Economist* (20/12/2003) comments that this work has been designed to appeal to the under-30s; an age group, it seems, that lacks either the will or the capacity to respond positively to more orthodox, analytical works.

Thus our third proposition suggests that:

> Recent changes in the market for guru texts, generally, and Peters' narrative experimentation, in particular, should be read as reflections of a market crisis for the gurus and their publishers insofar as younger readers seem disinclined to read the manifestos for business change prepared by the gurus.

A number of questions follow from this:

- Is it possible to validate this putative renewal crisis? If so is it a general problem or a local issue that reflects on Tom Peters in particular?
- Does Peters' position at the head of the market for guru wares place him outside the mooted trend or does his public recognition as the elder statesman of the gurus mean that he is now marked as 'old news' from a previous generation?

(4) Are Peters' concerns unfashionable?

A cursory review of the airport and high street bookshop shelves reveals a few things:

- Most of the Peters catalogue is unavailable to the casual browser.
- Those managerial texts that are generally available at the moment seem to be devoted either to the personal advantages that flow from 'self help' *or* to specific business processes and techniques.

From a reading of these market signals a fourth proposition is formed:

> Within the current marketplace for guru ideas Peter's key texts are too vague to 'add value'. His works are, of course, unremittingly galvanic but, beyond a simple faith in personal 'branding', they provide few concrete suggestions for the average white, male and skilled employee and they simply ignore the other groups that constitute the workforce.

A number of questions follow from this:

- Is Peters' market profile declining? Is his work really unavailable to the casual browser?
- Are those who are currently prospering in the guru market actually selling texts concerned with technique?
- Is Peters' account of the business of management – by omission – elitist, sexist and/or racist? If so is this recognized and does it blunt his appeal in particular markets and/or market segments?

(5) Have recent movements in the business of management made things more difficult for Peters?

As I draft this chapter statisticians are announcing a further growth in unemployment in Britain. This same group of statisticians told me yesterday that inflation remains 'above target'. Meanwhile other market commentators have suggested that this failure to achieve the target rate for inflation will force the Bank of England's Monetary Policy Committee to raise interest rates.

On the eve of the party that will celebrate Tom Peters' 25 years as a business guru there is something familiar about this constellation of data. Of course none of these indicators is quite as bad as the double-digit figures that scarred the 1980s (see Chapter 1). All things, however, are relative. And in relative terms these figures are troubling for they suggest future problems brewing; the sort of problems that, once upon a time, propelled Peters to the head of the guru industry. And yet 'the noughties' are different from 'the eighties'.

In 1982 Peters reassured us that America and other struggling economies could become great again and he insisted that Americans could learn to manage their way 'out of the crisis' because beacons of excellence, at home, would show the changes required to secure America's future. In 2007, however, Peters' message is less appealing.

In 1982 the beacons of excellence that Peters' highlighted were focused upon values, stories, customers, commitment and quality. These excellent companies employed American workers in America within a renewing, but distinctly American, system of management. In 2007, however, only the so-called American *system* remains. The work and the workers are increasingly to be found elsewhere.

This reading of 'the noughties' provokes our fifth and final proposition:

> Tom Peters is increasingly cut-off from the realities and insecurities of the modern workplace. His willingness to genuflect before the twin imperatives of globalization and market liberalization means that he offers those workers who must deal with the fall-out of these changes few reasons to applaud his headline support for initiatives such as 'out-sourcing' and 'off-shoring'.

A few questions follow from this:

- Do Peters' narratives of business enjoy general public recognition?
- Do current trends in business (and Peters' endorsement of such trends) act to separate this guru from the concerns and aspirations of the more general working population who once bought (and bought into) his work?
- Are there countervailing voices and perspectives that might enjoy greater public support?
- Can new narratives and new narrators be found?

Notes

Introduction

1 In this story, which is set in the years just prior to the Second World War, George Bowling laments the changes in English society that he has experienced in his lifetime and longs for a return to the simpler life of his childhood which he recalls imperfectly and in fragments.

2 We should observe that Micklethwait and Wooldridge (1997) and Purves (2006) suggest that these lists are potentially unreliable as indicators of reading habit and preference because they are open to the manipulation of larger commercial interests.

3 Information on the non-fiction books that have topped the *New York Times* best sellers lists may be found at www.hawes.com/no1_nf_d.htm

4 We should acknowledge that there is also a smaller, but growing market for books, which present the business of management in far less glowing terms. See for example George Monbiot (2001) and Joel Bakan (2005).

5 In 1999 the English footballer Paul Merson – a recovering alcoholic – announced that he was quitting Middlesbrough football club. Explaining this decision he complained that this club was an unsuitable place for a man with his problem because it amounted to a culture centred on booze. See archives.tcm.ie/breaking news/2001/08/21/story 21445.asp. A similar debate on cultural matters also took place at this time in the English police constabularies when it was suggested that policing had become a 'compensation culture'.

6 The eponymous stars of the film *Bill and Ted's Excellent Adventure.*

7 Peter Drucker (who died in 2005) and Michael Porter were ranked first and second respectively.

8 The renowned management commentator Peter Drucker quipped that the term guru is employed by those who, in being too polite to speak more plainly, shy away from using a term that is more appropriate. Thus Drucker has suggested that guru is a modern synonym for 'charlatan' (see Micklethwait and Wooldridge, 1997).

9 Those unfamiliar with this case may find Professor David Boje's web pages offer a useful source of information. The information may be accessed at: cbae.nmsu.edu/~dboje/enron/boje.

10 Andrew Robbins, the (unfeasibly) square-jawed guru of personal development, acted as a personal advisor to Bill Clinton during his impeachment crisis. Michael Porter, the guru of strategy, has similarly advised those at the centre of the UK government on the management of the British Higher Education sector.

2 The later works of Tom Peters

1 I should point out that this is a quip often repeated by my colleague at the University of Essex, Dr Martin Harris – albeit in a slightly different context.

2 Recently a number of commentators have suggested that Peters has lost touch with his congregation and now derives his insights on business and management, second hand, from a library of press clippings. This charge has some truth. Peters' recent texts and seminars are liberally sprinkled with quotations and more general insights derived from his habit of taking clippings from journals, books and magazines. Yet this criticism has a hollow ring when it is voiced by business journalists since many of those who have reviewed Peters' life and career in the popular press, and who have attacked him for his reliance on press clippings, have clearly based their own reviews on a battery of clippings. For example Blackhurst (2003) launches an attack on Peters as 'a propagator of twaddle', yet Blackhurst is sloppy in the conduct of his own research, and so produces a fair amount of twaddle himself. For example, in an attempt to demonstrate this guru's market worth and influence Blackhurst quotes Peters' lecturing fee. However, Blackhurst's clippings library provides figures that are 11 years out-of-date. Peters is a self-confessed compulsive clipper of magazines but at least his files remain up-to-date!

3 In fairness to William Fotheringham we should point out that he is a well-respected sporting journalist who has written a number of books that really are worth reading (see for example Fotheringham, 2003b, 2005).

3   Crazy days call for crazy ways?

1 This is a revised and enlarged version of a paper that first appeared in *Management Decision*. The full citation for the original paper is: Collins D and Watkins C (2006) 'Crazy Days Call for Crazy Ways? Narrating Tom Peters', *Management Decision*, 44 (5): 658–673.

2 In fairness we should concede that Peters would probably regard 'strategy by serendipity' as something to encourage and celebrate.

3 I am grateful to Robert Heller, founding editor of *Management Today*, for this observation.

4 As I write this chapter I am approximately one-third of the way through my term of office as Associate Dean of Academic Partnerships, which is by certain metrics the largest faculty of the University of Essex.

5 I would merely cite what might be termed the Keynesian defence strategy: challenged by his opponents on the question of supposed inconsistencies in his arguments over time the economist J. M. Keynes responded that in situations where/when he found that he had previously been in error he simply changed his mind. Furthermore he pointedly asked his detractors what they chose to do when they found themselves in similar predicaments.

4   Stories and storytelling in the work of Tom Peters

1 Goldman (2001) captures the writer's need for economy rather well. Discussing the craft of screen-writing he notes: 'In a screenplay you always attack your story as late as possible. You enter each scene as close as you can to the end ... you also enter the story as late as you can' (280–281).

2 Taylor argues that the appendix portion of *1984* is often overlooked. However, he protests that the appendix is important to this tale and is, in fact, to be regarded as a continuation of Winston Smith's story of resistance. Taylor is also keen to remind us that the project to develop a Newspeak dictionary has been beset by problem and delay and may, in time, be shelved completely.

3 Extracts from *Of Mice and Men* © John Steinbeck 1937, reproduced by permission of Curtis Brown Group Ltd., London and Penguin Books Ltd., London.

Bibliography

Abrahamson, E. (1996) 'Management Fashion', *Academy of Management Review*, 16 (3): 254–285.

Abrahamson, E. and Eisenman, M. (2001) 'Why Management Scholars must Intervene Strategically in the Management Knowledge Market', *Human Relations*, 54 (1): 67–75.

Abrams, F. (2002) *Below the Breadline: Living on the Minimum Wage*, Profile Books: London.

Ackman, D. (2002) 'Excellence Sought – And Found', *Forbes*, www.forbes.com/2002/10/10/1004excellent.html.

Ackroyd, S. and Thompson, P. (1999) *Organizational Misbehaviour*, Sage: London.

Anonymous (1999) 'Confessions of a Ghost', *Inc.com*, pf.inc.com/magazine/19990515/4708.html.

Aupperle, K. E., Acar, W. and Booth, D. E. (1986) 'An Empirical Critique of *In Search of Excellence*: How Excellent are the Excellent Companies?', *Journal of Management*, 12 (4): 499–512.

Bakan, J. (2005) *The Corporation: The Pathological Pursuit of Profit and Power*, Constable: London.

Barter, R. F. (1994) 'In Search of Excellence in Libraries: The Management Writings of Tom Peters and Their Implications for Library and Information Services', *Library Management*, 15 (8): 4–15.

Baskerville, S. and Willett, R. (eds) (1985) *Nothing Else to Fear: New Perspectives on America in the Thirties*, Manchester University Press: Manchester.

Blackhurst, C. (2003) 'Master of Reinvention', *Evening Standard* (London), 1/10/2003.

Boje, D. (1991) 'The Storytelling Organization: A Study of Performance in an Office Supply Firm', *Administrative Science Quarterly*, 36: 106–126.

Boje, D. (1998) 'Amos Tuck's post-sweat Nike Spin Story', Paper Presented in The International Academy of Business Disciplines Conference, San Francisco.

Boje, D. (2001) *Narrative Methods for Organizational and Communication Research*, Sage: London.

Boje, D. , Alvarez, R. and Schooling, B. (2001) 'Reclaiming Story in Organization: Narratologies and Action Sciences' in Westwood, R. and Linstead, S. (eds).

Boyce, M. E. (1995) 'Collective Centring and Collective Sense-making in the Stories and Storytelling of One Organization, *Organization Studies*, 16 (1): 107–137.

Brawer, R. A. (1998) *Fictions of Business: Insights on Management from Great Literature*, John Wiley and Sons: New York.

Brown, A. D. (2000) 'Making Sense of Inquiry Sensemaking', *Journal of Management Studies*, 37 (1): 45–75.

Brown, A. D. (2003) 'Authoritative Sensemaking in a Public Inquiry Report', *Organization Studies*, 25 (1): 95–112.

Buchanan, D. (2003) 'Getting the Story Straight: Illusions and Delusions in the Organizational Change Process', *Tamara: The Journal of Critical Postmodern Organizational Science*, 2 (4): 7–21.

Bunz, U. K. and Maes, J. D. (1998) 'Learning Excellence: Southwest Airlines' Approach', *Managing Service Quality*, 8 (3): 163–169.

Burnes, B. (2004) 'Kurt Lewin and the Planned Approach to Change: A Re-appraisal', *Journal of Management Studies*, 41 (6): 977–1002.

Burnes, B. (2005) 'Complexity Theories and Organizational Change, *International Journal of Management Reviews*, 7 (2): 73–90.

Burrell, G. and Morgan, G. (1979) *Sociological Paradigms and Organisational Analysis: Elements of the Sociology of Corporate Life*, Heinemann: London.

Burrell, G. (1997) *Pandemonium*, Sage: London.

Business Week (5/11/1984) 'Who's Excellent Now?': 46–54.

Byrne, J. A. (1992a) 'Ever In Search of a New Take on Excellence', *Business Week*, 31/08/1992, www.businessweek.com/archives/1992/b328144.arc.htm.

Byrne, J. A. (1992b) 'Tom Peters' Mantra for "Nutty Times"', *Business Week*, 16/11/1992, businessweek.com/archives/1992/b32939.arc.htm.

Cappelli, P. (1995) 'Rethinking Employment', *British Journal of Industrial Relations*, 33 (4): 563–602.

Carroll, D. T. (1983) 'A Disappointing Search for Excellence', *Harvard Business Review*, Nov.–Dec.: 78–82.

Carter, P. and Jackson, N. (2000) 'An-aesthetics' in Linstead, S. and Höpfl, H. (eds) *The Aesthetics of Organization*, Sage: London.

Charters, A. (1991) 'Introduction' in Kerouac, J., *On the Road*, Penguin: Harmondsworth.

Chia, R. and King, I. (1998) 'The Organizational Structuring of Novelty', *Organization*, 5 (4): 461–478.

Clark, T. (2004) 'The Fashion of Management Fashion: A Surge too Far?', *Organization*, 11 (2): 297–306.

Clark, T. and Fincham, R. (eds) (2002) *Critical Consulting: New Perspectives on the Management Advice Industry*, Blackwell: Oxford.

Clark, T. and Greatbatch, D. (2002) 'Knowledge Legitimation and Affiliation Through Storytelling: The Example of Management Gurus' in Clark, T. and Fincham, R. (eds) *Critical Consulting: New Perspectives on the Management Advice Industry*, Blackwell: Oxford.

Clark, T. and Greatbatch, D. (2003) 'Collaborative Relationships in the Creation and Fashioning of Management Ideas: Gurus, Editors and Managers' in Kipping, M. and Engwall, L. (eds) *Management Consulting: Emergence and Dynamics of a Knowledge Industry*, Oxford University Press: Oxford.

Clark, T. and Salaman, G. (1996) 'The Management Guru as Organizational Witchdoctor', *Organization*, 3 (1): 85–107.

Clark, T. and Salaman, G. (1998) 'Telling Tales: Management Gurus and the Construction of Managerial Identity', *Journal of Management Studies*, 35 (2): 137–161.

Collins, D. (1996) '*No Such Thing As . . .* A Practical Approach to Management', *Management Decision*, 34 (1): 66–71.

Collins, D. (1998) *Organizational Change: Sociological Perspectives*, Routledge: London.

Collins, D. (2000) *Management Fads and Buzzwords: Critical-Practical Perspectives*, Routledge: London.

Collins, D. (2001) 'The Fad Motif in Management Scholarship', *Employee Relations*, 23 (1): 26–37.

Collins, D. (2003) 'Review Article: Management Gurus and Management Fashions', *Management Communication Quarterly*, 26 (3): 459–462.

Collins, D. (2004a) 'Who put the Con in Consultancy? Fads, Recipes and "Vodka Margarine"', *Human Relations*, 57 (5): 553–572.

Collins, D. (2004b) 'X-Engineering: *ex cathedra?*', *Personnel Review*, 35 (1): 127–142.

Collins, D. (2005) 'Pyramid Schemes and Programmatic Management', *Culture and Organization*, 11 (1): 33–44.

Collins, D. (2006) 'Assaying the Advice Industry', *Culture and Organization*, 12 (2): 139–152.

Collins, D. and Rainwater, K. (2005) 'Managing Change at Sears: A Sideways Look at a Tale of Corporate Transformation', *Journal of Organizational Change Management*, 18 (1): 16–30.

Crainer, S. (1997) *Corporate Man to Corporate Skunk: The Tom Peters Phenomenon, A Biography*, Capstone: Oxford.

Crainer, S. (1998a) *The Ultimate Business Guru Book: 50 Thinkers Who Made Management*, Capstone: Oxford.

Crainer, S. (1998b) 'In Search of the Real Author', *Management Today*, May: 50–54.

Crick, B. (1982) *George Orwell: A Life*, Penguin: Harmondsworth.

Czarniawska, B. (1997) *Narrating the Organization: Dramas of Institutional Identity*, The University of Chicago Press: Chicago IL.

Czarniawska, B. (1999) *Writing Management: Organization Theory as a Literary Genre*, Oxford University Press: Oxford.

Czarniawska, B. and Gagliardi, P. (eds) (2003) *Narratives We Organize By*, John Benjamins Publishing Company: Amsterdam.

Czarniawska, B. and Mazza, C. (2003) 'Consulting as a Liminal Space', *Human Relations*, 56 (3): 267–290.

Deal, T. E. and Kennedy, A. A. (1982) *Corporate Cultures*, Penguin: Harmondsworth.

De Cock, ?. and Hipkin, I. (1997) 'TQM and BPR: Beyond the Beyond Myth', *Journal of Management Studies*, 34 (5): 659–675.

Dunford, R. and Jones, D. (2000) 'Narrative and Strategic Change', *Human Relations*, 53 (9): 1207–1226.

Durman, P. (1997) 'Fading Fame of a Management Guru', *The Times* (London) 10/04/1997.

Drucker, P. (1955) *The Practice of Management*, Heinemann: London.

Economist, The (15/6/1985) 'The Joy of Business'.

Economist, The (5/12/1992) 'A Mess of Parables'.

Economist, The (24/9/1994) 'Tom Peters, Performance Artist'.

Economist, The (20/12/2003) 'Excellence Revisited': 125–126.

Ehrenreich, B. (2002) *Nickel and Dimed: Undercover in Low-wage USA*, Granta Books: London.

Ehrenreich, B. (2006) *Bait and Switch: The Futile Pursuit of the Corporate Dream*, Granta Books: London.

Fairclough, N. (2000) *New Labour, New Language?*, Routledge: London.

Fincham, R. and Clark, T. (2002) 'Introduction: The Emergence of Critical Perspectives on Consulting', in Clark, T. and Fincham, R. (eds) (2002).

Fine, M. (1994) 'Working the Hyphens: Reinventing Self and Other' in Denzin, N. K. and Lincoln, Y. S. (eds) *Handbook of Qualitative Research*, Sage: London.

Finkelstein, D. (2004) 'Blair's Story is Coming to an End', *The Times* (London), 18/5/2004.

Follett, M. P. (1987) *Freedom and Co-ordination: Lectures in Business Organization*, Garland Publication: New York.

Foltz, K. and Resener, M. (1985) 'A Passion for Hype', *Newsweek*, 27/5/1985.

Fotheringham, W. (2003a) *A Century of Cycling*, Mitchell Beazley: London.

Fotheringham, W. (2003b) *Put me Back on my Bike: In Search of Tom Simpson*, Yellow Jersey Press: London.

Fotheringham, W. (2005) *Roule Britannia: A History of Britons in the Tour de France*, Yellow Jersey Press: London.

French, W. (1975) *John Steinbeck*, 2nd Edition, Bobbs-Merrill: Indianapolis.

Fucini, J. J. and Fucini, S. (1990) *Working for the Japanese: Inside Mazda's American Auto Plant*, MacMillan: Basingstoke.

Fukuda, J. (1988) *Japanese Management Transferred: The Experience of East Asia*, Routledge: London.

Furusten, S. (1999) *Popular Management Books: How they are Made and what they Mean for Organizations*, Routledge: London.

Gabriel, Y. (1995) 'The Unmanaged Organization: Stories, Fantasies and Subjectivity', *Organization Studies*, 16 (3): 477–501.

Gabriel, Y. (1998) 'Same Old Story or Changing Stories? Folkloric, Modern and Post-modern Mutations' in Grant, D., Keenoy, T. and Oswick, C. (eds) (1998).

Gabriel, Y. (2000) *Storytelling in Organizations: Facts, Fictions and Fantasies*, Oxford University Press: Oxford.

Gabriel, Y. (2004) 'Narratives, Stories and Texts' in Grant, D., Hardy, C., Oswick, C. and Putnam, L. (eds).

Gabriel, Y., Fineman, S. and Sims, D. (1992) *Organizing and Organizations*, Sage: London.

Gabriel, Y., Fineman, S. and Sims, D. (2000) *Organizing and Organizations*, 2nd Edition, Sage: London.

Gates, B. (1985) 'Business Needs its "Skunks"', *Financial Post* (Canada), 12/10/1985.

Geneen, H. and Moscow, A. (1986) *Managing*, Grafton Books: London.

Gioia, D. A. and Chittipeddi, K. (1991) 'Sensemaking and Sensegiving in Strategic Change Initiation', *Strategic Management Journal*, 12: 433–448.

Goldberg, E., Notkin, D. and Dutcher, R. F. (1995) *The Tom Peters Business School in a Box*, Macmillan: London.

Goldman, W. (2001) *Adventures in the Screen Trade: A Personal View of Hollywood and Screenwriting*, Abacus: London.

Grant, D., Hardy, C., Oswick, C. and Putnam, L. (eds) (2004) *The Sage Handbook of Organizational Discourse*, Sage: London.

Grant, D., Hardy, C., Oswick, C. and Putnam, L. (2004) 'Introduction: Organizational Discourse: Exploring the Field' in Grant, D., Hardy, C., Oswick, C. and Putnam, L. (eds).

Grant, D., Keenoy, T. and Oswick, C. (eds) (1998) *Discourse and Organization*, Sage: London.

Grant, D., Michelson, G., Oswick, C. and Wailes, N. (eds) (2005a) 'Discourse and Organizational Change' Special Issue of *Journal of Organizational Change Management*, 18 (1): 6–104.

Grant, D., Michelson, G., Oswick, C. and Wailes, N. (eds) (2005b) 'Discourse and Organizational Change: Part Two' Special Issue of *Journal of Organizational Change Management*, 18 (4): 309–390.

Gribbin, J. (1993) *In Search of the Edge of Time*, Black Swan: London.

Grint, K. (1994) 'Reengineering History: Social Resonances and Business Process Reengineering', *Organization* 1 (1): 179–201.

Grint, K. (1997a) 'TQM, BPR, JIT, BSCs and TLAs: Managerial Waves or Drownings?, *Management Decision*, 35 (10): 731–738.

Grint, K. (1997b) *Fuzzy Management*, Oxford University Press: Oxford.

Guardian (27/8/1998).

Guardian (27/3/2002).

Guest, D. (1992) 'Right Enough to be Dangerously Wrong: An Analysis of the *In Search of Excellence* Phenomenon' in Salaman, G. (ed.) *Human Resource Strategies*, Sage: London.

Hales, C. (1993) *Management Through Organization: The Management Process, Forms of Organization and the Work of Managers*, Routledge: London.

Hamilton, P. (2003a) 'The Saliency of Synecdoche: The Part and the Whole of Employment Relations', *Journal of Management Studies*, 40 (7): 1569–1585.

Hamilton, P. (2003b) ' "The Vital Connection": a Rhetoric on Equality', *Personnel Review*, 32 (6): 694–710.

Hammer, M. (1990) 'Reengineering Work: Don't Automate, Obliterate', *Harvard Business Review*, July–August: 104–112.

Hamper, B. (1992) *Rivethead: Tales from the Assembly Line*, Fourth Estate: London.

Heller, R. (2000) *Tom Peters: The Bestselling Prophet of the Management Revolution*, Dorling Kindersley: London.

Heller, R. (2002) *In Search of European Excellence: The 10 Key Strategies of Europe's Top Companies*, Profile Books: London.

Hilmer, F. and Donaldson, L. (1996) *Management Redeemed: Debunking the Fads that Undermine our Corporations*, Free Press: New York.

Hitt, M. A. and Ireland, R. D. (1987) 'Peters and Waterman Revisited: The Unended Quest for Excellence', *Academy of Management Executive*, 1 (2): 91–98.

Hopkinson, G. C. (2003) 'Stories from the Front-line: How they Construct the Organization', *Journal of Management Studies*, 40 (8): 1943–1969.

Huczynski, A. A. (1993) *Management Gurus: What Makes them and How to Become one*, Routledge: London.

Hyatt, J. (1990) 'How to Write a Business Best-Seller, *Inc.com*, pf.inc.com/magazine/19900301/5074.html.

Hyatt, J. (1999) 'When Everyone Was Excellent', *Inc.com*, pf.inc.com/magazine/19990515/4703.html.

Iacocca, L. and Novak, W. [1986 (1984)] *Iacocca*, Bantam Books: London.

Jackson, B. (1996) 'Re-engineering the Sense of Self: The Manager and the Management Guru', *Journal of Management Studies*, 33 (5): 571–590.

Jackson, B. (2001) *Management Gurus and Management Fashions: A Dramatistic Inquiry*, Routledge: London.

Jackson, N. and Carter, P. (1998) 'Management Gurus: What are We to Make of Them?' in Hassard, J. and Holliday, R. (eds) *Organization-Representation: Work and Organization in Popular Culture*, Sage: London.

Kahn, H. (1970) *The Emerging Japanese Superstate*, Harper and Row: London.

Kahn, H. and Pepper, T. (1978) *The Japanese Challenge: The Success and Failure of Economic Success*, Harper and Row: London.

Kanter, R. M. (1984) *Change Masters: Corporate Entrepreneurs at Work*, Routledge: London.

Keenoy, T. and Anthony, P. (1992) 'HRM: Metaphor, Meaning and Reality' in Blyton, P. and Turnbull, P. (eds) *Reassessing Human Resource Management*, Sage: London.

Kennedy, C. (1996) *Managing with the Gurus: Top Level Guidance on 20 Management Techniques*, Century Books: London.

Kennedy, C. (1998) *Guide to the Management Gurus: Shortcuts to the Leading Ideas of Leading Management Thinkers*, Century Books: London.

Kerouac, J. (1991) *On the Road*, Penguin: Harmondsworth.

Kieser, A. (1997) 'Rhetoric and Myth in Management Fashion', *Organization*, 4 (1): 49–74.

Kieser, A. (2003) 'Managers as Marionettes? Using Fashion Theories to Explain the Success of Consultancies' in Kipping, M. and Engwall, L. (2003) (eds).

Kipping, M. and Engwall, L. (2003) 'Introduction' in Kipping, M. and Engwall, L. (eds) (2003).

Kipping, M. and Engwall, L. (eds) (2003) *Management Consulting: Emergence and Dynamics of a Knowledge Industry*, Oxford University Press: Oxford.

Knights, D. and Wilmott, H. (1999) *Management Lives: Power and Identity in Work Organizations*, Sage: London.

Latour, B. (1987) *Science in Action*, Harvard University Press: Cambridge MA.

Leonard, C. (1992) 'Millionaire Marketing Guru Who Reigns Supreme', *The Times* (London), 5/12/1992.

Letiche, H. (2000) 'Phenomenal Complexity Theory as Informed by Bergson', *Journal of Organizational Change Management*, 13 (6): 545–557.

Lewin, K. (1947) 'Group Decisions and Social Change' in Macoby, E. E., Newcomb, T. M. and Hartley, E. L. (eds) *Readings in Social Psychology*, Henry Holt: New York.

Lewis, J. (ed.) (1992) *The Chatto Book of Office Life or Love Among the Filing Cabinets*, Chatto and Windus: London.

Lewis, S. (1922) *Babbit*, Jonathan Cape: London.

Lilley, S. (1997) 'Stuck in the Middle with You?', *British Journal of Management*, 8: 51–59.

Lorenz, C. (1986a) 'The Guru Factor', *Financial Times* (London), 2/7/1986.

Lorenz, C. (1986b) 'The Passionate and Unrepentant Crusader', *Financial Times* (London), 18/08/1986.

Lorenz, C. (1992) Untitled, *Financial Times* (London), 6/11/1992.

Maidique, M. A. (1983) 'Point of View: The New Management Thinkers', *California Management Review*, 26 (1): 151–161.

Marshak, R. J. (1998) 'A Discourse on Discourse: Redeeming the Meaning of Talk' in Grant, D., Keenoy, T. and Oswick, C. (eds) (1998).

Martin, J. (1992) *Cultures in Organizations: Three Perspectives*, Oxford University Press: Oxford.

Micklethwait, J. and Wooldridge, A. (1997) *The Witch Doctors: What the Management Gurus are Saying and How to Make Sense of it*, Mandarin: London.

Miller, W. C. (1993) 'Still Searching for Excellence: Using Past Performance to Predict Future Success, *Executive Research Project S95*, The Industrial College of the Armed Forces, Fort McNair: Washington DC.

Mitchell, T. R. (1985) 'In Search of Excellence versus the 100 Best Companies to Work for in America: A Question of Perspective and Values', *The Academy of Management Review*, 10 (2): 350–355.

Mohrman, S. A. (2001) 'Seize the Day: Organizational Studies can and should Make the Difference', *Human Relations*, 54 (1): 57–65.

Monbiot, G. (2001) *Captive State: The Corporate Takeover of Britain*, Pan: London.

Monin, N. and Monin, J. (2003) 'Re-navigating Management Theory: Steering by the Star of Mary Follett' in Czarniawska, B. and Gagliardi, P. (eds).

Moorhouse, H. F. (1981) *Driving Ambitions: A Social Analysis of the American Hot Rod Enthusiasm,* Manchester University Press: Manchester.

Nobbs, D. (1976) *The Fall and Rise of Reginald Perrin*, Penguin: Harmondsworth.

Nobbs, D. (1977) *The Return of Reginald Perrin*, Penguin: Harmondsworth.

Orwell, G. (1968) *Nineteen Eighty-Four*, Penguin: Harmondsworth.

Orwell, G. (1983) *Animal Farm*, Penguin: Harmondsworth.

Orwell, G. (1988) *Decline of the English Murder and Other Essays*, Penguin: Harmondsworth.

Orwell, G. (1990) *Coming up for Air*, Penguin: Harmondsworth.

Orwell, G. (2000) *George Orwell: Essays with an Introduction by Bernard Crick*, Penguin: Harmondsworth.

Parini, J. (1994) *John Steinbeck: A Biography*, Heinemann: London.

Pascale, R. T. and Athos, A. G. (1986 [1981]) *The Art of Japanese Management*, Sidgwick and Jackson: London.

Pattison, S. (1997) *The Faith of the Managers: When Management Becomes Religion*, Cassell: London.

Peter, P. J. and Hull, R. (1969) *The Peter Principle*, Souvenir: London.

Peters, T. (1987) *Thriving on Chaos: Handbook for a Management Revolution*, Guild Publishing: London.

Peters, T. (1989) 'Doubting Thomas', *Inc.com*, pf.inc.com/magazine/19890401/5599.html.

Peters, T. (1992) *Liberation Management: Necessary Disorganization for the Nanosecond Nineties*, MacMillan: London.

Peters, T. (1993) *The Tom Peters Seminar: Crazy Times Call for Crazy Organizations*, MacMillan: London.

Peters, T. (1994) *The Pursuit of Wow! Every Person's Guide to Topsy Turvy Times*, MacMillan: London.

Peters, T. (1997) *The Circle of Innovation: You can't Shrink your Way to Greatness*, Hodder and Stoughton: London.

Peters, T. (1999a) *Reinventing Work: The Project 50*, Alfred A Knopf: New York.

Peters, T. (1999b) *Reinventing Work: The Professional Service Firm 50*, Alfred A Knopf: New York.

Peters, T. (1999c) *Reinventing Work: The Brand You 50*, Alfred A Knopf: New York.

Peters, T. (2001) 'Tom Peters's True Confessions', *Fast Company*, Issue 53. www.fastcompany.com/magazine/53/peters.html.

Peters, T. (2003) *Re-imagine: Business Excellence in a Disruptive Age*, Dorling Kindersley: London.

Peters, T. (not dated) *Project 04: Snapshots of Excellence in Unstable Times*, Tom Peters Group: Boston MA.

Peters T Peters, T. Peters Group: Boston MA.

Peters T (not dated) *The Death Knell for 'Ordinary': Pursuing Difference*, Tom Peters Group: Boston MA.

Peters, T. (not dated) *We Are in a Brawl with No Rules*, Tom Peters Group: Boston MA.

Peters, T. (not dated) *Women Roar: The New Economy's Hidden Imperatives*, Tom Peters Group: Boston MA.

Peters, T. and Austin, N. (1985) *A Passion for Excellence: The Leadership Difference*, Fontana: London.

Peters, T. and Barletta, M. (2005a) *Tom Peters Essentials. Innovate, Differentiate, Communicate*, Dorling Kindersley: London.

Peters, T. and Barletta, M. (2005b) *Tom Peters Essentials. Develop it, Sell it, Be it*, Dorling Kindersley: London.

Peters, T. and Barletta, M. (2005c) *Tom Peters Essentials. Inspire, Liberate, Achieve*, Dorling Kindersley: London.

Peters, T. and Barletta, M. (2005d) *Tom Peters Essentials. Recognize, Analyze, Capitalize*, Dorling Kindersley: London.

Peters, T. and Waterman, R. (1982) *In Search of Excellence: Lessons from America's Best Run Companies*, Harper and Row: New York.

Peterson, W. C. (1995) *The Silent Depression: The Fate of the American Dream*, W. W. Norton and Co: London.

Pettigrew, A. M. (1985) *Awakening Giant: Continuity and Change in ICI*, Blackwell: Oxford.

Postrel, V. I. (1997) 'The Peters Principle, *reason online*, www.reason.com/9710/int. peters.shtml.

Purves, L. (2006) 'Reader you're a Dimwit', *The Times* (London), 30/5/2006.

Read, T. (2001) *Mr Benn's Little Book of Life*, Arrow Books: London.

Reingold, J. (2003) 'Still Angry After All These Years', *FastCompany*, 75 pf.fastcompany.com/magazine/75/angry.html.

Roberts, J. (2005) 'The Ritzerization of Knowledge', *Critical Perspectives on International Business*, 1 (1): 56–63.

Roethlisberger, F. J. and Dickson, W. J. (1964) *Management and the Worker: An account of a Research Program Conducted by the Western Electric Company, Hawthorne Works, Chicago*, John Wiley and Sons: New York.

Ryan, C. (1975) *A Bridge Too Far*, Book Club Associates: London.

Salzer-Mörling, M. (1998) 'As God Created the Earth ... A Saga that Makes Sense?' in Grant, D., Keenoy, T. and Oswick, C. (eds) (1998).

Sennett, R. (1998) *The Corrosion of Character: The Personal Consequences of Work in the New Capitalism*, Norton: New York.

Sims, D. (2003) 'Between the Millstones: A Narrative Account of the Vulnerability of Middle Managers' Storying', *Human Relations*, 56 (10): 1195–1211.

Sinclair, U. (1965) *The Jungle*, Penguin: Harmondsworth.

Sloan, A. P. with McDonald, J. and Stevens, C. (1965) *My Years with General Motors*, Sidgwick and Jackson: London.

Søderberg, A. (2003) 'Sensegiving and Sensemaking in an Integration Process: A Narrative Approach to the Study of an International Acquisition' in Czarniawska, B. and Gagliardi, P. (eds) (2003).

Steinbeck, J. (1970) *The Pearl*, Pan Books: London.

Steinbeck, J. (1974) *Of Mice and Men*, Pan Books: London.

Steinbeck, J. (1990) *Log from the Sea of Cortez: The Narrative Portion of the Book Sea of Cortez with a Profile 'About Ed Ricketts'*, Mandarin Paperbacks: London.

Swofford, A. (2006) *Jarhead: A Soldier's Story of Modern War*, Scribner: London.

Taylor, D. J. (2003) *Orwell: The Life*, Chatto and Windus: London.

Taylor, F. W. (1911) *The Principles of Scientific Management*, Harper and Row: New York.

Thackray, J. (1993) 'Fads, Fixes and Fictions', *Management Today*, June: 40–42.

Tietze, S., Cohen, L. and Musson, G. (2003) *Understanding Organizations through Language*, Sage: London.

Torrington, J. (1996) *The Devil's Carousel*, Secker and Warburg: London.

Townsend, R. (1970) *Up the Organization: How to Stop the Corporation from Stifling People and Strangling Profits*, Joseph: London.

Tsoukas, H. (2005) 'Afterword: why Language Matters in the Analysis of Organizational Change' *Journal of Organizational Change Management* 18 (1): 96–104.

Tsoukas, H. and Chia, R. (2002) 'Organizational Becoming: Rethinking Organizational Change', *Organization Science*, 13 (5): 567–582.

Van der Merwe, R. and Pitt, L. (2003) 'Are Excellent Companies Ethical? Evidence from an Industrial Setting', *Corporate Reputation Review*, 5 (4): 343–355.

Vonnegut, K. (1973) *Breakfast of Champions or Goodbye Monday*, Delacorte Press: New York.

Wallemacq, A. and Sims, D. (1998) 'The Struggle with Sense' in Grant, D., Keenoy, T. and Oswick, C. (eds) (1998).

Waterhouse, K. (1960) *Billy Liar*, Penguin: London.

Waterhouse, K. (1978) *Office Life*, Michael Joseph: London.

Watson, T. (2001) *In Search of Management: Culture, Chaos and Control in Managerial Work*, Thomson Learning: London.

Weick, K. (1995) *Sensemaking in Organizations*, Sage: London.

Weick, K. (2004) 'A Bias for Conversation: Acting Discursively in Organizations' in Grant, D., Hardy, C., Oswick, C. and Putnam, L. (eds).

Westwood, R. and Linstead, S. (eds) (2001) *The Language of Organization*, Sage: London.

Williams, K., Williams, J. and Haslam, C. (1987) *The Breakdown of Austin Rover: a Case-study in the Failure of Business Strategy and Industrial Policy*, Berg: Leamington Spa.

Wright-Mills, C. (1978) *The Sociological Imagination*, Pelican: Harmondsworth.

Index